The Infinite Omni
The Unending All Behind All Things

Volume I

Lance D. VanTine

© 2025 by Lance D. VanTine

The right of Lance D. VanTine to be identified as the author of this work has been asserted by him in accordance with the Copyright, Designs, and Patents Act 1988.

Published by Ascend Publishing LLC

All rights reserved. No part of this publication may be reproduced, stored in a retrieval system, or transmitted in any form or by any means – for example, electronic, photocopy, or recording – without the publisher's prior written permission. The only exception is brief quotations in printed reviews.

ISBN-13: 979-8-9926324-0-8

Unless otherwise indicated, Scripture quotations are from the New King James Version.

Scripture taken from the New King James Version®. Copyright © 1982 by Thomas Nelson. Used by permission. All rights reserved.

Scripture quotations taken from the (NASB®) New American Standard Bible®, Copyright © 1960, 1971, 1977, 1995, 2020 by The Lockman Foundation. Used by permission. All rights reserved.

Scripture has been italicized to distinguish it from the author's thoughts. Brackets in Scripture indicate the author's descriptors. Scripture that contains bold font is intended to highlight the author's emphasis.

No part of this publication may be reproduced or transmitted in any form or by any means, electronic or mechanical, including photocopy or recording of any information storage and retrieval system without prior permission in writing from the publisher.

This book is solely dedicated...

To the One True, Living God,

The Trinity — the Father, the Son, and the Holy Spirit,

The One Who ascends beyond the Heaven of Heavens and the Earth,

The One Who created all and sustains all,

The One Who offers salvation to all who are humble enough to put their faith, hope, and trust in Jesus Christ as Lord and Savior and repent of their sons,

The God of Love, Light, and Life,

The Infinite Omni.

A special thanks to my Wife,

Who has never doubted me, always believed in me, continually encourages me, and was part of the entire process of this book — even giving me a couple of ideas of God's Characteristics!

I love you and cherish you, and without you, I would not have written this life work of mine.

Thank you for being mine and continually pushing me to be better. You have taught me much and made me a better man.

May God forever bless you, My Love, and give you length of days, decades of years, and joy in every season.

I love you, Jackie VanTine.

"That the God of our Lord Jesus Christ, the Father of glory, may give to you the spirit of wisdom and revelation in the knowledge of Him."

— ***Ephesians 1:17 NKJV***

"But as for me, I would seek God, And to God I would commit my cause— Who does great things, and unsearchable, Marvelous things without number."

— ***Job 5:8-9 NKJV***

"He Who is the blessed and only Potentate, the King of kings and Lord of Lords, Who alone has immortality, dwelling in unapproachable light, Whom no man has seen or can see, to Whom be honor and everlasting power. Amen."

— ***I Timothy 6:15-16 NKJV***

Contents

Preface — xiii
Introduction — xv

1. Omnipresent — 1
   In All Places at the Same Time
2. Omnipraesens — 7
   All-Present – Present at Every Moment – Readily Available to Speak & Be With Us
3. Omnidimensent — 12
   All-Dimension – To Be in All Dimensions
4. Omniregnument — 20
   All-Realm – To Be In All Realms
5. Omniscient — 29
   All-Knowing – Knows All Things
6. Omniretinent — 36
   All-Remembering – Remembers All Things
7. Omnimemorient — 42
   All-Memory – Ability to Store All Facts & Data Within His Mind
8. Omniadmonitent — 49
   All-Warning — Can Forewarn of All Future Events & Consequences
9. Omniprovident — 62
   All-Provident – Prepared for the Future
10. Omniprophetent — 71
    All-Prophesying — Can Prophesy All Things
11. Omniinvulgent — 81
    All-Informing
12. Omniclairvoyant — 91
    All-Foreknowing — Can Perceive All Events that Will Happen in the Future
13. Omniaudient — 97
    All-Hearing – Hears All Things
14. Omniconscient — 105
    All-Aware – Aware of Everything at Any & Every Moment
15. Omniresponderent — 111
    All-Answering – Answers All Things

16. Omnijustificus 117
   All-Right — Always Right & Incapable of Being Wrong

17. Omnirespondent 124
   All-Responding – Always Knows How to Respond

18. Omnicomprehendent 132
   All-Comprehending – God Comprehends All Things

19. Omnisapient 139
   All-Wise

20. Omniintellegent 149
   All-Understanding

21. Omnidiscretent 155
   All-Discerning – God Discerns the Motives, Intentions & Thoughts of the Heart

22. Omniprocessent 161
   All-Processing – Can Process All Things

23. Omnicogitament 166
   All-Thought — Able To Think All Things

24. Omnicertus 173
   All-Certain — Always Sure of What, When & How to Do Something

25. Omniconfident 180
   All-Confident – Confident in Who He Is, What He Can Do & What He Has Declared

26. Omniconsiliument 188
   All-Counseling

27. Omnipotent 195
   All-Powerful

28. Omniperfunctent 203
   All-Performing – God Can Perform & Carry Out Anything

29. Omnicompletus 211
   All-Completing — Can Complete All Things

30. Omnivires 219
   All-Strength

31. Omnidefendent 226
   All-Defending – Capable of Defending & Protecting All Things

32. Omniratio 233
   All-Reason – Reason For All Things

33. Omniultimus 241
   All-Ultimate

Afterword	247
Let's Connect	249
About Lance D. VanTine	251
Also by Lance D. VanTine	253

Preface

As one progresses through this book series, it is important to note that I have taken the time to correlate words that exalt God while simultaneously seeking to resurrect the dead language of Latin.

I have chosen to create the words in a way that references the Latin language without using it ideally. Since I do not have a degree in Latin, at the expense of controversy, I have chosen to follow suit by creating specific names of God's Attributes to reference what they portray (based on my own viewpoint and use of the words).

I, therefore, am not attempting to use the Latin language perfectly to create the words. Instead, I am choosing to create unique words that portray some of the Latin language but are solely focused on giving each Attribute of God its meaning.

Those specializing in Latin may see accurate representations of words, while others may be used differently. I have chosen these words to exemplify each attribute. I am, therefore, not attempting to use the Latin language ideally, only to follow suit with the four common characteristics of God that have been known through the centuries, specifically referencing God as omnipotent, omniscient, omnipresent, and omnibenevolent.

With this being said, 98% of the Attributes listed (based upon the words given) throughout this multi-volume series of *The Infinite Omni* have never been written or seen.

I look forward to growing with you in Him Who indeed cannot be compared, duplicated, or replicated. Truly, God alone stands as *The Infinite Omni*, Who has always *Been* and will always *Be*.

"Behold, heaven and the heaven of heavens cannot contain You" (1 Kings 8:27 NKJV).

Lance D. VanTine

Author

Introduction

"Indeed heaven and the highest heavens belong to the Lord your God, also the earth with all that is in it."
— ***Deuteronomy 10:14 NKJV***

God is *The Infinite Omni*. He is the Unending All of all that is. Nothing assails or ascends beyond Him. He is forever the Highest, Most Potent, Ineffable Being. He alone is Immortal, Eternal, and Immutable.

Wherever we go, God is there. Whatever we come to understand, He reveals. Whatever is made is forever below Him, Who rules and reigns far beyond the Heavens.

It is a great wonder to meditate on Him Who has no bounds. It is a glorious exercise to think about the deeper truths of the One True God, the Trinity – the Father, the Son, and the Holy Spirit.

No more incredible being has existed or can exist outside of God. Nothing will ever reach a point that overthrows God in power, gains deeper understanding and knowledge than God, and reaches a point where God is not present. For God is Himself Power, Presence, Knowledge, Wisdom, and Truth.

When we allow the Holy Spirit to rule our human faculties; when we reach a point where we no longer are focused on the things of this earth, but the Holy Spirit Himself leads our spiritual man, we will find God in the deep secrets of the Unknown.

What we thought we knew about God will forever be an introduction. What we learn about God will forever be a beginning point.

God is All, and all things come by Him, reside in Him, exist for Him, and live because of Him. Without God, there is nothing. With God, there is everything.

Whatever we can imagine or think, God is beyond. Whatever we can conjure up with vocabulary and understanding is merely a glimpse of Him Who is *The Infinite Omni*. Just as infinity cannot reach a peak, The Infinite God cannot be fully understood, known, comprehended, revealed, described, or seen.

This beautiful, magisterial truth illuminates the soul and humbles the inner man. We are not as mighty as we believe. We are not as wise as we think. We cannot begin to comprehend what we do not know, and he who thinks he knows all is he who knows the least.

God is the Revealer of many things but is also the Concealer of infinite things. There are things we know that we do not know. More significant still, there are things we do not know that we do not know.

When meditating on the realm of infinity, there are words, places, and realms beyond our finite, limited capacities. There are visions, beauties, creations, and modes of existence that we have not yet understood. More remarkable still, there are infinite things we will never come to know. For just as God is an Infinite Mind, so His Infinite Mind can think of an innumerable, unending amount of creations and truths that have yet to be known to man – indeed, creations and truths that will never be known to man.

"*It is* the glory of God to conceal a matter, But the glory of kings *is* to search out a matter" (Proverbs 25:2 NKJV). God equally enjoys concealing as much as He enjoys revealing. Even if God desired to reveal everything to us, everything could not be everything. For by the nature of infinity itself, infinity cannot be everything that one comes to know.

We may understand infinity in part and by function but not by way of reality. Only God can contain an infinite amount of knowledge without forgetting, becoming overwhelmed, and dying from mental overload. Just as God is the Creator of all things, His revealed creation never fulfills what He can fully do.

As we read this book, we will realize how little we know of God. As we explore His "Omni" attributes, may we worship Him and bless His Holy Name. God is greater than any being, higher than any entity, above every dimension, and beyond every realm. He is the Great I AM, the Alpha and Omega. The Uncreated Creator cannot be contained, cannot be triumphed over, can never cease to exist, and can never be ascended beyond.

As we drink from the River of Life, may He continue to replenish us, restore us, and give us the strength, energy, joy, and desire to know Him more.

Our Great God is *The Infinite Omni*, and He will forever rule, reign, exist, dwell, and Be beyond all. Glory be to the King of kings and Lord of lords. Let us Praise the Father. Let us submit to the Holy Spirit. Let us leave behind all we believed we knew in full, for what is considered to be fully known in God is but a touch of His Divine Splendor.

God be with you, equip you, and touch you with His Divine Hand. May our minds explore the Unending All of that which God is and does by the guidance, wisdom, and knowledge of the Holy Scriptures and the Holy Spirit.

God in Heaven, Who is The Infinite Omni, Who revealed Himself in this life through His Son, the Lord Jesus Christ, we praise Thee. O God, You are Mighty in Power. By You, all things exist and continue to exist. Without You, there is nothing, but in You is Life, and Life abundantly. O God, we humble ourselves before Thy Holy Throne. Touch us with the knowledge that can only come from Your Divine Mind. Teach us the deeper truths of You. Reveal to us in part the unsearchable mysteries of Your Divine Nature, Divine Attributes, and Divine Existence. O Great and Awesome God, be our All in All. May You save our souls as we believe in Christ and repent of our sins. May You rule our hearts, touch our minds, and uplift our spirits. We come before You in humble adoration, seeking Your Glory, and Your Glory alone. We love You, O Creator and Maker. We Bless Your Holy Name, O Holy One of Israel. In Jesus' name, Amen.

Omnipresent
In All Places at the Same Time

"*Where can I go from Your Spirit? Or where can I flee from Your presence?*"
— ***Psalm 139:7 NKJV***

God is everywhere at all times.

No place exists where God is not. God is the Creator of "place," and He has full access to what He creates.

None of us can go anywhere and escape from God's Presence. He is there, watching, seeing, discerning, and knowing everything occurring. God is never unsure of what is happening. Continually, He is in a state of knowing and being present.

Everything that exists resides within God (Acts 17:28). Though it resides within God, God resides within everything (insofar as His Power and Will is what sustains everything moment by moment (Revelation 4:11)). Since God's Power and Will sustains all, He therefore is present everywhere in some degree.

Of course, when looking at unbelievers, God is not present within them, though His Presence *surrounds* them, and by God's Will, they continue to exist moment by moment. "You are worthy, O Lord, To receive glory and honor and power; For You created all things, And by Your will they exist and were created" (Revelation 4:11 NKJV).

God is always everywhere, and there is not a place we can hide from His Presence. In the darkest cave, God is there. In our room, God is watching. In our deepest heartbreak, God is present. On top of the mountain, God stands beside us. Going on an airplane, He is with us. God is present Everywhere "here" and "there" are.

God's Omnipresence does not go from place to place, for He is always in every place. He does not transition from one place to the next. God, in His collectivity, is simultaneously at the ocean's depths as He is in the stars in the universe.

"Can anyone hide himself in secret places, So I shall not see him?" says the Lord; "Do I not fill heaven and earth?" says the Lord" (Jeremiah 23:24 NKJV). For God, there is no distance from one place to the next. Since God fills all, and all things reside in Him, He is always where "there" is. He is equally present in the farthest place away from us as He is beside us.

When we believe Jesus Christ is Lord and Savior and repent of our sins, we become born-again. The Holy Spirit comes to reside within. We no longer are merely sustained in this life by God's Power and Will; we now have God living within us.

When God's Spirit lives within us, He comes to reside within the sea of our soul. As He touches our spirit, our spiritual man begins to change. What God loves, we begin to love. What God hates, we begin to hate.

Our desires change, our minds renew, and our spiritual state is restored. We recognize that we are redeemed and begin walking in the Power of the Spirit and the Light of the Holy Scriptures.

Truly, there is nothing more remarkable than to have God not merely present all *around* us but having God living *within* us. "Are not two sparrows sold for a copper coin? And not one of them falls to the ground apart from your Father's will. But the very hairs of your head are all numbered" (Matthew 10:29-30 NKJV). If God cares about the number of hairs on our heads, He most certainly cares about our eternal destiny throughout all eternity.

The beautiful reality of God being present everywhere is that nothing escapes His Omnipresent Eye. God is everywhere and is fully aware of all that is occurring in this life. God knows the times of joy and happiness as well as the times of depression and sadness. "In the day of prosperity be joyful, But in the day of adversity consider: Surely God has appointed the one as well as the other, So that man can find out nothing *that will come* after him" (Ecclesiastes 3:14 NKJV).

What God permits and allows is always meant to be worked out for a greater good (Genesis 50:20). We know that God "has made everything beautiful in its time. Also He has put eternity in their hearts, except that no one can find out the work that God does from beginning to end" (Ecclesiastes 3:11 NKJV). Indeed, "The end of a thing *is* better than its beginning" (Ecclesiastes 7:8 NKJV).

Whatever season we, as born-again believers, go through, God is with us and for us. He is not against us; instead, He walks beside us.

He is just as present in our good times as in our trying times. Just as the Father was with Christ, so Christ is with us. He is our Mediator to the Father, and our Heavenly Father loves us and is ever-present.

"For the eyes of the Lord run to and fro throughout the whole earth, to show Himself strong on behalf of those whose heart is loyal to Him" (2 Chronicles 16:9 NKJV). As we remain consistently loyal to God, God will continue to make Himself known. Of course, "If we are faithless, He remains faithful; He cannot deny Himself" (2 Timothy 2:13 NKJV). Nevertheless, we must not forget "*This is* a faithful saying: For if we died with *Him,* We shall also live with *Him.* If we endure, We shall also reign with *Him.* If we deny *Him,* He also will deny us" (2 Timothy 2:11-12 NKJV).

The places that *only* reside in God's Being, but where God's Presence is not, are Hell and the Lake of Fire. These places do not consist of God's Presence. These places are tormenting places of self absorption where eternal punishment for sin will be given.

God's Presence cannot be there because God's very Nature is Holy, Good, Perfect, Loving, Faithful, and Pure. Whoever rejects God rejects these Attributes of God's Nature and, therefore, will reside where they ultimately send themselves.

To reject these realities of God is to reject God. Love and Goodness cannot be recreated. Whatever attempts to be *as* God is not God; whatever attempts to be of God but is not God is a counterfeit and not real. When something is not real, it does not pertain to reality. When something does not correspond with reality, it is falsehood, deceptive, and a fraud.

Thanks be to God, however, that "The Lord is not slack concerning *His* promise, as some count slackness, but is longsuffering toward us, not willing that any should perish but that all should come to repentance" (2 Peter 3:9 NKJV). Thank God that He "desires all men to be saved and to come to the knowledge of the truth" (1 Timothy 2:4 NKJV).

"O Lord, You have searched me and known me. You know my sitting down and my rising up; You understand my thought afar off. You comprehend my path and my lying down, And are acquainted with all my ways. For there is not a word on my tongue, But behold, O Lord, You know it altogether" (Psalm 139:1-4 NKJV). God's Omnipresence and Omniscience (All-Knowing) always work in tandem with each other. There are subtle differences we will review as we proceed in different chapters of God's Omniscience (All-Knowing) and His Omnivoyance (All-Seeing). For now, it is essential to know that just as God knows what we are doing, He sees us all the same.

Truly, we need not fear what a day may bring when we know Him Who created it. Since God counts our days, we need not worry about *when* we will die but *how* we live.

Too many are living to die. Not many are dying to live. We know that Christ tells us: "If anyone desires to come after Me, let him deny himself, and take up his cross daily, and follow Me" (Luke 9:23 NKJV). We must be willing to die to self and live for God, Who is our Ultimate Help.

If God is present *in* us, then we know He is forever *with* us. If He is forever present *with* us, we need not fear any man or demon. "Behold, I give you the authority to trample on serpents and scorpions, and over all the power of the enemy, and nothing shall by any means hurt you" (Luke 10:19 NKJV).

God is always Present everywhere and at all times. No place exists where He does not exist.

"Where can I go from Your Spirit? Or where can I flee from Your presence? If I ascend into heaven, You are there; If I make my bed in hell, behold, You are there. If I take the wings of the morning, And dwell in the uttermost parts of the sea, Even there Your hand shall lead me, And Your right hand shall hold me. If I say, 'Surely the darkness shall fall on me,' Even the night shall be light about me; Indeed, the darkness shall not hide from You, But the night shines as the day; The darkness and the light are both alike to You" (Psalm 139:7-12 NKJV).

No amount of darkness can escape God. To hide sin before God is like attempting to hide the sky before man. Evil and sin do not escape the *Knowledge* of God. Literal darkness from the nighttime and the universe shines like the day before God. Truly, "even the moon does not shine, And the stars are not pure in His sight" (Job 25:5 NKJV).

God alone dwells in Unapproachable Light (1 Timothy 6:16). All things are fully and wholly exposed before Him. "And there is no creature hidden from His sight, but all things *are* naked and open to the eyes of Him to Whom we *must give* account" (Hebrews 4:13 NKJV).

We can rest assured that because God is Omnipresent, He will bring forth appropriate justice. Many times, we only know the story in part. We don't always see all the details and facts behind certain situations, circumstances, and relational conflicts. Only God knows all because He is always present. He not only can *see* and know all that is done, but He is the only One Who *remembers* all that is done.

God's Mind is Infinite. Therefore, His memory is unlimited. Truly, He will do right in all things because He has always been there to see, discern, know, and monitor every event and motion occurring. Even before a word is on our tongue or a thought is on our mind, God knows it altogether.

"But all things that are exposed are made manifest by the light, for whatever makes manifest is light. Therefore He says: 'Awake, you who sleep, Arise from the dead, And Christ will give you light'" (Ephesians 5:13-14 NKJV). May we seek Christ to be the Light within and know that even when our friends forsake us, our relatives distance themselves from us, and we are betrayed, God will always be with us.

Christ Himself has told us, "and lo, I am with you always, *even* to the end of the age." Amen" (Matthew 28:20 NKJV). The next time we feel lonely, may we understand that faith is not a feeling but an endurance in the Truth. God is Omnipresent, and He is forever present, even when it does not *feel* like He is.

Let us never be ruled by our emotions and feelings but allow the Truth of God and His Word to flood our minds and souls. Only then will we walk by faith and not by sight. Only then will we praise and give glory to the One Who is Omnipresent and is always Transcendently Far and Immanently Near.

―――

God of Glory, Who is Omnipresent and is everywhere, Who created "place" and "location", nothing escapes You. Your Presence, O God, captivates us. The Truth that You are always everywhere compels us to trust in You. God, we can do nothing without You. God, we are nothing without You. Truly, Your Power and Will must sustain us moment by moment. O God, whatever is to come in life, instill in us the Truth that You are with us. God, we know that You are both far and near. We know that when we draw near to You, You will draw near to us. God, help us to see Your Invisible Attributes and Divine Power throughout all creation. Open our eyes to the Truth of You and Your Word. Be glorified and magnified, O Infinite Omni, for You alone are God. In Jesus' name, Amen.

OMNIPRAESENS
ALL-PRESENT – PRESENT AT EVERY MOMENT – READILY AVAILABLE TO SPEAK & BE WITH US

"*So that they should seek the Lord, in the hope that they might grope for Him and find Him, though He is not far from each one of us; for in Him we live and move and have our being, as also some of your own poets have said, 'For we are also His offspring.'*"
— ***Acts 17:27-28 NKJV***

While Omnipresence signifies God is everywhere present, God's Omnipraesens reveals He is present, everywhere.

Something can *be* everywhere but not present everywhere. Atoms are everywhere, but they do not have a personal relationship with other atoms. They may be the building blocks of everything, but they do not present themselves as *understanding* and emotionally present within creation. They are *part* of creation everywhere but are not *relational* properties (talking, communicating, loving, etc.).

Only God is Omnipresent and Omnipraesent. God alone is not only everywhere at all times, but He is an ever-present God Who is near to the broken-hearted. He is One Who wants to meet us where we are and guide us into all that is good, joyful, peaceful, and loving. Even when these are not occurring, He wants us to go to Him amid our adversity, trouble, doubt, and anxiety: "casting all your anxieties on Him, because He cares for you" (1 Peter 5:7 ESV).

Whatever we are enduring, God is there, extending His Loving Hand. He desires to wrap His arms around us, but to receive a hug we must be willing to be embraced. If we neglect the arms extending out of those who love us, we withdraw the hands that would otherwise comfort us.

God wants to uplift our spirits. He wants to be our Encourager and Comforter. He wants to not only bless us with His Holy Spirit, but He wants us to be embraced by Him Who is the Alpha and Omega, our Comforter and Advocate, the Rock of our Salvation – the Trinitarian God.

As we go through life, friends come and go. Relationships and family dynamics change. People move out and move away. Those we used to be close with relocated or no longer desired our friendship. Everything that comes by way of God can also leave our hands. Everything that is will eventually cease to exist in this life.

The more we recognize that not everyone is for us and that we will be judged, ridiculed, mocked, or heavily inflicted by the opinions of those closest to us, the more we will run to God. "Stop regarding man in whose nostrils is breath, for of what account is he?" (Isaiah 2:22 ESV).

Man is never always present for us – not even our mother, father, best friend, or spouse. Only God is always present and readily available to speak, listen, comfort, teach, and give a listening ear.

How many times have we desired to share our heart with another, only to find it be brushed aside and have the conversation turned to be about them? How often have we become zealous and shared our heart about what interests us, only to be shot down by those closest?

People are not as present as they believe themselves to be. They use phrases such as "I am always here for you," "Call me whenever," or "Whatever I can do to help, know that I am here." Ironically, when this is tested, it turns out to be nothing but empty words.

Though people are this way, God is not, and we must not allow what man has done to us to dictate our view of God. We must not be led by the pain of the past and pin upon God a false image created in our minds that He is the same. No, God is Omnipraesent and is willing to be there for us at any moment.

Who else is Timeless? Who else has created all that is? Who else cares and loves perfectly at all moments? Who else treats us as if we were the only person in the world to be loved? We do not deserve God's love, yet He extends it freely. For God loves one soul more than all the angels of Heaven.

We are created in God's image and can, therefore, have the most intimate relationship with God. "Draw near to God and He will draw near to you. Cleanse your hands, you sinners; and purify your hearts, you double-minded" (James 4:8 NKJV). Sin is the gap to knowing Christ. Self is the gap to experiencing Christ.

When we draw near to God, we must do so with a repentant, contrite heart. "The Lord is near to those who have a broken heart, And saves such as have a contrite spirit" (Psalm 34:18 NKJV). God is always present to hear our prayers. However, we may believe He doesn't care about them or that He is too busy to listen to us.

Maybe we had a father who was never present in our lives—always going to work and away from home. Perhaps he was home, but his mind would be elsewhere. He wouldn't be present with us in the moment. Though his *body* was near, his *mind* was far. It isn't so with God.

God is not only Omnipresent regarding His Being, but also Omnipraesent in His Presence. God is present both in Being and Presence. He truly is not only with us at every moment but readily willing to hear our prayers.

"The Lord is near to all who call upon Him, To all who call upon Him in truth" (Psalm 145:18 NKJV). God does not answer prayers from those who remain unconverted. He wants to help them, but first they must accept Christ as Lord and Savior and repent of their sins. Then, and only then, will God hear their prayers.

"For *there is* one God and one Mediator between God and men, *the* Man Christ Jesus" (1 Timothy 2:5 NKJV). "The Lord *is* far from the wicked, But He hears the prayer of the righteous" (Proverbs 15:29 NKJV). We become righteous when the Blood of Christ covers us. Only then will God's desire be met for us to be born again and hear our prayer.

God wants us to depend on Him, to go to Him when we are happy, sad, confident, or afraid. He wants to speak to us, reveal more profound revelations of Himself, and show us His Will for our lives. God desires to do more than we could ever ask or think, but we must recognize that He is not only Omnipresent and Omnivoyant—He is Omnipraesent.

Christ promises He is always with us, "even to the end of the age" (Matthew 28:20 NKJV). God cannot lie (Hebrews 6:18, Titus 1:2). He truly is for us and not against us. He wants to save us. He wants to sanctify us. He wants us to run to Him as a child to a loving father.

God is our Heavenly Father. Though our earthly father fails us, He will never fail. He is ready and available to have us pray to Him and listen to us. He speaks in more ways than one, just as much as He speaks by way of His Word.

God's Word is Truth and a guiding path to understanding God, for it is the Word of God that helps us know the God of the Word.

God is not confined by His Word. John 21:25 (NKJV) declares, "And there are also many other things that Jesus did, which if they were written one by one, I suppose that even the world itself could not contain the books that would be written. Amen." Likewise, not all the books to be written from now through eternity could contain and captivate our Transcendent God.

God speaks to us through His Word and His Spirit. He speaks through Truth, a soundless whisper, a Ghostly Hug, and an enlarging vision within our minds. He truly is near and knows how to comfort and speak to us.

Just as God knows what we go through, He knows how to approach us. Though it is always in truth, His Omnipraesence is known, understood, recognized, and felt in different ways.

Let us never drift from God's Omnipraesence but rush into His Divine Love. He wants to embrace us more than we desire to be embraced, listen more than we want to speak, and give more than we are willing to receive.

May all understand that they are never alone. God is near and calling. May we be given ears to hear what the Spirit is saying. God is first and foremost our God, then our Father, then a Friend.

Let us live lives that always recognize Thee Omnipraesent One, that we may be present with the One Who created, formed, and knit us in our mother's womb.

———

God in Heaven, Him Who humbles Himself to look down upon His creation, You are the Omnipraesent One Who is always near us. O God, may we come to You in Truth, always. God, give us the humility not to attempt to live our lives in this life apart from You. May we not strive to make ourselves known by our courage and might, when Your Strength is not pressed into or recognized. O God, You are our Strength and our Song. You alone, God, are willing to hear and answer our prayers. Comfort those hurting. Uplift the hearts of those who are downcast. God, let those who suffer from poor in spirit know that they are loved. Let the meek know that they will inherit the earth. O God, guide and direct our steps. Make Your Presence known to us. May we see Thy Glory shine forth. You are Holy and Love, and Your Perfection does all things Purely. God, we love Thee and thank Thee for being always near to us. Teach us to draw near, that we might gain a heart of wisdom and greater reverence for Thee. In Jesus' name, Amen.

Omnidimensent
All-Dimension – To Be in All Dimensions

"The Lord is high above all nations, His glory above the heavens. Who is like the Lord our God, Who dwells on high, Who humbles Himself to behold The things that are in the heavens and in the earth?"
— **Psalm 113:4-6 NKJV**

For God to look upon His creation, He must always humble Himself and descend from His Infinite Ascension. What God creates is forever below Him, and to see what He has created, He must come down from Ineffable states that we know not.

Truly, God is Omnidimensent. He is in all dimensions since He created dimensions.

When we think of dimensions, we think of places that hold certain realms of existence. For simplicity's sake, dimensions consist of landscapes and boundaries. Realms consist of the modes of existence. An example of a dimension would be a Heavenly dimension, whereas a realm would be a spiritual realm. The spiritual realm resides in the Heavenly dimension but, as we see, can interact, and go outside of the Heavenly dimension (so long as it is permitted).

Let us take angels, for example. Angels exist within the Heavenly dimension (we can refer to this as the "fourth dimension"). When looking at dimensions, paper exists in a 2-dimension, we exist in a 3-dimension, and angels exist in a 4-dimension.

We may live in a 3-dimensional world, but we can interact with a 2-dimensional. We can feel and touch paper and write on paper with a pen or pencil. It is the same with angels. Angels can interact within our dimension, though their habitation is in the 4-dimensional. For we know, just as Hebrews 13:2 (NKJV) declares, "Do not forget to entertain strangers, for by so *doing* some have unwittingly entertained angels."

God allows angels to interact with us in the same way that He allows demons to interact with us. We know Satan is "the prince of the power of the air" (Ephesians 2:2 NKJV) and "the ruler of this world" (John 12:31 NKJV).

"Therefore submit to God. Resist the devil and he will flee from you" (James 4:7 NKJV). We are called to resist the devil. Christ declared, "And these signs will follow those who believe: In My name they will cast out demons; they will speak with new tongues" (Mark 16:17 NKJV). Clearly, those who inhabit the 4-dimensional can interact within our 3-dimensional.

"Is not God in the height of heaven? And see the highest stars, how lofty they are!" (Job 22:12 NKJV). God Immanently fills all that He exists in. No place is hidden from God. There is no dimension where He does not exist. "Where can I go from Your Spirit? Or where can I flee from Your presence? If I ascend into heaven, You *are* there; If I make my bed in hell, behold, You *are there*" (Psalm 139:7-8 NKJV).

Wherever a location, place, or dimension is, there is God. Of course, God's Being can contain all that is within Himself, since all things do exist within Him, "for in Him we live and move and have our being" (Acts 17:28 NKJV).

Just because God's *Being* is everywhere does not mean His *Presence* is everywhere. Of course, God's Presence will not be there in the Lake of Fire, though the Lake of Fire will reside within God's *Being* (since nothing can exist outside of God or apart from God).

God's Will will sustain those who rejected Him with a unique body that can endure the torments of the Lake of Fire for all eternity. Thankfully, however, God wants none to perish but wants all to be saved (1 Timothy 2:4, 2 Peter 3:9). May all believe in Christ to be saved from such a horrific, terrible dimension.

God is All-Dimension because all dimensions are created by Him. He is within every dimension, either by Being, Presence, Spirit, Power, or Will. Wherever a dimension is, God can be found directly in it or sustaining it, which automatically makes Him part of it since He is Power and Will. Both His Power and Will create and sustain a dimension and keep those within that dimension in existence.

God is truly associated with every dimension. This means that God exists within Heaven to the fullest degree we humans can *experience*. Of course, the fullness of God can never be taken in since "No one has seen God at any time" (1 John 4:12 NKJV). God even told Moses, "'You cannot see My face; for no man shall see Me, and live'" (Exodus 33:20 NKJV).

God cannot be fully seen, lest man die. Nonetheless, the fullest extent of *experience of God* that man can have will be found in Heaven.

Christ will be the Light of Heaven. Revelation 21:22-23 (NKJV) declares of Heaven: "But I saw no temple in it, for the Lord God Almighty and the Lamb are its temple. The city had no need of the sun or of the moon to shine in it, for the glory of God illuminated it. The Lamb *is* its light."

There will be no light since Christ is the Light of Heaven. Since He is the Light that shines throughout all of Heaven, we know that the highest *experience* of God will be in Heaven. However, this does not confine God to Heaven.

God not only dwells in the dimension of Heaven; He exists beyond it. ""But will God indeed dwell on the earth? Behold, heaven and the heaven of heavens cannot contain You. How much less this temple which I have built!" (1 Kings 8:27 NKJV). God dwells in the highest Heaven and beyond. God exists not only within the dimension of Heaven but beyond it.

When we look at dimensions, each dimension resides within another. The 2-dimension resides within the 3-dimension, and the 3-

dimension resides within the 4-dimension. As far as we know, there are an innumerable number of dimensions.

Many may think Heaven is the highest dimension, but it is only a touch and taste of God. Since God cannot be fully understood or grasped, even Heaven, in all its wonder and glory, is only a sample of God. It is the beginning of true understanding and growing in knowledge, but never arriving at an end.

As Christ is the true image of God and we will continue to grow in God, we will not experience or know the literal *fullness* of God. As permitted, we will *truly experience* the fullness of God in part, but we will not *literally experience* the fullness of God. For just as Moses would have died seeing the face of God, so we would be obliterated if we attempted to enter the Unapproachable Light where God resides (1 Timothy 6:16).

As we reflect on how Heaven dwells within the Highest Heaven, even the Highest Heaven must dwell in a higher mode of Heaven. God is Infinite; therefore, the dimension it takes to get to the Absolute, Transcendent Nucleus of Him is also infinite.

To get to God's Highest Ascending point is to begin a pursuit that can never be accomplished. For whatever new dimension we would enter, another one would be created. Since God has infinite dimensions, every dimension we enter into would be as if a billion more were made. For infinity has no ending, and neither does God.

When we reflect on this, we see how small we truly are. We are beings of a beginning who dwell only in a 3-dimensional. Is it any wonder, knowing God is Omnidimensent, that He sees and knows all things instantly? God not only created all dimensions but Also an innumerable amount of dimensions. Not only did He create an innumerable number of dimensions, He exists outside of dimension Himself.

This is a wonderful, mind-blowing reality. God dwells in every dimension He created. For Him, all things are as they are, instantly. Everything comes to be from its beginning and end, immediately. God has created innumerable dimensions, which *would* have made Him far out of reach and untouchable had it not been for Christ! It took Christ for us to truly come to know God. God can be known, experienced, loved, and enjoyed. This is His desire!

As we understand the Innumerable Dimensions the Logos came from to enter into the Virgin Mary, we should be amazed at the humility of Christ. Truly, He left what we cannot begin to fathom to become one of us but without sin. "For we do not have a High Priest who cannot sympathize with our weaknesses, but was in all *points* tempted as *we are, yet* without sin" (Hebrews 4:15 NKJV).

If every step was a number, and that number was a dimension, we can quickly see how we could never reach a finality in dimension. Every step would go from a 3-dimensional to a 4-dimensional, to a 5-dimensional, and so on. Even a trillion times a trillion would not even begin our pursuit of getting to the Transcendence of God.

This is a remarkable wonder – that God is All-Dimension. He is Infinite, and therefore exists within the innumerable amount of dimensions He has created for Himself. Of course, with an innumerable number of dimensions, there are infinite things known, going on, understood, and created at any given time. Within God, truly, "*It is* the glory of God to conceal a matter" (Proverbs 25:2 NKJV).

What is still a greater mystery is that even though God dwells within an infinite number of dimensions, since He created them, He still transcends dimensions. God is Omnidimensent, existing in all dimensions He has created.

Though God is Infinite, what is greater than infinity? Transcendence.

God's Transcendence can be found when we arrive at the Unending Finality of His Infinitude. Though God's Infinity has no end and peak, God's Transcendence still goes beyond infinity.

This is not hard to understand when we reflect on God. If He truly is the Creator of all things, then He is the Creator of dimensions. If God created infinite dimensions, then He is Omnidimensent – He exists within them all. If He exists *within* an infinite number of dimensions, then He also *transcends* them.

Though God is in infinite dimensions, He also transcends dimension. For God is simultaneously All-Dimension as well as Dimensionless. God cannot be bound by that which He creates, and not even dimensions can keep God contained.

"Thus says the Lord: "Heaven is My throne, And earth is My footstool. Where is the house that you will build Me? And where is the place of My rest?" (Isaiah 66:1 NKJV). God could have spoken on a much higher level, but to help us begin to grasp Him, He continually humbles Himself – not just in what He has done, but in how He speaks to us.

Every word of God is true, and God's Word is true, but that does not mean every word He has spoken to us has revealed everything about Himself. Just as John 21:25 (NKJV) declares, "And there are also many other things that Jesus did, which if they were written one by one, I suppose that even the world itself could not contain the books that would be written. Amen", so not even God's Word has revealed or described Him in full, since words have been created by Him Who is the Word.

Even if God's Holy Scriptures in the Bible were comprised of all the pages every book ever written or printed had, it would only begin to describe God. Truly, "No one has seen God at any time. The only begotten Son, Who is in the bosom of the Father, He has declared *Him*" (John 1:18 NKJV).

"But our God is in heaven; He does whatever He pleases" (Psalm 115:3 NKJV). God rules all dimensions since He created and resides in all dimensions.

"Who has measured the waters in the hollow of His hand, Measured heaven with a span And calculated the dust of the earth in a measure? Weighed the mountains in scales And the hills in a balance?" (Isaiah 40:12 NKJV). Since God is Omnidimensent, He knows everything about every dimension.

In our dimension, God knows all that exists. He knows every micro and macro happening that consists of movement, understanding, learning, growing, and strengthening. God possesses whatever can be known in any form of knowledge and information and has it instantly contained within His Infinite Mind.

Our 3-dimensional space-time is a mere introduction to what lies ahead. What we who are born-again are to see in Heaven will be so joyous and wonderful that only God could contain us and keep our minds from exploding with dopamine release. Heaven is a continual increase in experience, understanding, knowledge, enjoyment, peace, love, and fellowship with God.

"When I consider Your heavens, the work of Your fingers, The moon and the stars, which You have ordained, What is man that You are mindful of him, And the son of man that You visit him?" (Psalm 8:3-4 NKJV). Why God looks upon us and loves us the way He does is a mystery. The Omnidimensent One Who exists far beyond what our mind can grasp is truly longsuffering and patient with us.

If only we would grow to know God more every day and not be distracted by the petty cares and trifles of our day.

What an amazing reality it is to know that even dimensions themselves exist within God. Let us give praise to Him alone Who is Omnidimensent and Dimensionless. Let us marvel at how God alone is all that He is in His fullest and will never be beyond the reach of us knowing Him in this life.

May we all go to the Word of God and pray, asking that He would send His Holy Spirit to illuminate us within as we become born-again by putting our faith in Him Who died and rose again: The Lord Jesus Christ.

―――

O Great and Mighty One, Who created all dimensions and is All-Dimension, Who is not bound or confined by that which He creates but forever exists beyond all, Independently and Solely, Who is in need of nothing and no one, Who creates out of love and desires fellowship with those made in His image, You are worthy to receive all Glory, Honor, and Worship! O Omnidimensent God, what knowledge is stored within Your Infinite Mind? You alone, O God, are both Knowledge and Mind! Who can think beyond or above Your thoughts? Who can assail or go beyond Your Transcendence? You are Existence and go beyond that which even our minds can comprehend. You alone, O God, have no limitations. You alone, God, can do all things. You create by Logic. You declare Truth. You speak the Word. You form reality. You are Alpha and Omega, the Supreme Almighty Who will never bow before man. O God, take our minds into new realms of thinking. Push us beyond what we have always known. Show us hidden secrecies and bring forth revealed revelations that were once mysteries. Touch us with Thy Divine Light and fill us with Thy Spirit, we pray. In Jesus' name, Amen.

OMNIREGNUMENT
ALL-REALM – TO BE IN ALL REALMS

"*Yours, O Lord, is the greatness, The power and the glory, The victory and the majesty; For all that is in heaven and in earth is Yours; Yours is the kingdom, O Lord, And You are exalted as head over all.*"
— **1 Chronicles 29:11 NKJV**

God is All-Realm, and all realms dwell within Him.

God is head over all things because He created all things. When we look at the understanding of realm, we find a myriad of realms. *Realms* are modes of existence, whereas *dimensions* are the landscapes and boundaries where existence resides.

When we look at the afterlife, we see a spiritual realm. Each of us, with our soul, will stand before Almighty God. We who are born again and covered by the Blood of Christ will go to be with Him in everlasting life. Those who are not with God will be thrown into the Lake of Fire.

It is important to briefly understand that Hell and the Lake of Fire are separate places. The ungodly currently reside in Hell until that Final Day of Judgment. When that occurs, all of Hell will be thrown into the Lake of Fire. "Then Death and Hades were cast into the lake of fire. This is the second death. And anyone not found written in the Book of Life was cast into the lake of fire" (Revelation 20:14-15 NKJV).

These separate places (Heaven and Hell/the Lake of Fire) are the only two dimensions in which human beings can reside throughout all eternity. It all comes down to how they responded to God, based on the amount of appropriate truth He gave them to come to know Him.

Those who rejected God will reside in a place where God's Presence is not. Those who affirmed Christ will be in the perfection of His Presence. We know that a time is coming "when the Lord Jesus is revealed from heaven with His mighty angels, in flaming fire taking vengeance on those who do not know God, and on those who do not obey the gospel of our Lord Jesus Christ. These shall be punished with everlasting destruction from the presence of the Lord and from the glory of His power, when He comes, in that Day, to be glorified in His saints and to be admired among all those who believe, because our testimony among you was believed" (1 Thessalonians 1:7-10 NKJV).

Who will end up in the dimension of Hell? "But the cowardly, unbelieving, abominable, murderers, sexually immoral, sorcerers, idolaters, and all liars shall have their part in the lake which burns with fire and brimstone, which is the second death" (Revelation 21:8 NKJV). "Do you not know that the unrighteous will not inherit the kingdom of God? Do not be deceived. Neither fornicators, nor idolaters, nor adulterers, nor homosexuals, nor sodomites, nor thieves, nor covetous, nor drunkards, nor revilers, nor extortioners will inherit the kingdom of God" (1 Corinthians 6:9-10 NKJV).

Thanks be to God, however, that "The Lord is not slack concerning *His* promise, as some count slackness, but is longsuffering toward us, not willing that any should perish but that all should come to repentance" (2 Peter 3:9 NKJV)!

May all believe in Jesus as Lord and Savior and repent of their sins so that they may become born again! "I tell you, no; but unless you repent you will all likewise perish" (Luke 13:3 NKJV). "Jesus answered and said to him, 'Most assuredly, I say to you, unless one is born again, he cannot see the kingdom of God'" (John 3:3 NKJV).

Now that we have a basic understanding of the afterlife, we find that the Lake of Fire and Heaven are not places of *physicality* but places of *spirituality*. Although they are dimensions that are differentiated from each other, they share the same realm: the spiritual realm.

When we look at the reality of Heaven and the Lake of Fire, we find souls within each. The difference between each, however, is the reality of God's Presence.

Though God's Presence is fully *experienced* in Heaven, God's Presence is fully *extracted* in the Lake of Fire. This is the greatest form of *torment* in the Lake of Fire. It is the anguish of being apart from all that God is – His Love, His Peace, His life-giving joy, His Perfection, His Purity, His Holiness, His care, and His Presence.

When we look at Heaven and the Lake of Fire, each carries the spiritual realm within them. The Lake of Fire is *specifically* designed to harbor the ungodly and transgressors, though it was *formerly* and *initially* created for Satan and his demons.

Jesus "will also say to those on the left hand, 'Depart from Me, you cursed, into the everlasting fire prepared for the devil and his angels'" (Matthew 25:41 NKJV). Everlasting fire (the Lake of Fire) was not made for man, but for Satan and his demons; and those who go in the way of demons will suffer the same fate.

When we consider that God is Omniregnument, He created all realms and will give each person special bodies that appropriately fit the dimension where each person will spend eternity. Again, thanks be to God for being willing and wanting to save all from damnation and sin and have everyone enter into fellowship with Him!

This is the promise of those who become born-again in 1 Corinthians 15:40-49 (NKJV):

> "*There are* also celestial bodies and terrestrial bodies; but the glory of the celestial *is* one, and the *glory* of the terrestrial *is* another. *There is* one glory of the sun, another glory of the moon, and another glory of the stars; for *one* star differs from *another* star in glory. So also *is* the resurrection of the dead. *The body* is sown in corruption, it is raised in incorruption. It is sown in dishonor, it is raised in glory. It is sown in weakness, it is raised in power. It is sown a natural body, it is raised a spiritual body. There is a natural body, and there is a spiritual body. And so it is written, "The first man Adam became a living being." The

last Adam *became* a life-giving spirit. However, the spiritual is not first, but the natural, and afterward the spiritual. The first man *was* of the earth, *made* of dust; the second Man *is* the Lord from heaven. As *was* the *man* of dust, so also *are* those *who are made* of dust; and as *is* the heavenly *Man*, so also *are* those *who are* heavenly. And as we have borne the image of the *man* of dust, we shall also bear the image of the heavenly *Man*."

Glory be to God that those of us in Heaven will have spiritual bodies within the spiritual realm that cannot suffer or experience pain! "God will wipe away every tear from their eyes; there shall be no more death, nor sorrow, nor crying. There shall be no more pain, for the former things have passed away" (Revelation 21:4 NKJV).

From these Scriptures, we understand that God is the Creator of "realm" itself. We have focused on the *spiritual* realm and see that there are only two *dimensions* in the afterlife by which men might be sent. God will not force people into Heaven in the same way He does not force people to love Him. True love is freely given and freely received. It is not infringed upon a person – true love can only be free.

As we freely love the One True God, we experience more of Him. The spiritual realm begins to open to us – not only a recognition of the afterlife, but also in this life.

There is a battle between Light and darkness, Truth and deception, the Way and self, Life and death. We know that Christ is the Way, the Truth, and the Life (John 14:6). When we become born again and receive God's Holy Spirit to live within us, He begins to make spiritual truths and the spiritual realm more real and known to us.

"For we do not wrestle against flesh and blood, but against principalities, against powers, against the rulers of the darkness of this age, against spiritual *hosts* of wickedness in the heavenly *places*" (Ephesians 6:12 NKJV).

There are battles taking place in the spiritual realm that we know not, and we must receive the Holy Spirit to make us alert of what is occurring. Just as a person grows up to be a certain way, it is not just due to the person but also their upbringing and what they were exposed to, as well as a plethora of other aspects. Therefore, the way things are and what we see in the physical are not just due to the physical. There is an Enemy, and we as born-again believers are in a constant spiritual battle (for more on understanding the spiritual realm, see my book *The Realm Beyond: Spiritual Truths, Tongues, Demons, & Deliverance* and *Spiritual Gifts: What Only Come From The Holy Spirit*).

If God is Spirit (John 4:24), then of course, there are higher realities in this life that we cannot perceive with mere sensory input from our physical nature and structure. The Holy Spirit must be present to help us understand more about the spiritual realm that can invade our three-dimensional space-time continuum.

"But the manifestation of the Spirit is given to each one for the profit *of all:* for to one is given the word of wisdom through the Spirit, to another the word of knowledge through the same Spirit, to another faith by the same Spirit, to another gifts of healings by the same Spirit, to another the working of miracles, to another prophecy, to another discerning of spirits, to another *different* kinds of tongues, to another the interpretation of tongues. But one and the same Spirit works all these things, distributing to each one individually as He wills" (1 Corinthians 12:7-11 NKJV).

The spiritual realm can only be understood and perceived by the Holy Spirit Himself. We must seek to cultivate a relationship with Him continually and pray that He would open our spiritual eyes. We are body and soul, not just body (Matthew 10:28). We are part of the spiritual realm, even within these earthly vessels.

Dimensions are the way by which things can be seen. *Realms* are that which things reside in. We live in this 3-dimension, but there is more to us than our physical make-up. When we begin to see that God is the Creator of all realms, we come to find just how much we do not know.

I used to ask and ponder the question, "What did God do before creation?" Eventually, I realized that He did what He continues to do now—only it was that which was always; before anything else *was*.

God's Supra-Eternality is the mode in which He exists only where He is. As He brought things into being, they were created in created dimensions. God's Supra-Eternality is in an Undimensioned-Dimension. It is a Realmless-Realm filled with only God, since God alone is within Himself. It is a "place" and mode of existence where there is no place but God.

This Domain, which only God knows, resides, and where He oversees all (as God remains in the fullness of all He is), is a continuation of a Perpetual, Unending Coming Out and Returning of God to God. What God is doing in His Supra-Eternality in the Unending Future, is the same as the Unbegotten Beginning.

God is the Creator of realms and is, therefore, not bound by them. Just as He created the *physical* and *spiritual* realms, He also created the *mental* realm. When we have thoughts, imagination, wonder, awe, mystery, creativity, and can envision what could be, these all exist within the mental realm that God created.

All our minds are independent from one another, and they all exist within the metaphysical realm of the mind created by Him Who is Divine. Just as we exist in the physical realm and can see each other independently, so it is in the spiritual realm. We will exist independently of each other in the spiritual realm, but within one of the two dimensions (Heaven or Hell/the Lake of Fire) in the afterlife.

As we recognize these truths, we find that God has also created the realm of mind. We each have independent minds that surf across the sea of Him Who is the Infinite, Unlimited, Boundless Mind. God alone is the True and Sole Independent. His Mind is not in need of anything, but our minds can only exist, think, and function because God wills and allows them to do so.

"'For My thoughts are not your thoughts, Nor are your ways My ways,' says the Lord. 'For as the heavens are higher than the earth, So are My ways higher than your ways, And My thoughts than your thoughts'" (Isaiah 55:8-9 NKJV). God's thoughts are limitless, whereas ours are limited. We can think of various thoughts within the mental realm through the ability allotted to us. Still, we cannot imagine what other realms exist apart from the physical, spiritual, and mental. God, however, can.

Since God is the Creator of all, He knows all. Since God knows all, He can think of all that can be done. This is the magnificent wonder: Not everything that God *thinks*, He *creates*.

God could create many other realms that are known to us if He wanted to. He could also create other realms in the future when we exist in eternity. God knows of all the different realms He could create, and He, in fact, has the ability to create an infinite number of realms.

We don't know what this would be like, because we are finite. God, however, is *The Infinite Omni*. He does all things easily and effortlessly, and there are truths for Him that we do not know. For we cannot know all that is or all that God can do. We can only grasp a touch of His Divine Splendor and Glory.

Therefore, we can understand that there are other realms created by God and known by God. There are other realms of reality that are not known to us. For just as everything dwells within God's Being, so everything has a foundation—namely, it is sustained by Him Who is the Ultimate Foundation.

The spiritual realm not only exists *because* of God, but the spiritual realm also resides *within* God. There is something outside of Heaven that God knows. There is something to God that is a higher reality and a more profound realm of Incorporeality and Hiddenness that we cannot fathom.

Truly, this is the beauty of God. He knows all, and all the knowledge that we come to know of Him and what He can do, is forever at the basic level. Though we reach higher, and God gives us deeper revelations, God is the All, Unlimited Revelation. God is always out of reach for us when attempting to understand Him in full.

God guides us along the path to knowing and understanding Him more, even though He knows He cannot give us all understanding and knowledge. We cannot handle it, we cannot contain it, and we cannot come to know Him, Who is Infinite, in His *entirety*.

God, indeed, will forever transcend all we know. Nonetheless, our pursuit of Him should continually be, for it is the greatest pursuit known to man. This path alone of striving to know Him more is Inexhaustible and will never end. What a glorious truth!

Truly, "the Lord Most High is awesome; He is a great King over all the earth" (Psalm 47:2 NKJV). This is why Christ teaches us, "In this manner, therefore, pray: Our Father in heaven, Hallowed be Your name" (Matthew 6:9 NKJV).

God is Holy and to be revered. He is Omniregnument. He alone is

All-Realm and exists within all realms while also existing outside of them altogether. For that which God creates, He is not bound by, and what He is not bound by is Himself existing and Being within Himself.

"The Lord has established His throne in heaven, And His kingdom rules over all" (Psalm 103:19 NKJV). How wonderful are God's signs, "And how mighty His wonders! His kingdom is an everlasting kingdom, And His dominion is from generation to generation" (Daniel 4:3 NKJV)!

Though we only discussed the physical, spiritual, and mental realms in part, all of these exist within the realm of existence. All that is and comes to be, whether seen or unseen, exists within the realm of Existence. This is God, since He is Omniexistent (God is Existence and gives existence to all things).

We will review this later in *The Infinite Omni* series. For now, we must humbly and reverently meditate on the truth and reality that "by Him all things were created that are in heaven and that are on earth, visible and invisible, whether thrones or dominions or principalities or powers. All things were created through Him and for Him" (Colossians 1:16 NKJV).

May we be as the Psalmist and declare, "Such knowledge is too wonderful for me; It is high, I cannot attain it" (Psalm 139:6 NKJV)!

God is the Omniregnument One Who has created all realms and in which all realms reside.

―――

O Omniregnument One, Who created all realms and Who is All-Realm, Who is the Highest Being and is Existence Himself, Who gets nothing from anyone and to Whom belong all things, You are to be revered, glorified, and honored. You, O God of the Heavens and the Earth, deserve all the praise and worship! Who is like You, O God? Who has lived a perfect life like You, Lord Jesus? Who has created a realm in which entities and beings operate? Who can make a realm that has never been? Who understands and knows everything about a particular realm? O God, You are Mighty and Awesome! You are Magnificent and Wonderful! You are the God of all realms and the Creator of all things! God, may we live lives that glorify You. May we be living sacrifices, holy and acceptable to You. God, give us the power to be righteous and live purely physically and spiritually. Give us discernment to recognize when the Enemy is fighting us and tempting us. Give us the courage to pray to You and believe that You will answer, for You reward those who are faithful and believe that You Are and are a rewarder to those who seek You. Fight our battles, Lord God. Give us the strength and courage to press on into the good fight. May we finish the race in Your Power and Might, for Your Spirit alone is the One Who is our Advocate, Comforter, and Protector. We trust in You, O God of all realms. In Jesus' name, Amen.

Omniscient
All-Knowing – Knows All Things

"*For if our heart condemns us, God is greater than our heart, and knows all things.*"
— *1 John 3:20 NKJV*

God knows all things because He created all things.

When God knows something, He knows it before it is knowledge that we can know. God's Timeless Mind consists of all knowledge. God Himself is the Highest Form of Knowledge because He Himself is Knowledge.

Just as there is no wisdom without God, since God is Wisdom, there is no knowledge apart from God, since God is Knowledge.

Whatever God is, He is in His Ultimate, Unending state. Since God is Knowledge, He is the Highest form of Knowledge, which is unattainable. Since He is the Transcendent Knowledge behind all knowledge, He therefore has all knowledge within Him.

Everything dwells in the Being of God. It does not matter if it is visible or invisible; physical or metaphysical; natural or spiritual; in time or eternity, all things dwell within God's Being. Whatever dwells within something can be known by that thing in which it resides.

We as humans know that we have a heart and lungs. We have knowledge of what is within our vessels. We are familiar with the fact that we have a brain and a flow of blood. Though our knowledge is proper, it is not in its most whole form. We *all* are not familiar with *how* the brain works, what specific arteries pump blood to our heart (coronary arteries), or how many breaths we take within each given day. We know *what* things are and have a surface-level knowledge, but our knowledge is not to its fullest form in any way – not even about ourselves.

We know we have hairs on our arms and legs, but how many do we have at any given time? We know we are made up of muscle and bone, but how do muscles and bones interact? What happens if one bone is broken? How do the muscles overcompensate to help with a broken bone? How long does it take certain bones to heal, compared to others? Why are some people's bones more fragile than others? We all know we have bones in our frame and makeup, but our knowledge is always at a surface level.

With any knowledge we may possess, we do not think beyond our current knowledge—of course, not until the right questions are asked. We have an innate hunger to learn more, and we have the discipline to study to gain more knowledge. Until these all come together, we will never acquire all the knowledge about one thing.

The more we learn about something, the more we come to understand that we do not know much at all. Of course, we may learn more about the bones, but do we know when our bones will move in a specific direction? Do we know when we (God-forbid) may need surgery on one of our bones? Do we know what specific foods will aid our bone health as we age? Do we understand *how* bones lose their strength or density? Do we know the leading causes of decreased bone strength or density? Do we precisely know what will happen to our strength and what our bones and muscles will be able to lift ten years from now?

When we begin to think about the knowledge of one matter, we find that the matter we know is just a fraction of what we truly know and what can be known. For knowledge is like a web, and whatever point we pick on the web of knowledge, there is a multitude of interconnections and information to be gathered and learned that we cannot fully come to know. Of course, for God, He knows all things at once.

God knows all the above for us and for every individual on the face of this earth. He has all this knowledge that is easily accessible and readily available to Him since He is the Creator of knowledge itself.

When we come to know something, we know it because God created it to be as such. God created the facts and reality behind the truthful knowledge that can be acquired. God's declaration of what is, is knowledge to be gathered.

"Oh, the depth of the riches both of the wisdom and knowledge of God! How unsearchable are His judgments and His ways past finding out! 'For who has known the mind of the Lord? Or who has become His counselor?' 'Or who has first given to Him And it shall be repaid to him?' For of Him and through Him and to Him are all things, to Whom be glory forever. Amen" (Romans 11:33-36 NKJV).

Knowledge cannot exist without God being the Declarer of what is. When God declares by His Word, He creates. When God creates, He brings forth knowledge within what He creates that we can understand as human beings. Knowledge is a metaphysical principle by which the world operates, how humans live and grow, and an expansion of deeper realities to those who dare to press into knowledge.

When seeking more knowledge, we must not seek after man's intellect first, but God's Infinite Mind. "The fear of the LORD *is* the beginning of wisdom, And the knowledge of the Holy One *is* understanding" (Proverbs 9:10 NKJV). To know God is better than to know all things apart from God. To know God is to know Him Who knows all.

When we know Him Who knows all, we can ask Him anything and everything, and He can and will answer. He will speak to the born-again believer of deeper revelations and understanding and will give knowledge and insight.

When we walk in the Way of Him Who is Wisdom, we will receive wisdom from On High. The Father will give the Holy Spirit His thoughts, and the Holy Spirit will make them known to us. "For what man knows the things of a man except the spirit of the man which is in him? Even so no one knows the things of God except the Spirit of God. Now we have received, not the spirit of the world, but the Spirit Who is from God, that we might know the things that have been freely given to us by God" (1 Corinthians 2:11-12 NKJV).

When we know Him Who knows all we honestly "can do all things through Christ Who strengthens me" (Philippians 4:13 NKJV). We can know all that can be known – things revealed and concealed, made known and hidden, common knowledge and knowledge that could only come from God, directly.

When we say God is Omniscient, He truly knows everything about everything. Everything is instantly known by Him Who is All-Knowing.

When God declares to Jeremiah, "Before I formed you in the womb I knew you" (Jeremiah 1:5 NKJV), He also had this knowledge for all people. Before God created, He knew what we would eventually do. His foreknowledge saw what *was going to be* before it *actually happened.* Greater still, before God knew what was to be, He saw what *ought* to be.

God did not randomly place us within time and space and then begin to think, "O no, I should have made them born in this family instead of that family" or "I should have created them one-thousand years ago in a different generation rather than this one." God does not create and then figure out. Instead, God has already figured it out and known what needs to be done, based on the infinite number of possibilities He has before Him (for more on understanding just how many endless possibilities are accessible to God in any given moment, see my book *The Infinite Day: Insight Into God's Middle-Knowledge*).

Before He creates, God knows what should be done and what decision is the most beneficial. He knows that even amid chaos, evil, and suffering, He can work all of it out for the greater good (Genesis 50:20).

God knows what is to happen before it happens. Since He is Omniconscient (All-Aware), He knows what leads to a particular scenario and what will occur if allowed and permitted. If what would be allowed and permitted by God cannot in any way lead toward a greater good, it will not be allowed and permitted to happen. If it will lead toward a greater good, then God will allow and permit it to happen. This can be easily seen in the life of His Son, the Godman, the Lord Jesus Christ.

Christ was Perfect and did not deserve to be crucified. Yet, it was God allowing that terrible evil of torture and torment of His Son to die on a cross for our sins that led toward opening the door of salvation to all men who will believe in Christ and repent of their sins. Even amid this terrible evil that Christ did not deserve, it was permitted to work out a greater good.

If God did this for His Son, He is doing it for everything else we see (even if we cannot understand or see how a certain evil could be worked out for a greater good). We are not all knowledge, but God is. We do not understand everything, but God does. We cannot be aware of and comprehend everything at all times, but God does and always will. We must learn to trust in Him, Who alone is Omniscient.

"Listen to this, O Job; Stand still and consider the wondrous works of God. Do you know when God dispatches them, And causes the light of His cloud to shine? Do you know how the clouds are balanced, Those wondrous works of Him Who is perfect in knowledge? Why *are* your garments hot, When He quiets the earth by the south *wind?* With Him, have you spread out the skies, Strong as a cast metal mirror?" (Job 37:14-18 NKJV).

We all need to be rebuked like Job and understand the second greatest form of knowledge; namely, God being first, and second being the knowledge of knowing how much we do not know. This knowledge leads us to go toward Him Who is Knowledge, All-Knowing, and has all the answers (Omniresponderent).

Without knowing we do *not* know, we cannot come to a place of ignorance that leads us to humbly seek God for counsel, knowledge, and wisdom. "If any of you lacks wisdom, let him ask of God, Who gives to all liberally and without reproach, and it will be given to him. But let him ask in faith, with no doubting, for he who doubts is like a wave of the sea driven and tossed by the wind. For let not that man suppose that he will receive anything from the Lord; *he is* a double-minded man, unstable in all his ways" (James 1:5-8 NKJV).

When we allow the second most excellent knowledge to lead us to the First, we must not go with doubt but fully confident that God will answer us who are born-again and have His Spirit. "For the Spirit searches all things, yes, the deep things of God" (1 Corinthians 2:10 NKJV).

God can be known in a more profound, intimate way. God can

bestow upon us deeper revelations and make them known to us by His Holy Spirit. God can guide and direct our paths and make them straight. "Trust in the LORD with all your heart, And lean not on your own understanding; In all your ways acknowledge Him, And He shall direct your paths" (Proverbs 3:5-6 NKJV). We simply need to surrender our will and intellect to God and allow Him to bestow godly counsel and knowledge that can only come from Him, Who knows all.

"Do not boast about tomorrow, For you do not know what a day may bring forth" (Proverbs 27:1 NKJV). We do not know what a day may bring forth, but God does. He knows what will occur, and He is already in the future and is equally present there as He is within the actual present.

God is Timeless, and therefore all knowledge for Him is eternal. It is forever known by God, given by God, created by God, and Is God. Even knowledge of our thoughts is before Him. "The Lord knows the thoughts of man, That they are futile" (Psalm 94:11 NKJV).

Let us begin to reflect on our thoughts and how we think. Let us take seriously the fact that God perceives and knows our thoughts as clearly as He sees the day in which we live. Let us take heed to the counsel of David to Solomon in 1 Chronicles 28:9 (NKJV): "As for you, my son Solomon, know the God of your father, and serve Him with a loyal heart and with a willing mind; for the Lord searches all hearts and understands all the intent of the thoughts. If you seek Him, He will be found by you; but if you forsake Him, He will cast you off forever."

God knows our thoughts, intentions, motives, and the like. He knows everything about us – even more than we know ourselves. We must be willing to seek, serve, and "love the LORD your God with all your heart, with all your soul, with all your mind, and with all your strength" (Mark 12:30 NKJV).

When we seek Him Who is Knowledge and knows all, we will walk in the way of wisdom. We will learn the art of simplicity.

Man does not give the greatest knowledge, but God; it is not read in books, but Thee Book; it is not in listening to many podcasts, but in listening to His Voice.

Let us all go to the Omniscient One in all things, knowing that He will provide the knowledge, wisdom, and understanding necessary to know what is expected of us, to know God more, and to understand His Will.

Let us all be led by God's Word, God's Spirit, and God's Voice.

To understand God's different types of knowledge, see my book *Maximum Mind: Understanding the Knowledge & Wisdom of God.*

———

God of Omniscience, Who alone possesses all knowledge and is the Creator of knowledge, Who is Knowledge Himself and the Highest Form of all reality, Who alone dictates what knowledge should be revealed and what knowledge should be concealed, we worship You, the Sovereign Lord over all. Truly, God, You know all things and can do all things. In You is Reason, Wisdom, and Understanding. In You, O God, is a continuation of Perfect and Pure Knowledge. God, there is nothing in You that is evil or tainted. God, You truly are Holy and Just. You alone are Righteous and bestow righteousness to Your people who turn to You with a lowly spirit and a contrite heart. O God, may we go to You in all things. Speak to us and reveal Thy faithfulness. Keep us from placing secular intellect over Your Divine Mind. God, You desire to speak and are always speaking. May we listen and have ears to hear what the Spirit is saying. Enhance our spiritual gifts and spiritual senses. May we run to You when we are unsure, doubting, and have questions. You alone, O God, know all and provide the answers to all things. We submit ourselves to You and trust in You, the All-Knowing God. In Jesus' name, Amen.

Omniretinent
All-Remembering – Remembers All Things

"He is the Lord our God; His judgments are in all the earth. He remembers His covenant forever, The word which He commanded, for a thousand generations"
— **Psalm 105:7-8 NKJV**

Everyone knows something, but not everyone remembers the something that they know at any time of the day.

We do not think and process everything we know when we go through life. Even worse, we do not remember everything that occurs to us. When we read a book, we quickly forget most of what is written (hopefully, that is not the case for this book). We may remember specific quotes or big concepts, but we cannot retain and remember all things because we are not God.

God alone is Omniretinent and can remember all things. Not only does He know everything, but everything is equally, wholly, and instantly remembered. Like a video and voice recorder following us wherever we go, so is it within God's Transcendent Mind.

God knows all that is and occurs, remembers it, and it is forever at the forefront of Thee Almighty. Again, Psalm 105:8 (NKJV) declares,

"He remembers His covenant forever, The word which He commanded, for a thousand generations."

When God remembers, He not only remembers what happens externally, but He remembers what He declares.

How many people do not keep their word? How many flake out and quickly forget? How many people negate fulfilling their promises? How many say only what is right but fail to follow through in action?

Only God perfectly remembers His declarations and perfectly acts out on what He declares and has promised.

At this point, one may argue that in the Old Testament, God would declare how He would destroy a people, yet He didn't. He would speak on how His wrath would be poured out, but Prophets would stand in the gap.

"Then Moses pleaded with the LORD his God, and said: "LORD, why does Your wrath burn hot against Your people whom You have brought out of the land of Egypt with great power and with a mighty hand? Why should the Egyptians speak, and say, 'He brought them out to harm them, to kill them in the mountains, and to consume them from the face of the earth'? Turn from Your fierce wrath, and relent from this harm to Your people. Remember Abraham, Isaac, and Israel, Your servants, to whom You swore by Your Own self, and said to them, 'I will multiply your descendants as the stars of heaven; and all this land that I have spoken of I give to your descendants, and they shall inherit *it* forever.' " So the LORD relented from the harm which He said He would do to His people" (Exodus 32:11-14 NKJV).

When God relents, it is not that He *literally* changes His Mind. God knew what He would do before the world's foundations. Just as Ephesians 1:4 (NKJV) declares, "just as He chose us in Him before the foundation of the world, that we should be holy and without blame before Him in love", and Jeremiah 1:4-5 (NKJV) states, "Then the word of the LORD came to me, saying: 'Before I formed you in the womb I knew you; Before you were born I sanctified you; I ordained you a prophet to the nations'", so God knows what He will do before He does it.

It seems that God changes His Mind and "does not remember His Word" to show us the power of prayer. When we cease to pray, God ceases to complete His *entire* will through us (since our disobedience stunts His Spirit from moving). "And do not grieve the Holy Spirit of God, by Whom you were sealed for the day of redemption" (Ephesians 4:30 NKJV).

Of course, God's *Ultimate Will* will occur regardless of how we act since God is Sovereign. However, disobedience can ruin what God was otherwise willing to do in our lives.

As we understand that God does not *literally* not remember what He says He will do, but He shows us the power of what prayer can do and how God will respond to prayer, we see that God is truly Good. He reveals what we must do and can do so that the Holy Spirit may flow through us like a river.

God, therefore, does not forget but remembers all things. "Then God remembered Noah, and every living thing, and all the animals that were with him in the ark. And God made a wind to pass over the earth, and the waters subsided" (Genesis 8:1 NKJV).

"Then God spoke to Noah and to his sons with him, saying: "And as for Me, behold, I establish My covenant with you and with your descendants after you, and with every living creature that *is* with you: the birds, the cattle, and every beast of the earth with you, of all that go out of the ark, every beast of the earth. Thus I establish My covenant with you: Never again shall all flesh be cut off by the waters of the flood; never again shall there be a flood to destroy the earth'" (Genesis 9:8-11 NKJV).

God remembers His promises to us, and He truly keeps His Word. Never again has there been or will there be a Flood. God holds to what He declares because He is Omnibenevolent (All-Good) and will never renege on what He promises and declares.

God is the One "Who remembered us in our lowly state, For His mercy endures forever" (Psalm 136:23 NKJV). When we are low, God remembers, sees, and loves us through our adversity and suffering. He does not forget us or cast us aside when life gets difficult. He will not leave us to our own devices and see us as a means to His end. God created us as ends, wanting us to know Him, Who is the Ultimate End.

When life gets difficult, some find satisfaction and fulfillment in others' misery and suffering. They see others as charity cases and make themselves feel good by attending to their needs. Few truly empathize with and have compassion for others and what they go through. God, of course, is not like this.

God is the Ultimate Empathizer. He cares for those who are hurting and lost. God Almighty does not leave the marginalized and those perceived as weak by the world. No, God remembers them as He remembers those of status. God sees what every person does and how they behave. God remembers what each person has gone through and endures. God does not forget the difficulty, joy, times of sorrow, and times of gladness. God has the entirety of all information readily available to Him since all things reside in Him (Colossians 1:16).

"For God is not unjust to forget your work and labor of love which you have shown toward His name, in that you have ministered to the saints, and do minister" (Hebrews 6:10 NKJV). Never is our work in vain before God. Employers may rob us. The wicked may swindle us, but God sees it all. God will have justice done because He does not forget. What is done in darkness will be brought into the light (Luke 12:2-3). What is intended in the chambers of the heart, God knows altogether (Jeremiah 17:9-10 NKJV); and what God knows, He remembers.

Again, we may experience, read, or learn some information from books, people, and life, but we cannot remember everything that happens. Even though we lived it in the current moment, we quickly forget. The stranger we met a few months ago, we forgot their name. As years go by, we forget the people we did business with. Each day, we walk past certain buildings and different faces, but we do not remember what every building and face looked like that we saw.

Even when it comes to experiences, we may know we were excited about one of our favorite days from the past, but we don't remember everything that happens in sequential order. We still don't remember everything about our favorite day or the next day that came after our favorite day! We don't remember every detail, and this is because we are finite.

God, however, is Infinite. He is Omniretinent, and He remembers all things. God remembers everything that happens. Whether it be what happens to us, what happens through us, how we felt, what we said, how we did our work, the attitude we had behind our work, the people we met, the experiences we had, the memories we made, what we remember and what we forget, and what we will eventually forget, God knows and remembers it! He has all the knowledge, and His Omniretinent dwells within His Omniscient Mind.

God's Infinite Mind makes Him Omniretinent, and His Omniretinent is the eternal stamp behind His Omniscience. Whatever God knows, He will never forget. Whatever is done, is what will be done, and God will forever remember.

"For her sins have reached to heaven, and God has remembered her iniquities" (Revelation 18:5 NKJV). God does not forget the sins of the ungodly. God "does not forget the cry of the humble" (Psalm 9:12 NKJV).

God will have justice done for those who have wronged us and done injustice: Ultimate Justice for those who do not repent—conviction and calamity in this life for those who need to be woken up.

"Then he said to Jesus, "Lord, remember me when You come into Your kingdom." And Jesus said to him, "Assuredly, I say to you, today you will be with Me in Paradise"" (Luke 23:42-43 NKJV). God will not forget us when we are born-again and found in Christ. He will remember us as we ascend into Heaven. We will be found under the Banner of Christ when the Blood of Christ covers us.

Praise God that He never forgets. We may remember facts and forget about them at a later time, but God forever remembers all facts. All information is laid out before God. All that can be known is forever known by God.

This is the majestic wonder of God being Omniretinent: His Knowledge is forever. When knowledge is forever known, there is an eternal remembering. All facts, information, experiences, creations, events, unfoldings, insight, equations, sets, adversity, seasons, knowledge, understanding, mechanisms, and reasons are known, stored, and remembered within His Infinite Mind.

Praise God that He never forgets and can judge, act, speak, and do appropriately. Praise God that He alone rules and reigns over the Heavens and the earth!

"Some trust in chariots, and some in horses; But we will remember the name of the Lord our God" (Psalm 20:7 NKJV). We remember God because He remembers us. We come to know God because He knows us. We love Him because He first loved us (1 John 4:19).

Therefore, "Let your conduct be without covetousness; be content with such things as you have. For He Himself has said, 'I will never leave you nor forsake you'" (Hebrews 13:5 NKJV). Knowing this, "we may boldly say: 'The LORD *is* my helper; I will not fear. What can man do to me?'" (Hebrews 13:6 NKJV).

"'Can a woman forget her nursing child, And not have compassion on the son of her womb? Surely they may forget, Yet I will not forget you'" (Isaiah 49:15 NKJV). God will never forget us. He will be with us who are born-again and provide for every one of our needs.

Let us trust Him in all things and for all things, knowing that He is with us to the very end.

May the God Who is Omniretinent be exalted. May He Who remembers all things be forever glorified.

———

God in Heaven, He Who does not forget and cannot forget, You are Great and worthy of praise. You alone, O God, know all things, remember all things, do all things, provide, preserve, and sustain all things. You alone, Almighty One, cannot be triumphed and overthrown. You alone can perform the impossible, effortlessly. You take care of Your people, continually. You exist forever, eternally. May You alone, O God, be exalted throughout our lives. Expand our minds that we may receive more of You and wield greater understanding of You, the King of kings and Lord of lords. Keep us from pride. Build in us minds that can remember Your Word. God, help us always to know You are with us. Help us not forget the truth that You see all and remember what people have done to us. God, those who touch Your anointed will experience Your justice and wrath, unless they repent. We pray they would turn to You before their last breath, lest they endure throughout Hell forever. God, thank You for remembering us and remaining faithful, even when we fail You and are unfaithful. Holy Spirit, rule us. Touch us. Mold us and shape us into the image of Christ. We love You, O Holy One, Who alone is Thee Omniretinent God. In Jesus' name, Amen.

Omnimemorient
All-Memory – Ability to Store All Facts & Data Within His Mind

"'These things I have spoken to you while being present with you. But the Helper, the Holy Spirit, Whom the Father will send in My name, He will teach you all things, and bring to your remembrance all things that I said to you.'"
— *John 14:25-26 NKJV*

God alone can store all facts and data within His Mind.

Though metaphysical in nature, our mind operates only based on the functioning capacities of the brain. If the brain is damaged, the mind cannot think appropriately. If we lack sleep, the mind becomes foggy. Suppose the brain does not receive the proper oxygen levels from deep diaphragmatic breathing or balanced hips that allow the lungs to appropriate the level of oxygen to the brain. In that case, we have difficulty thinking and being clear.

Our minds are dependent upon the features of the body and how they are currently functioning. If something is damaged or not functioning at its peak, our minds cannot function to the highest level or degree. With God, however, it is different.

God stores an infinite amount of information within His Mind, which is all equally accessible to Him at any given moment. Everything is at once for Him and all facts and data are easily and conveniently available.

When we declare something through our mouths, we tend to forget what we declare. We do not remember everything we say. Our lives are filled with so many distractions, temptations, projects, and "to-dos", that we find it difficult to remember even everything that happened yesterday! With God, however, He has a Perfect, Unending Memory that always knows exactly what He declares to others.

"Then God remembered Rachel, and God listened to her and opened her womb" (Genesis 30:22 NKJV). "He remembers His covenant forever, The word which He commanded, for a thousand generations" (Psalm 105:8 NKJV). "So God heard their groaning, and God remembered His covenant with Abraham, with Isaac, and with Jacob" (Exodus 2:24 NKJV). What God has already declared He does not forget.

God's memory is forever at the forefront. When He declares He will come, bless, help, aid, deliver, and give us strength, He will follow through, for God follows through with everything He declares. He always accomplishes what He says He will do.

"Nevertheless I will remember My covenant with you in the days of your youth, and I will establish an everlasting covenant with you" (Ezekiel 16:60 NKJV). "The Lord has been mindful of us; He will bless us; He will bless the house of Israel; He will bless the house of Aaron" (Psalm 115:12 NKJV). "He has helped His servant Israel, In remembrance of His mercy, As He spoke to our fathers, To Abraham and to his seed forever" (Luke 1:54-55 NKJV).

Though it is a study in and of itself to see everything God promises, we see on an elementary and fundamental level that God's Word proves God true. The Word declares, "it *is* impossible for God to lie" (Hebrews 6:18 NKJV). What God declares He will do, He will do.

When we get older, we tend to forget what happened throughout our lives. Our ability to remember everything we ever did and said is limited. Of course, there are highlighted moments that stand out, but we do not remember everything that happened. In fact, we can only recall a very minute amount of data and information.

When people get older, they also suffer with the *possibility* of getting Alzheimer's or Dementia. This also does not aid in our memory, but only depletes our capability to recall past times and events. God, however, does not in age or grow old. If He is the same and has always remained the same (Hebrews 13:8), He cannot grow old or young. He simply Is Timeless and Eternal.

God's Word is meant to reveal to us all the times that God promised and spoke what He would do, what He *would* allow, and how He would act *if* something happened. Ironically, all of God's Word reveals precisely how things would (and are to) unfold. Why? Because God works backward the same way we live our lives forward. He already knows what will happen and what He will do, because it has already been done and seen by Him (Ecclesiastes 3:15).

Therefore, God's Word is a blessing and gift for understanding the reality that God is Omnimemorient. God possesses all memory and never falters or waivers. He is always willing to perform and do as He declares. When He speaks, what is communicated is sealed. It is within His Infinite Mind and remains there.

Just as we recognized that our brains limit our minds, God's Mind is Limitless. God's Mind is not hindered by anything. Nothing can damage or destroy It. Nothing can overthrow or exhaust It. Truly, God's Mind is Boundless, Borderless, Unlimited, and Beyond. God's Memory can never unlearn or unknow something. It simply is information and data that He will always know.

Even before we see God act or declare something, it is already within His Mind to do and perform. The data He *already* knows, He has *always* known. A Being that does not have a beginning already contains all that is.

It is God "Who remembered us in our lowly state, For His mercy endures forever" (Psalm 136:23 NKJV). "For God is not unjust to forget your work and labor of love which you have shown toward His name, in that you have ministered to the saints, and do minister. And we desire that each one of you show the same diligence to the full assurance of hope until the end, that you do not become sluggish, but imitate those who through faith and patience inherit the promises" (Hebrews 6:10-11 NKJV)

When referencing the true meaning of the rainbow, God declares, "'and I will remember My covenant which is between Me and you and every living creature of all flesh; the waters shall never again become a flood to destroy all flesh. The rainbow shall be in the cloud, and I will look on it to remember the everlasting covenant between God and every living creature of all flesh that is on the earth'" (Genesis 9:15-16 NKJV). Never has there been a worldwide flood again since that day of God's declaration and promise. We see that God holds to His Word, and reveals He holds to His Word within the Holy Scriptures!

"If we are faithless, He remains faithful; He cannot deny Himself" (2 Timothy 2:13 NKJV). Even when our memory fails us, God's memory never fails. That is why "When you make a vow to God, do not delay to pay it; For *He has* no pleasure in fools. Pay what you have vowed — Better not to vow than to vow and not pay" (Ecclesiastes 5:4-5 NKJV).

God's Memory never forgets the promises we make to Him. He will hold us accountable for every word we speak. "'But I say to you that for every idle word men may speak, they will give account of it in the day of judgment. For by your words you will be justified, and by your words you will be condemned'" (Mathew 12:36-37 NKJV).

We must never forget that God forever Remains and remembers everything. As we covered in Omniretinent (All-Remembering), God does not *literally* forget anything, lest there be a realm of knowledge to which He does not have access. He just does not hold us responsible for our sins (to the point that we are sent to Hell and the Lake of Fire) when we are born again.

Creations remain as such because God declares and remembers them to be as such. If God's Memory were not all-encompassing in every realm about anything and everything, nothing would remain as it is. For nothing can exist on its own. Everything takes God to exist. If God were not Omnimemorient, then everything would fall and crumble.

Life would be like a businessman who casts the vision and works on a business for a few months, only to give up and move on to the next business. As time goes on, that particular businessman forgets all the promises and declarations he made to himself and others about that business. Over time, that business fades and flops, and it does not last.

The same is valid with God being All-Memory. If God did *not* remember anything and everything and did *not* have the ability to store any and all facts, information, and data within His Mind, things would quickly fade and crumble. Nothing would be concrete. Eventually, all that we know would not remain. However, things remain as they are because God declared how they should be and He is Omnimemorient and remembers how He permits, allows, sustains, and preserves everything in existence.

Nothing can remain as it is if there is no capability to access data and information. If God did not have a Perfect, Infinite Mind, nothing would be fine! It is because He has a Mind of All-Memory that everything we know to be, is. God's declaration is simply the revealment of what is in His Mind, and what is in His Mind forever remains.

Like a computer with a hard drive, so is God's Mind. What is on the hard drive for a computer is forever remembered and accessible (so long as everything else is functioning and working appropriately). Since God is Perfect in all realms and in all ways, His Mind cannot unlearn or *literally* forget. God can't do so, since that act would not make Him God.

Sometimes we may cry to God and say, "How long, O Lord? Will You forget me forever? How long will You hide Your face from me? How long shall I take counsel in my soul, Having sorrow in my heart daily? How long will my enemy be exalted over me?" (Psalm 13:1-2 NKJV). When this occurs, we must "Be strong and of good courage, do not fear nor be afraid of them; for the Lord your God, He is the One Who goes with you. He will not leave you nor forsake you" (Deuteronomy 31:6 NKJV).

"The Lord knows the thoughts of man, That they are futile" (Psalm 10:11 NKJV). We know God declares, "'Can a woman forget her nursing child, And not have compassion on the son of her womb? Surely they may forget, Yet I will not forget you'" (Isaiah 49:15 NKJV).

God knows everything about us and what happens to us, and He will deliver and protect us. "Beloved, do not avenge yourselves, but *rather* give place to wrath; for it is written, "Vengeance *is* Mine, I will repay," says the Lord" (Romans 12:19 NKJV).

God's Memory forever stores everything about us and what happens to us. God will repay, in His time, if people do not hear the call to repent of their sins and turn to Christ.

Let us never forget that everything about life has a hidden DNA. This is a Heavenly Stamp of "Invisible Information". At the root of all things is information, which is brought about by God, allowed to be known by others because of God, cannot be *literally* forgotten by God, and reveals that God is God.

Nothing exists without information, and information is invisible in nature. Information comes from the memory and Mind of God, and it is what is behind all things.

Some may argue that the tiniest particles are electrons or quarks. Others may say string theory, the quantum level, and wavelengths are the tiniest aspects known to man. In reality, even these aspects have information behind them. God is the Ultimate Informer, and He delivers all information. This information comes from His Infinite Mind and cannot be literally forgotten; it can only be given out, created, made known, and established.

"For there are Three that bear witness in heaven: the Father, the Word, and the Holy Spirit; and these Three are One" (1 John 5:7 NKJV). Let us praise the Trinity, Who cannot forget and stores all data, information, and facts within Their Divine Mind. God alone has perfect access to everything in His memory, and not one thing dwells outside His memory.

Truly, "in Him we live and move and have our being" (Acts 17:28 NKJV). God alone will never forget what He declares. His Infinite Mind possesses and knows more than we will ever come to know. He does not grow exhausted from knowing and remembering everything. His memory is Perfect and He can recall anything about everything.

Everything is before Him at once Who is *The Infinite Omni* and Instant All.

Blessed be the God and Father of our Lord Jesus Christ, Who alone is Omnimemorient.

O God in Heaven, Who contains and knows all facts, Who stamps a Heavenly code of Invisible Information behind everything, Who stands apart and above all, and in Whom all things exist, You are the Great Unending One Who is All-Memory. You alone, O God, remember everything and can store unlimited information. Not even information can be known or come to exist on its own. Only because of You, God, there is such a thing as information. Truly, You cannot be triumphed over. You cannot be outwitted or taught. You alone hold the keys to Death and Hades. If Hell and Destruction are before your eyes, how much more our hearts? O God, bless us and touch us with Thy Divine Light. May we search Your Holy Word and see that You are Good. You hold to Your promises and blessings. You will have justice done on that Final Day. O God, You alone are Omnimemorient. We trust Thee and Thy Word, knowing You are the God of Truth. In Jesus' name, Amen.

Omniadmonitent
All-Warning — Can Forewarn of All Future Events & Consequences

"*I tell you, no; but unless you repent you will all likewise perish.*'"
— **Luke 13:5 NKJV**

God alone can forewarn all future events and consequences that would occur or will occur if we continue in the way we are going.

How often throughout Scripture do we see God forewarning a nation to repent? Continually, God would send His Prophets to warn a people to turn from their sins, lest they receive God's Justice and Wrath and perish. "Surely the Lord God does nothing, Unless He reveals His secret to His servants the prophets" (Amos 3:7 NKJV).

Jeremiah 25:3-7 (NKJV) declares:

""From the thirteenth year of Josiah the son of Amon, king of Judah, even to this day, this *is* the twenty-third year in which the word of the Lord has come to me; and I have spoken to you, rising early and speaking, but you have not listened. And the Lord has sent to you all His servants the prophets, rising early and sending *them,* but you have not listened nor inclined your ear to hear. They said, 'Repent now everyone of his evil way and his evil doings, and dwell in the land that the Lord has given to you and your fathers forever and ever. Do not go after other gods to serve them and worship them, and do not provoke Me to anger with the works of your hands; and I will not harm you.' Yet you have not listened to Me," says the Lord, "that you might provoke Me to anger with the works of your hands to your own hurt."

God always sends his Prophets to warn people of what will occur if they do not repent. When a nation, people, or person refuses to repent, God's anger is aroused. It breathes down upon the necks of the sons of disobedience. God, of course, does not want to damn and destroy others and bring them to nothing in this life. However, when He is rejected, His Word despised, and He is not revered, His anger grows like a rising tempest.

Jeremiah 35:12, 15-17 (NKJV) reveals again:

"Then came the word of the Lord to Jeremiah, saying, ...

"I have also sent to you all My servants the prophets, rising up early and sending *them,* saying, 'Turn now everyone from his evil way, amend your doings, and do not go after other gods to serve them; then you will dwell in the land which I have given you and your fathers.' But you have not inclined your ear, nor obeyed Me. Surely the sons of Jonadab the son of Rechab have performed the commandment of their father, which he commanded them, but this people has not obeyed Me."'

"Therefore thus says the Lord God of hosts, the God of Israel: 'Behold, I will bring on Judah and on all the inhabitants of Jerusalem all the doom that I have pronounced against them; because I have spoken to them but they have not heard, and I have called to them but they have not answered.'"

This is one of God's many beautiful realities—He always warns before He acts, and He is always longsuffering before He pours out His justice.

"Turn at my rebuke; Surely I will pour out my spirit on you; I will make my words known to you" (Proverbs 1:23 NKJV). If we listen to the Voice of God and obey, the judgment that would have otherwise happened in our lives will be prevented. Only God can interrupt God and keep Himself from acting out what He declared He would do if we continued in the way He is warning us about and remain in disobedience.

God is always giving allotted time and the opportunity to repent. He is not hasty nor in a rush. He is not quick to damn, but slow to have justice done.

God is Omniadmonitent. He can forewarn of all future events and consequences that will occur and would occur. He makes known where we are headed if we continue in the way we are going. He reveals to us how He will respond and what He will do if we do not turn from our sins and run to Him for Mercy.

Deuteronomy 30 gives further insight into how God is All-Warning. God's Word declares in certain parts of Deuteronomy 30 (NKJV):

"'Now it shall come to pass, when all these things come upon you, the blessing and the curse which I have set before you, and you call *them* to mind among all the nations where the Lord your God drives you, and you return to the Lord your God and obey His voice, according to all that I command you today, you and your children, with all your heart and with all your soul, that the Lord your God will bring you back from captivity, and have compassion on you, and gather you again from all the nations where the Lord your God has scattered you'" (Deuteronomy 30:1-3 NKJV).

"'The Lord your God will make you abound in all the work of your hand, in the fruit of your body, in the increase of your livestock, and in the produce of your land for good. For the Lord will again rejoice over you for good as He rejoiced over your fathers, if you obey the voice of the Lord your God, to keep His commandments and His statutes which are written in this Book of the Law, *and* if you turn to the Lord your God with all your heart and with all your soul'" (Deuteronomy 30:9-10 NKJV).

"'For this commandment which I command you today *is* not *too* mysterious for you, nor *is* it far off. It *is* not in heaven, that you should say, 'Who will ascend into heaven for us and bring it to us, that we may hear it and do it?' Nor *is* it beyond the sea, that you should say, 'Who will go over the sea for us and bring it to us, that we may hear it and do it?' But the word *is* very near you, in your mouth and in your heart, that you may do it'" (Deuteronomy 30:11-14 NKJV).

"'See, I have set before you today life and good, death and evil, in that I command you today to love the Lord your God, to walk in His ways, and to keep His commandments, His statutes, and His judgments, that you may live and multiply; and the Lord your God will bless you in the land which you go to possess. But if your heart turns away so that you do not hear, and are drawn away, and worship other gods and serve them, I announce to you today that you shall surely perish; you shall not prolong *your* days in the land which you cross over the Jordan to go in and possess. I call heaven and earth as witnesses today against you, *that* I have set before you life and death, blessing and cursing; therefore choose life, that both you and your descendants may live; that you may love the Lord your God, that you may obey His voice, and that you may cling to Him, for He *is* your life and the length of your days; and that you may dwell in the land which the Lord swore to your fathers, to Abraham, Isaac, and Jacob, to give them'" (Deuteronomy 30:15-20 NKJV).

God is quick to bless and forgive, but only when we are walking in His Way. If we do not walk in the Way of the Word and what He has declared, we walk in disobedience.

Any good parent will warn their child what will occur if they continue to do what they do. They will let their children know that what they are doing is not the way, and if they continue to do what is not right, they will suffer consequences. These consequences will come by way of punishment from them directly, self-harm from oneself, getting in trouble at school, or even with the law.

True love warns of what will occur from bad behavior and rebukes when bad behavior is done. How might we know? God does the same. "My son, do not despise the chastening of the Lord, Nor detest His correction; For whom the Lord loves He corrects, Just as a father the son *in whom* he delights" (Proverbs 3:11-12 NKJV).

True love disciplines their children to correct them, just as God does with us. "He who spares his rod hates his son, But he who loves him disciplines him promptly" (Proverbs 13:24 NKJV). "FOR WHOM THE LORD LOVES HE DISCIPLINES, AND HE PUNISHES EVERY SON WHOM HE ACCEPTS" (Hebrews 12:6 NASB).

Some may argue against spanking a child, but this is Biblical. It is to be done in the same nature as God when He chastises, rebukes, and disciplines us. It must always be done out of love, never in wrath. Why the punishment is occurring must be explained. There must be an embrace afterward, allowing a child to know they are loved.

If we don't discipline our kids, the law will punish them. If they aren't found out and punished by the law and do not repent, God will ultimately judge them on that Final Day.

Discipline teaches us what is right and wrong, what is of God, and what is contrary to His Nature and Word. Without consequence, men would continue to do whatever they wanted, ultimately ending in ruin, loss of reputation, and death.

"It is for discipline that you endure; God deals with you as with sons; for what son is there whom *his* father does not discipline? But if you are without discipline, of which all have become partakers, then you are illegitimate children and not sons. Furthermore, we had earthly fathers to discipline us, and we respected *them*; shall we not much more be subject to the Father of spirits, and live? For they disciplined *us* for a short time as seemed best to them, but He *disciplines us* for *our* good, so that we may share His holiness. For the moment, all discipline seems not to be pleasant, but painful; yet to those who have been trained by it, afterward it yields the peaceful fruit of righteousness" (Hebrews 12:7-11 NASB).

Discipline is a gift. Though it is difficult, it must be done. For what good is acquired without adversity? What virtue gained without difficulty? What salvation is received without admitting we are sinners and repenting?

To receive the good, we must acknowledge the bad. Doing bad, yet having a heart willing to correct and be corrected, serves great merit and provides excellent gain.

When we understand this is God's way, we will see that His warning often comes in a tough word—a word of rebuke, an exhortation, a correction.

"I charge *you* therefore before God and the Lord Jesus Christ, Who will judge the living and the dead at His appearing and His kingdom: Preach the word! Be ready in season *and* out of season. Convince, rebuke, exhort, with all longsuffering and teaching. For the time will come when they will not endure sound doctrine, but according to their own desires, *because* they have itching ears, they will heap up for themselves teachers; and they will turn *their* ears away from the truth, and be turned aside to fables" (2 Timothy 4:1-4 NKJV).

Anyone who denies God's chastening and correction is headed for an eternally bounded descent.

"But I want to remind you, though you once knew this, that the Lord, having saved the people out of the land of Egypt, afterward destroyed those who did not believe. And the angels who did not keep their proper domain, but left their own abode, He has reserved in everlasting chains under darkness for the judgment of the great day; as Sodom and Gomorrah, and the cities around them in a similar manner to these, having given themselves over to sexual immorality and gone after strange flesh, are set forth as an example, suffering the vengeance of eternal fire" (Jude 1:5-7 NKJV).

God warns many times through His Prophets, His people, and also directly through His Word. If we continue in a way that is not the Way of God, we will suffer and eventually reach the end that God warned us about from the beginning.

When people become too prideful, they don't want to listen to the Voice of God. They don't want to acknowledge He is Omniadmonitent. They don't want to accept that His warning is meant for our good. Instead, they see it as an unnecessary or unwanted command to give up what they want to continue to possess. Ironically, what they possess is not worth having or fulfilling. "'For what will it profit a man if he gains the whole world, and loses his own soul?'" (Mark 8:36 NKJV).

Due to God being outside the reality of dimension itself, He can provide the help and means necessary of communicating where our current road is heading. If we are continually looking at pornography, God can reveal to us the damage it not only is doing, but what it is keeping us from; He can not only speak of what it is keeping us from, but what it is leading us toward; He can not only speak what it is leading us toward, but how it is changing our very being.

No rapist or sex-craved addict willing to go to the lengths and pay for sex starts out that way. Little by little, we make inroads that we venture down. When one is ventured down, we create another. With every inroad ventured down, there is another. When we go to the next one, we keep walking further away from the Path we are to take. As we venture further and further away from the Way, we proceed into darkness.

"Your word *is* a lamp to my feet And a light to my path" (Psalm 119:105 NKJV). We will go into darkness if we do not listen to the Word and abide by God's warning. The more we venture into darkness, the greater the depravity, evil, and vileness. With pornography, what was once images, is now videos. What is now videos, turns into other aspects of polygamy, incest, homosexuality, beastiality, transgender porn and even deeper and darker areas.

"Now the works of the flesh are evident, which are: adultery, fornication, uncleanness, lewdness, idolatry, sorcery, hatred, contentions, jealousies, outbursts of wrath, selfish ambitions, dissensions, heresies, envy, murders, drunkenness, revelries, and the like; of which I tell you beforehand, just as I also told *you* in time past, that those who practice such things will not inherit the kingdom of God" (Galatians 5:19-21 NKJV).

"Do you not know that the unrighteous will not inherit the kingdom of God? Do not be deceived. Neither fornicators, nor idolaters, nor adulterers, nor homosexuals, nor sodomites, nor thieves, nor covetous, nor drunkards, nor revilers, nor extortioners will inherit the kingdom of God" (1 Corinthians 6:9-10 NKJV).

"But we know that the law *is* good if one uses it lawfully, knowing this: that the law is not made for a righteous person, but for *the* lawless and insubordinate, for *the* ungodly and for sinners, for *the* unholy and profane, for murderers of fathers and murderers of mothers, for manslayers, for fornicators, for sodomites, for kidnappers, for liars, for perjurers, and if there is any other thing that is contrary to sound doctrine, according to the glorious gospel of the blessed God which was committed to my trust" (1 Timothy 1:8-11 NKJV).

This may be difficult to hear, but it is true. God warns who will not inherit His Kingdom. God has a say in this and has provided the Way through Christ Jesus for us to be saved from our sins and sanctified by His Holy Spirit. If we put our faith in Jesus as Lord and Savior and repent of our sins, we will become born again and receive newness of life. The Holy Spirit will reside within us and give us the strength to endure to the very end.

It was 1 Corinthians 6:9-10 that woke me up to the reality that I was not headed down the road of eternal life. I was amongst the sexually immoral with my porn addiction and being addicted to masturbation (and yes, masturbation is a sin – see Matthew 5:27-30. There is a reason why it is better to cut off the hand than to enter Hell in full, and why this is mentioned in the section on adultery and lust).

I was habitually stuck in this for 10 years. God revealed these Scriptures, and it put the fear of God in me! I began to take my walk seriously and make it my own. I became "re-born", and God set a fire inside me to repent and seek Him wholeheartedly.

He can do the same for anyone else stuck in any sin. Think about this for a moment... what are you currently struggling with? What are you going through? Is it gluttony? Envy? Hate? Bitterness? Gossip? Narcissism? Lying? Cheating? Ungodly fantasy? Whatever it is, God knows it; and yet, He has not smitten you down. You are still living and breathing because God is patient and longsuffering.

"The Lord is not slack concerning *His* promise, as some count slackness, but is longsuffering toward us, not willing that any should perish but that all should come to repentance" (2 Peter 3:9 NKJV).

God does not want you to go to Hell, so He warns of the consequences of sin, where we are headed if we don't repent, and who does not make it. He has made it explicitly clear – not just the consequences of the wrong way but how to get on the right path. This path is not in our strength or by our own doing. "For by grace you have been saved through faith, and that not of yourselves; *it is* the gift of God, not of works, lest anyone should boast" (Ephesians 2:8-9 NKJV).

Truly, "whatever things were written before were written for our learning, that we through the patience and comfort of the Scriptures might have hope" (Romans 15:4 NKJV). "If we confess our sins, He is faithful and just to forgive us *our* sins and to cleanse us from all unrighteousness" (1 John 1:9 NKJV).

Isaiah 43:18-21 (NKJV) declares:

> "'Do not remember the former things,
>   Nor consider the things of old.
>   Behold, I will do a new thing,
>   Now it shall spring forth;
>   Shall you not know it?
>   I will even make a road in the wilderness
>   *And* rivers in the desert.
>   The beast of the field will honor Me,
>   The jackals and the ostriches,
>   Because I give waters in the wilderness
>   *And* rivers in the desert,
>   To give drink to My people, My chosen.
>   This people I have formed for Myself;
>   They shall declare My praise.'"

When we are born-again, we may claim this promise. We need not remember the former things of old or condemn ourselves for our past. When we become born-again, we are new! "Therefore, if anyone *is* in Christ, *he is* a new creation; old things have passed away; behold, all things have become new" (2 Corinthians 5:17 NKJV).

""Come now, and let us reason together," Says the LORD, "Though your sins are like scarlet, They shall be as white as snow; Though they are red like crimson, They shall be as wool. If you are willing and obedient, You shall eat the good of the land; But if you refuse and rebel, You shall be devoured by the sword"; For the mouth of the LORD has spoken" (Isaiah 1:18-20 NKJV).

We only have two options in this life: either we repent or we rebel. God's warnings are not just for us, currently, but where our current actions and decisions are leading us.

We must not become prideful and believe God does not mean what He says. We must not excuse His warnings simply because we do not like them. God always convicts in love, and it is intended to get us following Him – building our relationship through obedience to His Word, fellowship with Him, and being led by the Spirit.

If we continue to disobey and neglect God, we can "be sure your sin will find you out" (Numbers 32:23 NKJV). "For the wages of sin is death, but the gift of God is eternal life in Christ Jesus our Lord" (Romans 6:23 NKJV).

Let us listen to Joshua 24:14 (NKJV), and "Now therefore, fear the Lord, serve Him in sincerity and in truth, and put away the gods which your fathers served on the other side of the River and in Egypt. Serve the Lord!" (Joshua 24:14 NKJV). Let us obey the call of Deuteronomy 5:32-33 (NKJV): "'Therefore you shall be careful to do as the Lord your God has commanded you; you shall not turn aside to the right hand or to the left. You shall walk in all the ways which the Lord your God has commanded you, that you may live and *that it may be* well with you, and *that* you may prolong *your* days in the land which you shall possess.'"

God can and will forewarn of future events and consequences. He has already spoken in the Book of Revelation. When we grow in our walk with Him, He will even answer us directly, just as He did with David in 1 Samuel 23:9-13 (NKJV):

"When David knew that Saul plotted evil against him, he said to Abiathar the priest, "Bring the ephod here." Then David said, "O Lord God of Israel, Your servant has certainly heard that Saul seeks to come to Keilah to destroy the city for my sake. Will the men of Keilah deliver me into his hand? Will Saul come down, as Your servant has heard? O Lord God of Israel, I pray, tell Your servant." And the Lord said, "He will come down." Then David said, "Will the men of Keilah deliver me and my men into the hand of Saul?" And the Lord said, "They will deliver *you*." So David and his men, about six hundred, arose and departed from Keilah and went wherever they could go. Then it was told Saul that David had escaped from Keilah; so he halted the expedition."

Though this Scripture reveals God's Middle-Knowledge (God knowing what *would* happen if David went to the men of Keilah), it also reveals God's willingness to forewarn.

God's Middle Knowledge told David that the men of Keilah would deliver him to Saul if he went to them. What does David do? He and his men flee Keilah. God made a truth claim about something that never came to pass.

God alone has this type of knowledge, and in this situation, it was paired with His Omniadmonitence. God warned David of the events that would occur, based on David's specific request.

How many of us go to God and ask Him specifically what will happen? Though learning the Voice of God takes time, patience, and a willingness to sit within His Presence, it is well worth it. We can get to the point where we clearly hear what God is speaking.

This is offered to anyone, but the path of acquiring this comes with a cost that few are willing to endure. There is sacrifice involved as one seeks to spend more time with God. This sacrifice is simply one of time – sacrificing time we could spend on leisure, entertainment, or whatever else. To give up what our flesh desires and press into what our spirit needs brings forth spiritual realities that cannot be otherwise spoken of but only experienced. They are blessings that come only from God that many may not relate to but are offered to anyone willing to be a Mary instead of a Martha. Luke 10:38-42 (NKJV) says:

> "Now it happened as they went that He entered a certain village; and a certain woman named Martha welcomed Him into her house. And she had a sister called Mary, who also sat at Jesus' feet and heard His word. But Martha was distracted with much serving, and she approached Him and said, "Lord, do You not care that my sister has left me to serve alone? Therefore tell her to help me." And Jesus answered and said to her, "Martha, Martha, you are worried and troubled about many things. But one thing is needed, and Mary has chosen that good part, which will not be taken away from her.""

Spending time with God is never in vain. We can get to the point where just as God spoke to David and David clearly heard God's warning, we can hear God's Voice. It requires time, effort, and patience, but the fruits that spring forth are beyond what any amount of work in the flesh could produce, for it is not the flesh that moves God, only the heart. If we desire Him and for Him to speak, He will.

Therefore, God's warnings come not just through conviction when we are wrong but directly from Him. Though many denominations will excuse this, they build their Theology on man's thoughts more than God's Word.

God will enlighten minds through His Holy Spirit about what is possible. Just because the Cannon is closed does not mean God's Spirit is limited. Revelation, experiential wisdom, and insight are open and offered to any man or woman who seeks God and does not limit God to what a denomination says. That is one of the many reasons I, Lance VanTine, will die by the Word as a non-denominational born-again believer.

God can and will warn. He does this with anything and everything. He warns us about our actions, thoughts, motives, deeds, and speech. He convicts, chastises, rebukes, and disciplines us. He is willing to answer us directly. He can do all these things because He is the Creator of all. If He wants to do it, no one can stop Him. If no one can stop Him, why are we not spending more time with Him?

Truly, the Greatest Being, Highest Mode of Existence, Ultimate Giver of Life, Unseen Sustainer of creation, and Omniadmonitent God is the Holy Trinity. He alone is *The Infinite Omni* Who can forewarn us of all future events and consequences, what will occur if we do not turn, where we are headed, what our habits and character have become by prior mistakes and sins, and who we are becoming from that which is not of Him.

God is for us, not against us. He wants us to believe in His Son, the Lord Jesus Christ, and repent of our sins. If we see that God's warnings are meant for our protection and eternal salvation, why would we not turn to His rebuke?

May all see the blessedness of God's Omniadmonitence and know that He warns us to keep us from consequences and turn us toward Him out of His Love and Goodness.

May all become born-again and be saved from sin. For only in Christ is newness of life. Hallelujah.

———

God of Glory and Magnificence, Who is not bound by anything or anyone, Who can warn at any time and is willing and able to set the captives free, Who does not want us to perish but to enter into fellowship with You, Who raises kings up and brings them down, Who is the Ruler over all, Who cannot be told He is in the wrong, Who does all things in Love, You alone are Omniadmonitent. God, we thank You for the times of warning us. We thank You for warning us to protect us from the future consequences and devastations that would otherwise arise had we not listened. God, help us to love conviction, knowing it will bear much fruit if we listen to the Holy Spirit. For we know He came into the world to convict the world of sin, righteousness, and judgment. God, thank You for keeping our foot from stumbling. Thank You for lifting us up when we fall. Thank You for being our Strength, our All-in-All. Truly, You desire to protect and save. You alone, Lord Jesus Christ, have conquered the grave. We worship You and lift Your Name High, Him Who sits at the Right Hand of the Father and Whom angels worship day and night. You are the Morning Star, the One Who shines forever, and Whose Light is Brighter and Purer than any gem or stone, moon or star, and cherubim or seraphim. To You be honor and praise, Lord God. Thank You for having Your best interest in mind toward us, the apple of Your eye, the ones made in Your image Who You desire to become Your children. May all listen to Your warning and rebuke, allowing You to chastise and convict, listening to Your discipline, knowing it is out of Love. In Jesus' name, Amen.

OMNIPROVIDENT
ALL-PROVIDENT – PREPARED FOR THE FUTURE

"*For we are His workmanship, created in Christ Jesus for good works, which God prepared beforehand that we should walk in them.*"
— **Ephesians 2:10 NKJV**

Before things come to be, God has thought of, known, and declared them.

When the future happens for us, it appears the way it appears. It is not brought about according to our wishes or what we believe will occur. Of course, there are moments when we prepare for what is to come, and that event happens.

If we are an athlete, we train for the next game. If we are about to give a presentation, we prepare for when we stand before others. Maybe we have a due date for a project, and we prepare for the submission. We prepare for the future in all these events, but we do not know what will occur during those specific moments.

Will there be an injury during our game? Will it be the best game we have ever played? Will we present well in our speech? Will there be distractions, people talking, and interruptions? When we submit the project due, will it meet our boss's or teacher's qualifications and standards?

We plan for all of these things in the future, but we don't know what the future will bring. This is why James 4:13-16 (NKJV) declares, "Come now, you who say, "Today or tomorrow we will go to such and such a city, spend a year there, buy and sell, and make a profit"; whereas you do not know what *will happen* tomorrow. For what *is* your life? It is even a vapor that appears for a little time and then vanishes away. Instead you *ought* to say, "If the Lord wills, we shall live and do this or that." But now you boast in your arrogance. All such boasting is evil."

We have plans for the future of what we know is coming up, but we don't even know of the micro-events that will occur in the large event we are aware of; let alone, if the large event will even come to pass or be as we believe it to be. That is why we must say "'If the Lord wills, we shall live and do this or that'" (James 4:15 NKJV).

God alone is Omniprovident. He prepares for the future in all matters. When we believe something is to occur, only He knows what will happen. This occurs not only based on His declaration (Isaiah 46:10) or His foreknowledge (Romans 8:29) but also from God's preparation of what He has already declared and what He foreknows will happen.

This may sound redundant, but it is essential to understand the Middle Providential Ground in between what God declares and what God foreknows. Things come to be, because God declared them to be. Things will occur because God foreknows they will happen as they do.

Between God's declaration and foreknowledge, we find a series of truths and events. We find freedom, mistakes, fulfillment of God's Perfect Will, times when mankind goes astray, and missed opportunities. All this occurs because we use our free will correctly, or fail to use it appropriately. It comes from operating with God in our minds or self in mind.

Though we play a role and part in this world, other forces are behind the scenes. "For we do not wrestle against flesh and blood, but against principalities, against powers, against the rulers of the darkness of this age, against spiritual *hosts* of wickedness in the heavenly *places*" (Ephesians 6:12 NKJV).

These other forces contribute to what occurs at times. However, everything that does come to be is permitted by God. If it does not aid in God's overarching story of working evil out for the greater good, it will not occur.

Greater still, we see that God being All-Provident is in charge of setting up the means and preparation of what He will do, based upon what He allows to occur. For example, 1 Corinthians 10:13 (NKJV) declares, "No temptation has overtaken you except such as is common to man; but God *is* faithful, who will not allow you to be tempted beyond what you are able, but with the temptation will also make the way of escape, that you may be able to bear *it*."

If God foreknows that we will be tempted at times, His Omnipotence acts upon that knowledge and provides a way to escape from every temptation.

Some of us who are tempted seek to find a way out of our temptation. Maybe we get into a bad business deal and want out because we didn't listen to God's voice. Maybe we are in a relationship that is not God-honoring, where we are abused (verbally, physically, mentally, or emotionally), or we are in misery. In these examples, we are trying to find the best way out because we have not listened to and gone to God.

In God's Omniprovidence, He was already prepared for our future mistakes, turning away from Him, and times of temptation. In our temptation, He provides a way of escape. In our mistakes, He is willing to forgive. In our lack of desiring Him and His Will, He convicts us. In wasting time, through our repentance and seeking Him, He can make up for what the locust has eaten (Joel 2:25). In not doing what He wanted within a given moment, He fills the gap by sending another person to do the job.

God is always seeking our best in mind. However, His best does not equal our happiness. His best is what He deems fit to make us more like Christ, draw us to Him, grows us in the faith and spiritual maturity, bear His Name with a testimony of His Strength and Faithfulness, and to get our eyes off this world and set upon Him, the Author and Finisher of our Faith.

God can do all of this, and He does it for those born again and possess a heart that is genuinely repentant when they fail Him. "And we know that all things work together for good to those who love God, to those who are the called according to His purpose" (Romans 8:28 NKJV).

"But my God shall supply all your need according to His riches in glory by Christ Jesus" (Philippians 4:19 NKJV). Before we have a need, God knows how to supply that need. He has prepared all things in advance before they come to pass for us. This is because even the future itself extends into the Eternality of God, preventing God from being shocked or surprised. Instead, God always knows what must be given, provided for, and done before it is actually given, provided for, or accomplished.

"Therefore do not worry, saying, 'What shall we eat?' or 'What shall we drink?' or 'What shall we wear?'" (Matthew 6:31 NKJV). Truly, we need not worry about our needs, for our God knows, is able, will bring forth, and provide what is needed. "For He satisfies the longing soul, And fills the hungry soul with goodness" (Psalm 107:9 NKJV).

"For the Lord God is a sun and shield; The Lord will give grace and glory; No good thing will He withhold from those who walk uprightly" (Psalm 84:11 NKJV). When we walk with God, God walks with us. When we obey His Commands, He will withhold nothing from His Divine Hand. He will give us everything pertaining to life and godliness (2 Peter 1:3).

"Oh, taste and see that the Lord is good; Blessed is the man who trusts in Him!" (Psalm 34:8 NKJV). Truly, God had provided and prepared before there was a need for preparation.

When an army goes to war, it is prepared and trained in advance. However, it does not know when the time will come. Maybe its training is a precaution against what *could* occur, but not what *will* happen.

God never *literally* prepares. He does not think, "I better store up such and such, just in case my creation fails at this point." No, Him Who can form whatever He desires by a Word does not prepare with precautionary measures. Instead, His preparation is definite and done due to Him foreknowing what *will* occur.

There is no guessing with God. There is never a time when He is unsure. God is always in a state of "Knowing". He lives in a Singular, Godlike Instant. His "Eternal Now" is always present at all moments where there is a moment. Even when moments or time do not exist, God continually exists. He is the One Who brought forth time and moments, and nothing can be or come to be without God first bringing it forth and knowing it.

"Of His Own will He brought us forth by the word of truth, that we might be a kind of firstfruits of His creatures" (James 1:18 NKJV). God by His Own Will brings forth what is, and God by His Omniprovidence has already prepared for what will be.

God simultaneously creates, prepares, knows, intervenes, allows, permits, and works out everything. He does nothing in successive moments from His Vision and Scope. God equally prepares for what shall come in tandem with the moment He creates. To God, there is no before or after; there just *is*. His Present is Always Present.

This should bring us great comfort, as God alone is the One and Only True Prudent. He shows great care and thought for the future. His thoughts of the future vary, based on what could happen, what would happen, what will happen, what should happen, what would occur if a particular event happened over another, how one action could lead to a rippling effect of an event He wants to happen ten years from now... God knows it all, and He is truly readily prepared for all moments in the future, because He is in the future as equally as the future unfolds from within Him.

Some may say, "Why did God allow Satan in the Garden?". God did so to reveal to us the Might, Magnificence, Love, and Care He Is and has in ways that He otherwise would not have shown before. Had Satan not been in the Garden, sin would not have entered into the world. If sin did not enter into the world, we would not know Satan as an Enemy. If we did not know what an "Enemy" was, we would not come to fully understand that God is Greater than any entity and Enemy.

Yes, we would know God as Creator, but we would not know Him as Defender. We would not come to understand what an Enemy was because we would not know evil. Enemies come forth by way of evil. Peace comes by way of perfection.

God has revealed to us many things from allowing Satan into the

Garden. His Love, to the point of sending His Son to die on a Cross for our sins! His Faithfulness in declaring what will occur in the end. His longsuffering patience with sinners such as us. His Might, from the standpoint that, if He so chose, God could obliterate Satan within a second. Even from Job 1, we know Satan can do nothing without going to God first.

It may seem misguided of God to allow Satan into the Garden. Still, Satan has aided in our ability to see God in ways we would have never known had Satan not turned himself into an Enemy of God and tempted man. There is beauty in Justice, and we will see Satan thrown into the Lake of Fire on that Final Day (Revelation 20:10).

In all the above, we find that God is truly Omniprovident. He prepared for the future, before the future came to be. Before Satan tempted Adam and Eve, God knew He would send His Son, the Lord Jesus Christ, to die upon that Tree at Calvary. Truly, God declares, "For I know the thoughts that I think toward you, says the Lord, thoughts of peace and not of evil, to give you a future and a hope" (Jeremiah 29:11 NKJV). Even though evil and sin occur, Christ's atoning sacrifice triumphs these. When we are born-again, we have promised hopes that we cannot even fathom or dream.

"'And behold, I am coming quickly, and My reward is with Me, to give to every one according to his work'" (Revelation 22:12 NKJV). "Then the King will say to those on His right hand, 'Come, you blessed of My Father, inherit the kingdom prepared for you from the foundation of the world'" (Matthew 25:34 NKJV). "'In My Father's house are many mansions; if it were not so, I would have told you. I go to prepare a place for you'" (John 14:2 NKJV). "But as it is written: 'Eye has not seen, nor ear heard, nor have entered into the heart of man the things which God has prepared for those who love Him'" (1 Corinthians 2:9 NKJV).

God "will swallow up death forever, And the Lord God will wipe away tears from all faces; The rebuke of His people He will take away from all the earth; For the Lord has spoken" (Isaiah 25:8 NKJV). He is the One "Who saved us and called us with a holy calling, not according to our works, but according to His own purpose and grace which was given to us in Christ Jesus before time began" (2 Timothy 1:9 NKJV).

Our works are a reflection of the Holy Spirit working within us and what God already knew would occur. Our salvation comes from our willingness to hear the call of God and be chosen by Him, based on our authenticity of responding to His call and choosing Him.

As this occurs, we see that predestination is simply God's foreknowledge of our free will decision to accept Him, based on His call and the amount of Truth He has given us to enter under the banner of Christ's atoning sacrifice.

Before time began, we were chosen. We are chosen because God is All-Provident. He prepared for the future salvation we would have through where He placed us, why He placed us where He placed us, the people who would come our way and share the Gospel, speaking to us through dreams and visions, revealing His invisible attributes, Power, and Godhead through creation (Romans 1:20), and giving us a "want" in our soul to thirst for more.

When we are born again, we can declare, "The Lord is my shepherd; I shall not want" (Psalm 23:1 NKJV). "To them God willed to make known what are the riches of the glory of this mystery among the Gentiles: which is Christ in you, the hope of glory" (Colossians 1:27 NKJV). We are saints of God because of God's Omniprovidence to bring forth, speak, reveal, and draw us to, based on His Love for us and His want of fellowship with us. He does not need us, but He wants us to know Him. Knowing Him means we receive salvation from sin and escape damnation.

God's Omniprovidence is readily prepared for anything and everything. Who can escape the One Who knows what will occur before it occurs? Who can outthink, outsmart, outwork, outstrategize Him Who is the God of Thought, Intellect, Work, and Strategy? God cannot be overthrown. He will never be minimized. He is the Supreme Mind Who alone is Divine.

God already provides for us before we need to be provided for. He saves us and protects us from so much, physically and spiritually. If He were not with us, we would be worse off than we could imagine. Truly, it is because of Him that we may live.

"For whatever things were written before were written for our learning, that we through the patience and comfort of the Scriptures might have hope" (Romans 15:4 NKJV). God's Word is equally for today as it was back then. God is the only Author Who possesses a Book for all generations, at all times, and speaks to every person in Truth, yet simultaneously bringing forth different revelations pertaining to each individual's stage of life, desire for deeper revelation, and insight into what others might not see. God alone has provided His Book for all generations, and it was written before we were, for the sake of us who had not yet existed.

Glory be to God for His Perfect Prudence and immediate preparation for all seasons, events, situations, circumstances, misfortunes, blessings, endeavors, pursuits, spiritual, emotional, physical, mental, Heavenly, and time-bound operations.

Truly, God alone is Omniprovident and is to be revered and loved. "We love Him because He first loved us" (1 John 4:19 NKJV). "Blessed *be* the God and Father of our Lord Jesus Christ, Who has blessed us with every spiritual blessing in the heavenly *places* in Christ, just as He chose us in Him before the foundation of the world, that we should be holy and without blame before Him in love, having predestined us to adoption as sons by Jesus Christ to Himself, according to the good pleasure of His will, to the praise of the glory of His grace, by which He made us accepted in the Beloved" (Ephesians 1:3-6 NKJV).

Omniprovident God, Who alone is Sovereign and prepares for what will be, before it is; Who alone possesses all Knowledge, Who created clairvoyance out of Thy Eternal Bossom, Who knows what shall be before it is even made, Who dwells in modes of Eternity too wonderful for the mind to grasp, Who is readily able, Faithful, and Just to forgive us our sins and cleanse us from all unrighteousness, You are Him Who provides for all of our needs. O God, if You take care of the birds of the air, the fish of the sea, and are willing to save our souls and bless us in eternity, will You not take care of us in our struggles and adversity? Will You not rise up and defend us against the Enemy? Will You not provide a way where there is no way, leading us upon level ground as You part the seas? O God, instill in us the child-like faith and the Vision of the Holy Spirit to see beyond and outside ourselves and to look and gaze upon the Beauty of Thy Love, Grace, and Mercy. O God, thank You for preparing all things for us in time and eternity. Thank You for blessing us with knowing You, the One True God, the Holy Trinity. God, we bless You and give You all we are so that we may live to be all we can be by the Power, Wisdom, Knowledge, Understanding, Love, and Strength of the Holy Spirit. In Jesus' name, Amen.

Omniprophetent
All-Prophesying — Can Prophesy All Things

"*And now I have told you before it comes, that when it does come to pass, you may believe.*"
— *John 14:29 NKJV*

God alone is Perfectly and Purely Omniprophetent. He alone predicts the future because the future itself dwells within Him.

When we think of prophets (or prophetesses), we think of a man or woman who comes with a message directly from the Throne of God. Typically, this message is a call to repentance and turning from our sins and toward God.

The road of a prophet is incredibly lonely and isolating. It is filled with heartache and turmoil. Why? Because a message from God to His creation is not always easy to accept.

Darkness does not mix with Light, just as the righteous are not of the wicked. "You cannot drink the cup of the Lord and the cup of demons; you cannot partake of the Lord's table and of the table of demons" (1 Corinthians 10:21 NKJV).

"Examine me, O Lord, and prove me; Try my mind and my heart.

For Your lovingkindness *is* before my eyes, And I have walked in Your truth. I have not sat with idolatrous mortals, Nor will I go in with hypocrites. I have hated the assembly of evildoers, And will not sit with the wicked" (Psalm 26:2-5 NKJV).

Prophets do not associate themselves with the wicked. For if they do so, they will be tainted. Their mind will not be clear to hear the voice and instruction of the Lord. They will be those who give into cowardice and fear, ultimately, neglecting to speak and say what God wants them to declare.

Prophets are bound to be ridiculed in their current generation but will be revered in future generations. Prophets bring a word from God, and they are to obey whether they feel like it or not.

As mentioned, this word is typically used to "repent", but it is many times also a declaration of what will happen *if* repentance of sin is not done before a Holy God. This prophetic declaration reveals what God is ready to do *if* there is not a change of heart, a hatred of sin, and a desire for holiness (for more on what it means to be a Prophet, see my book *The Prophetic Voice: When A Man Is Guided By The Holy Spirit*).

"Surely the Lord God does nothing, Unless He reveals His secret to His servants the prophets" (Amos 3:7 NKJV). God does not act or move without first sending a prophet (or prophets) to warn and tell a people, group, or nation what will occur if they continue wickedly.

God's remedy to relent from His anger is found in 2 Chronicles 7:14 (NKJV), where He declares: "if My people who are called by My name will humble themselves, and pray and seek My face, and turn from their wicked ways, then I will hear from heaven, and will forgive their sin and heal their land."

God is never in the wrong for unleashing His wrath, as the Scriptures validate time and time again that He sends His servants (the Prophets) to forewarn what He will do. "Yet He sent prophets to them, to bring them back to the Lord; and they testified against them, but they would not listen" (2 Chronicles 24:19 NKJV).

When a people do not want to listen to the voice of God, they will incur the wrath of God. This is why God always sends a Prophet – to speak and declare what most are too cowardly to say.

Therefore, God is Omniprophetent because the future dwells

within Him. He is entirely in control of what will happen, what He will permit and allow, and where He will intervene. God knows the means to achieve His desired end, and He knows the end of what will occur if He does not use particular means.

God is All-Predicting because He knows what is to occur before it occurs. "'It shall come to pass That before they call, I will answer; And while they are still speaking, I will hear'" (Isaiah 65:24 NKJV). God knows what will be done before it is done. God knows how He will respond to future events He is already aware of since He alone is Omnistatim (All-Instant).

"But there is a God in heaven Who reveals secrets, and He has made known to King Nebuchadnezzar what will be in the latter days. Your dream, and the visions of your head upon your bed, were these" (Daniel 2:28 NKJV). When God predicts what will happen, He does so by various means. We see He sends prophets. Other times, He will do so using dreams.

God gives dreams and visions to communicate and reveal hidden things that were not otherwise known. They can often be dreams of the future, where we are to proceed with caution, what someone is doing behind the scenes, and of Heaven and Hell. "But this is what was spoken by the prophet Joel: 'And it shall come to pass in the last days, says God, That I will pour out of My Spirit on all flesh; Your sons and your daughters shall prophesy, Your young men shall see visions, Your old men shall dream dreams'" (Acts 2:17 NKJV).

Joel declared this in B.C. and it was further discussed in A.D. by Peter. Clearly, "Jesus Christ is the same yesterday, today, and forever" (Hebrews 13:8 NKJV). What God's Word declares is validated not only by the continuation of what is declared from the Old Testament to the New Testament but also by our current and present reality.

There are too many testimonies that reveal God speaks through dreams and visions. Of course, we never want to believe everything we hear, as many do come with false dreams and visions.

"Thus says the Lord God: "Woe to the foolish prophets, who follow their own spirit and have seen nothing! O Israel, your prophets are like foxes in the deserts. You have not gone up into the gaps to build a wall for the house of Israel to stand in battle on the day of the Lord.

They have envisioned futility and false divination, saying, 'Thus says the Lord!' But the Lord has not sent them; yet they hope that the word may be confirmed. Have you not seen a futile vision, and have you not spoken false divination? You say, 'The Lord says,' but I have not spoken'" (Ezekiel 13:3-7 NKJV).

What is the consequence of false prophets? "Therefore thus says the Lord God: 'Because you have spoken nonsense and envisioned lies, therefore I *am* indeed against you,' says the Lord God. 'My hand will be against the prophets who envision futility and who divine lies; they shall not be in the assembly of My people, nor be written in the record of the house of Israel, nor shall they enter into the land of Israel. Then you shall know that I *am* the Lord God'" (Ezekiel 13:8-9 NKJV).

This is why when prophets speak or others share their dreams and visions, it is to be tested and weighed with Holy Ghost discernment. "Beloved, do not believe every spirit, but test the spirits, whether they are of God; because many false prophets have gone out into the world" (1 John 4:1 NKJV).

When we test what others say and the spirit behind what they say, the Holy Spirit will reveal what is of Him and what is not.

In knowing this, we come to find that when the Holy Spirit confirms a dream or vision, He truly is revealing what is of Him and what He has declared.

It is a sad reality that many *only* hold to the Word of God but deny that the Holy Spirit confirms God's Word and He Himself is also Unbounded and Unrestricted.

When the Holy Spirit falls upon man, religious folk often get scared. If they don't get scared, they instantly dismiss what the Spirit is saying. This, in turn, suppresses, grieves, and quenches the Spirit. "Do not quench the Spirit. Do not despise prophecies. Test all things; hold fast what is good. Abstain from every form of evil" (1 Thessalonians 5:19-22 NKJV).

We do not want to be of the Pharisees and follow a ritualistic routine merely because we were raised in it. We don't want to continue down the path of a denomination when we know that denominations are man-made. If they were of God, there would only be one (which is why I myself am a Non-Denominational Born-Again Believing Christian).

We must hold to the Holy Scriptures at all cost, but we must understand that the Holy Spirit is always doing something new. The Cannon is closed, but revelation from the Holy Spirit is not. If it were, we would think we know everything about God, but by the mere fact He is *The Infinite Omni*, we can rest assured there is always something new the Holy Spirit wants to speak and reveal about Who the Trinity *Is*.

Truly, our minds cannot comprehend the Incomprehensible God. Therefore, since He is the Uncreated Creator and we are created, we would do well to stop negating on what the Spirit is doing and denying Him in our minds what He is clearly able to do and is already doing. We worship Him Who is All-Revelation.

"For prophecy never came by the will of man, but holy men of God spoke as they were moved by the Holy Spirit" (2 Peter 1:21 NKJV). When we know that the Spirit is always speaking, we know that in prior times of the Holy Scriptures being written He was continually leading.

The Word of God was not written by man, but by the Spirit of God in men. It is the Holy Spirit Who confirms the Scriptures and never denies Them. The Holy Spirit is the One Who spoke to the Prophets of Old and revealed what would occur. That future has been revealed, as Christ Who is the Way, Truth, and Life died on the Cross for our sins and rose again the Third Day! Hallelujah!

"Surely He has borne our griefs And carried our sorrows; Yet we esteemed Him stricken, Smitten by God, and afflicted. But He *was* wounded for our transgressions, *He was* bruised for our iniquities; The chastisement for our peace *was* upon Him, And by His stripes we are healed" (Isaiah 53:4-5 NKJV).

All of Isaiah 53 foreshadows the time of Christ entering this world to die on the Cross for our sins. Truly, the Holy Scriptures are validated by God's Omniprophetence. What His Word declares, is what has happened. Not only does It declare what has happened; It declares what will happen.

All prophecy has *yet* to be fulfilled. This is clearly known through the Book of Revelation. Future events must unfold. A new Heaven and new earth have yet to be created (Isaiah 65:17). There is a coming Day when God will have Justice done (Ecclesiastes 3:17, Romans 12:19, Revelation 20:11-15). One Day, all things will be made new, redemption and restoration will occur for born-again believers, and we will be in Paradise with the King of kings and Lord of lords, forever (Revelation 21:5, Revelation 17:14).

God declares, "Remember the former things of old, For I am God, and there is no other; I am God, and there is none like Me, Declaring the end from the beginning, And from ancient times things that are not yet done, Saying, 'My counsel shall stand, And I will do all My pleasure'" (Isaiah 46:9-10 NKJV). What God has declared has already come to pass or has yet to come to pass; and if it has yet to come to pass, we can be sure it will indeed pass.

God can predict the future and declare what will happen because everything resides within Him. He alone knows the end from the beginning since He is the Beginningless Beginning and the Endless End.

"Pursue love, and desire spiritual *gifts,* but especially that you may prophesy. For he who speaks in a tongue does not speak to men but to God, for no one understands *him;* however, in the spirit he speaks mysteries. But he who prophesies speaks edification and exhortation and comfort to men. He who speaks in a tongue edifies himself, but he who prophesies edifies the church. I wish you all spoke with tongues, but even more that you prophesied; for he who prophesies *is* greater than he who speaks with tongues, unless indeed he interprets, that the church may receive edification" (1 Corinthians 14:1-5 NKJV).

When God's Spirit is leading, we can receive a word of knowledge about someone, their situation, what is currently going on, what they are curious about, what will happen, or their sin. Since God resides outside of time, He, of course, can do whatever He pleases within time.

If the Enemy seeks to duplicate all that God does (but does so in a perverted, twisted, empty way), then of course God can speak to someone to share that hidden information with someone else (since the Enemy copies God in this manner). If those who practice divination can gain insight into certain things from the Enemy, then of course we who walk with God and understand our spiritual gifting can receive a word of knowledge: "for to one is given the word of wisdom through the

Spirit, to another the word of knowledge through the same Spirit" (1 Corinthians 12:8 NKJV).

"'You have heard; See all this. And will you not declare *it?* I have made you hear new things from this time, Even hidden things, and you did not know them. They are created now and not from the beginning; And before this day you have not heard them, Lest you should say, 'Of course I knew them'"" (Isaiah 48:6-7 NKJV).

My wife has the gift of words of knowledge on a level I have not seen elsewhere (as of June 2024). When we go out for dinner, she receives a verse or word of knowledge from God. When she shares it, many people begin to cry.

There was this one time we went to a restaurant, and she spoke to three of the staff members at the same time! She shared a verse God gave her from Isaiah with one of them. As my wife shared it with the waitress, she said, "Thank you so much. You don't know how much that means to me. I'm trying not to cry right now, but it has been a year since my ex died as of yesterday and this really spoke to me. Thank you, truly." It was beautiful, but not uncommon when I am with my wife.

The beautiful thing is that a gift must be exercised in order to be activated. Some of us have spiritual gifts God has given us, but they are not active. Of course, the Holy Spirit must be present for them to be used appropriately. When my wife receives a word of knowledge, it is because she asks God for a word for that person—something that speaks to their situation, encourages them, or, if God leads, convicts them (for more on spiritual gifts, see my book *Spiritual Gifts: What Can Only Come From the Holy Spirit*).

God can give the right word at the right time. He is always on time, and His timing is perfect. He can work through vessels and speak through them to others at the appropriate time.

Ironically, my ex's father said to me upon my ex and I breaking up, "Lance, I don't think you two are a best fit. You want to find someone who will hold the camera for your YouTube videos." He said this after he bashed me for having a YouTube channel, declaring, "Who are you making these videos for anyways? My buddies and I were joking around, saying, 'he has thirty views, and half of them are from us watching it multiple times'. We think, 'What is Lance doing?'".

Though this hurt at the time, little did my ex's father know that God would give me someone to hold the camera; not just someone to hold the camera, but who would have the same calling and ministry to do YouTube videos together. To share God and His Word. Ironically, the greatest part, is we met on YouTube! God truly has a sense of humor and is mysterious in all His ways.

God allowed him to ridicule me because he very quickly in the future will, as my wife likes to put it, "be eating his words."

I digress from this story. The point is that God allows those made in His image (my ex's dad) and those born again (my wife) to prophecy. Some may have the gift without even knowing it. It is the spirit behind it that counts and gives us discernment as to what we are speaking and what we will speak, as well as understanding the gift(s) we have been given.

God is Omniprophetent. He predicts everything because everything has already been for Him (Ecclesiastes 3:15). God is never wrong or in error about what He says will occur. Of course, we know He sometimes warns people that He will unleash His wrath. However, many times, warnings are made because they are the warnings that will help others make course corrections. Without a warning, some of us would continue to do wrong, sin, and evil and believe we can get away with it and there is no consequence.

"Therefore, my brethren, desire earnestly to prophesy, and do not forbid to speak with tongues" (1 Corinthians 14:39 NKJV). We must desire to prophesy. Encouraging, exhorting, and rebuking others as the Spirit leads and speaks through us.

"But when He, the Spirit of truth, has come, He will guide you into all truth; for He will not speak on His Own authority, but whatever He hears He will speak; and He will tell you things to come" (John 16:13 NKJV).

The Holy Spirit can reveal whatever is to come. Many times, He has already done so. For some things, God has already told us what will occur, but we are waiting for the fulfillment of what He has declared.

Just because something has not happened yet does not mean it will not happen. Our future spouse is out there. We will be given the best job. God will reveal His plan and purposes for our lives. We need only be still and know He is God (Psalm 46:10).

Let us, therefore, listen when God speaks. There is not one bit of information, not one single event, and not an ounce of doubt that what God has spoken did not (or will not) occur. We can rest in *The Infinite Omni*, knowing He is Omniprophetent. Nothing can speak of the future but Him, Who both created the future and knows it.

God alone is Mighty and Powerful. He alone "changes the times and the seasons;

He removes kings and raises up kings; He gives wisdom to the wise And knowledge to those who have understanding" (Daniel 2:21 NKJV). God knows who will become king in this life because He raises up kings. God knows what a time and season will bring because He changes the times and seasons.

Let us go to God, seeking Him. Let us trust that what He has promised us will come true, whether in this life or the next. We need not worry about the "how," the "when," or the "why." We need only listen to His Voice, discern what others say, and trust that He has a beautiful plan for our lives.

Let us go to Him Who knows all things and predicts what will be before it comes to be.

"'I have declared the former things from the beginning; They went forth from My mouth, and I caused them to hear it. Suddenly I did them, and they came to pass'" (Isaiah 48:3 NKJV).

"'I, even I, have spoken; Yes, I have called him, I have brought him, and his way will prosper'" (Isaiah 48:15 NKJV).

Heavenly Father, God over all, Who speaks and it is created, Who declares and it is so, Who moves and it comes to life, Who accomplishes and it is finished, blessed be Thy Holy Name. O God, thank You for Your many blessings. Thank You for Your promises and revealing already that the Enemy will not prevail. Christ, we worship You, the One Who holds the keys to Death and Hades. We know You, O God, created Satan and his angels before they fell from Heaven. They went against You in their perfec-

tion, but You were not surprised. You were not caught off guard. For what You permit, You know. What You know, You have taken care of. What You have taken care of, You planned before events led to what You needed to plan for. O Great and Mighty God, You are Omniprophetent! You alone are all-predicting. Prophecy comes from You alone, O God. Thank You for already revealing much of prophecy coming to pass. We await Your return, Lord God, and trust in Your Divine Will for our lives. In Jesus' name, Amen.

Omniinvulgent
All-Informing

"*Surely the Lord God does nothing, Unless He reveals His secret to His servants the prophets.*"
— *Amos 3:7 NKJV*

God is not only Omniadmonitent; namely, All-Warning. He is also All-Informing.

Before God does something, He forewarns of what will occur—not only does He forewarn, but He foretells. He informs us of what will happen before something occurs. Even if it does not occur, He informs us of what *will* occur *if* we continue.

This informing is similar to warning, but it is also a means of notifying us of what reality is, not what we perceive it to be.

How often do we believe someone is for us, only to find out they are not? We enter into business deals, purchase a home, or marry a spouse, and sadly, many of us find that what was presented was not what actually was. We operate based on misinformation, not true information. We continue to believe what our senses are noticing and what additional externals are communicating, but we fail to listen to Him Who is Omniinvulgent.

The beautiful reality about God is He is always speaking. Through people, His creation... in all ways, God is communicating. However, the most excellent means of communicating that God does is speaking directly to our conscience.

How often are we guilty of *hearing* the Original Voice of God speak but neglecting to *listen* to what He is telling or warning us? How many times does God give us discernment behind something, but because we don't want to hear what it actually is, we allow deception to take place? We disguise the discernment given, which ultimately leads to a bankrupt ending.

Truly, when God speaks and informs us of what He is actually saying, we would do well to listen to Him the first time! If we do not, our discernment will weaken, and we will end up in the very position or place that God originally told us to avoid.

When people invest in the stock market, what do they desire? Information. Not just information, but the best, most sound, most predictable information. However, we tend not to desire the same regard when we go about our day-to-day lives. We hope to find confirmation of what we *want*, leading to a destructive end.

Let us go back to the example of the stock market. If we wanted a stock to soar, but everyone told us it would not happen, we would not invest in it. Why? Because we would lose out on much. If this is the case with the stock market, why are we not operating as such when it comes to the Voice of God and life matters? Why are we so quick to ignore what God speaks? Is it not our fault for marrying the wrong person? Moving into the wrong home? Befriending the wrong people? Trusting the wrong business partners? Purchasing the wrong used vehicle? Going into the wrong religion? Allowing society to direct our steps, instead of listening to the One and Only Omniinvulgent One?

Oh, what a great disservice we do to ourselves and those around us when *want* interrupts God's Voice. When we go after what we want, we will later wish we had not or want to get out of the very thing God was informing us about.

To be informed is to understand facts, which produces a responsibility to operate appropriately. When we suffer, many times, it is our own doing. Though God sometimes permits suffering and allows it to fan the flame of Christ-like virtue within us, much of the pain we experience is due to not listening to Him Who is All-Informing.

God is All-Informed because all information is derived and known by Him. There is not one bit of information outside of God. He is the Giver and Revealer of information. He is the Creator of Reality and Sustainer of Life. Whatever is, has come to be by way of Him Who speaks, and it is done.

"The secret things belong to the Lord our God" (Deuteronomy 29:29 NKJV). Every secret thing is concealed from us until God reveals it. Many things lie undetected and unknown until *The Infinite Omni* makes them known. "But there is a God in heaven Who reveals secrets, and He has made known to King Nebuchadnezzar what will be in the latter days" (Daniel 2:28 NKJV).

If God can reveal to King Nebuchadnezzar, the Prophets of Old, and others what is to come, He can do it to us, His modern-day saints. God still speaks by dreams and visions. "'And it shall come to pass in the last days, says God, That I will pour out of My Spirit on all flesh; Your sons and your daughters shall prophesy, Your young men shall see visions, Your old men shall dream dreams'" (Acts 2:17 NKJV).

I do not want to discuss if we are in the last days, as I believe we have been since Christ resurrected and ascended to be with the Heavenly Father. The point for Acts 2:17 is to reveal that God still speaks in various ways (which we will review further in the Chapter on Omnipolyglot (able to speak in all languages and in all ways)).

David Wilkerson, a mighty man of God and one of the greatest saints of the 20th century, wrote a book called "The Vision". In the early 1970s God gave him a vision of what was to come. Mind you, this was during a time when homosexuality was not accepted as it is by the world. He stated that there was going to come a time when homosexuality would be accepted by the "Church" and there would be homosexual "pastors" preaching from the pulpits saying God accepts homosexuality.

Fast forward 50 years, and this is absolutely true. However, he had a difficult time sharing what God revealed. Why? Because there was no sign or hint that would ever occur. It was foreign and thought foolish back then. Yet, God, being Omniinvulgent, spoke to one of His saints, revealing what was to come.

When we walk with God and seek to know what He has to say, we will grow in discernment, knowledge, and revelation. We will receive Divine insight into certain matters. For "those who honor Me I will honor" (1 Samuel 2:30 NKJV), declares the Lord God in Heaven.

> God still speaks in dreams and in visions. He can give knowledge through speaking directly to our conscience, implanting a thought within the mind, allowing us to feel what others feel, or through a prophetic word. Yes, all of this is possible. Why? God is Spirit (John 4:24). If Spirit cannot be seen, neither can spiritual gifts.

Yes, spiritual gifts can be exercised and done in the physical realm, but it is difficult for the carnal man to understand spiritual gifts. As a matter of fact, he cannot. 1 Corinthians 2:10-14 (NKJV) declares:

> "But God has revealed *them* to us through His Spirit. For the Spirit searches all things, yes, the deep things of God. For what man knows the things of a man except the spirit of the man which is in him? Even so no one knows the things of God except the Spirit of God. Now we have received, not the spirit of the world, but the Spirit Who is from God, that we might know the things that have been freely given to us by God. These things we also speak, not in words which man's wisdom teaches but which the Holy Spirit teaches, comparing spiritual things with spiritual. But the natural man does not receive the things of the Spirit of God, for they are foolishness to him; nor can he know *them*, because they are spiritually discerned."

Sadly, due to believing more in denominations than God's Word entirely, many have perpetually missed out and negated gifts of the Spirit. They do not understand because they have chosen to believe man's word about God's Word over God's Voice regarding God's Word.

1 Corinthians 12:4-10 (NKJV) speaks on spiritual giftings as follows:

"There are diversities of gifts, but the same Spirit. There are differences of ministries, but the same Lord. And there are diversities of activities, but it is the same God Who works all in all. But the manifestation of the Spirit is given to each one for the profit *of all:* for to one is given the word of wisdom through the Spirit, to another the word of knowledge through the same Spirit, to another faith by the same Spirit, to another gifts of healings by the same Spirit, to another the working of miracles, to another prophecy, to another discerning of spirits, to another *different* kinds of tongues, to another the interpretation of tongues."

Spiritual gifts cannot be understood by carnal means. They can be described, but they cannot be understood. It is not until God brings forth revelation, understanding, and blesses one with a particular spiritual gift, that one begins to understand (I have written more on the gifts of the Spirit in my book, *Spiritual Gifts: What Can Only Come From The Holy Spirit*).

This is one of the many reasons why studying the metaphysical nature of our being is imperative (For more on understanding our invisible nature, see my book *The Metaphysical Trichotomy of Persons*).

Just because the Cannon is closed, does not mean revelations are. The Word of God is closed, but revelations of His Word are not. The Holy Spirit is able and willing to reveal deeper truths within God's Word, and I hope that this seven-volume series of *The Infinite Omni* reveals this.

God can give spiritual gifts and inform us of the reality around us or the future. Since the future exists within Him Who is Self-Existent, it makes sense that God can speak within our present the reality to come. He does this by way of His Spirit speaking through particular spiritual gifts, directly to our mind, conscience, or soul, and giving us spiritual discernment, knowledge, and understanding.

Most denominations do not understand this because most denominations have suppressed this. In my life, I believed in these realities, because they were in the Word. However, I did not begin understanding them until my late 20s. Though the Pentecostals who are truly born-again do well with the gifts, there is a dependency on the gifts and a lack of going to God's Word. We need both to be informed in all matters. For God's Word speaks equally to the proportion that God's Spirit speaks. We just need to have ears to hear above all and allow the Spirit's guiding and directing to lead us into all Truth.

We must always pray "That the God of our Lord Jesus Christ, the Father of glory, may give to you the spirit of wisdom and revelation in the knowledge of Him" (Ephesians 1:17 NKJV). We must know that "nothing is secret that will not be revealed, nor anything hidden that will not be known and come to light" (Luke 8:17 NKJV). God is at full liberty to reveal the intentions of the heart to others. He alone discerns the heart, but that does not mean He does not speak what is in the hearts of men to His servants.

It truly is a wonderful thing to walk with God. He reveals, speaks, shares, and allows us to understand, discern, and feel the intentions of others. He informs us of what is actually going on behind the scenes. He brings us to our knees in praise and thanksgiving. For when we are informed, we can make appropriate decisions. When we make the right decision, we save ourselves from a multitude of trouble, based on God first speaking to us and allowing us to decide if we will listen.

Our conscience is so important. It is the metaphysical tool where God's Spirit brings conviction and correction; where we are directed and guided. If we listen immediately to our conscience, we will grow in discernment. If we do not listen to our conscience, we will suffer. For it is not us who is telling us where to go; it is God's Spirit convicting our conscience, but ultimately allowing our consciousness (the intermediate state between what the mind thinks and the soul wills) to make the decision (again, more of this can be found in my book, *The Metaphysical Trichotomy of Persons*).

Truly, God "reveals deep and secret things; He knows what is in the darkness, And light dwells with Him" (Daniel 2:22 NKJV). God is always informed because all information dwells within Him and comes from Him. God is All-Informing, but the question is whether or not we are listening.

The next time we enter a building and tension arises from within our spirit, may we know it is the Holy Spirit speaking and not confirming where we are going. When we are about to do something and the consequences of what might, could, would, or will occur from our actions are presented, the Holy Spirit is convicting us. When a random thought comes from nowhere about a person, place, or situation, may we go to God and see that His Spirit could be leading us to pray about that very thing. If a word of knowledge about someone's intentions comes forth, may we not automatically excuse it away and give people "the benefit of the doubt". Nowhere in Scripture is that suggested or implied.

We must always be discerning and know that people are inherently sinful and evil. "Behold, I was brought forth in iniquity, And in sin my mother conceived me" (Psalm 51:5 NKJV). "And you *He made alive,* who were dead in trespasses and sins, in which you once walked according to the course of this world, according to the prince of the power of the air, the spirit who now works in the sons of disobedience, among whom also we all once conducted ourselves in the lusts of our flesh, fulfilling the desires of the flesh and of the mind, and were by nature children of wrath, just as the others" (Ephesians 2:1-3 NKJV).

"Therefore, just as through one man sin entered the world, and death through sin, and thus death spread to all men, because all sinned— (For until the law sin was in the world, but sin is not imputed when there is no law. Nevertheless death reigned from Adam to Moses, even over those who had not sinned according to the likeness of the transgression of Adam, who is a type of Him who was to come. But the free gift *is* not like the offense. For if by the one man's offense many died, much more the grace of God and the gift by the grace of the one Man, Jesus Christ, abounded to many. And the gift *is* not like *that which came* through the one who sinned. For the judgment *which came* from one *offense resulted* in condemnation, but the free gift *which came* from many offenses *resulted* in justification. For if by the one man's offense death reigned through the one, much more those who receive abundance of grace and of the gift of righteousness will reign in life through the One, Jesus Christ.) Therefore, as through one man's offense *judgment came* to all men, resulting in condemnation, even so through one Man's righteous act *the free gift came* to all men, resulting in justification of life. For as by one man's disobedience many were made sinners, so also by one Man's obedience many will be made righteous. Moreover the law entered that the offense might abound. But where sin abounded, grace abounded much more, so that as sin reigned in death, even so grace might reign through righteousness to eternal life through Jesus Christ our Lord" (Romans 5:12-21 NKJV).

God informs us of who we are apart from Him and who we are in Him. He reveals the mysteries of what is hidden in the darkness. He makes known the chambers of other people's hearts. He gives spiritual discernment behind certain matters. He helps us understand if something is of the flesh or demonic. He gives us wisdom to recognize what is of Him and what is not of Him. He speaks to us about His Will for our lives on a moment-by-moment basis and on a widespread scale.

We must allow ourselves to be guided by Him Who is Omniinvulgent. For God is All-Informing and always speaking. We must be willing to learn and be trained in the inner life, for it is there that our spiritual man and woman will shine forth. There, we will learn how the Spirit moves, speaks, operates, protects, and guides.

"So Jesus answered and said to them, 'My doctrine is not Mine, but His Who sent Me. If anyone wills to do His will, he shall know concerning the doctrine, whether it is from God or whether I speak on My own authority'" (John 7:16-17 NKJV). Miracles happen, doors open, spiritual insight is bestowed, and hidden things are made known when we walk with Him Whom no man has seen or can see. "No one has seen God at any time. The only begotten Son, Who is in the bosom of the Father, He has declared *Him*" (John 1:18 NKJV).

"Jesus answered and said to him, 'Blessed are you, Simon Bar-Jonah, for flesh and blood has not revealed this to you, but My Father Who is in heaven'" (Matthew 16:17 NKJV). Not everything is revealed by flesh and blood. Not everything that is to be known only comes from the physical realm, our senses, or information that can be gathered by communicating with other people. No, God in Heaven can speak to us and give us the capacity to learn His Voice and receive insight that could not be obtained in any other manner.

Blessed are we when the Heavenly Father speaks to us directly. I have seen this happen. Though it may be rare and far between, He can and will. All Three Persons of the Trinity continually communicate with Each Other and with us. They are continuously engaged and involved with Their creation and Their creatures. We are made in God's image, and He loves us.

Will not the God of all do right? Will He not protect us and reveal what must be shown to keep us from going in the way of harm?

May we never lean on the arms of the flesh, but on God alone, for He will never fail us. He has never failed us.

Truly, when we are in Christ, He is with us, from now into eternity. Blessed be the One and Only God, the Trinity.

———

God in Heaven, Who is Omniinvulgent, Who informs man of what is to come, what is being done, what will occur, what man intends toward us, whether for us or against us, You alone are the Great Discerner of the hearts and the God of Love. Truly, You desire to do more for us and in us than we desire in ourselves. God, You alone are the Great Sovereign and Blessed Sustainer Whose Glory can be seen throughout all creation. You speak in the depths of the soul and see the deep creatures of the sea. You rise the humble up and You see the caps of every mountain. You give breath to our lungs, and You guide the winds that breeze upon the lilies of the valley. Your Presence is upon us who are born-again, and we bless You for continually consecrating us and saving us from our sin. God, open our ears to Thy Divine instruction. Teach us Your movement, speaking, and directing. Guide us into all truth and may we listen to the Spirit. Touch our mind and soul to think and will what is of You. God, give us the strength to listen to the Spirit speaking to our conscience and may we continually make the right decision. Not in our own might, but by the Power of the Holy Spirit. Thank You for showing us what reality is and not allowing us to be misguided with what we think it is. For You are Truth and You are for us. May we listen to You alone, O God, the Revealer of the hidden things of life, the chambers of men's hearts, the future to come, the intentions of others, and spiritual matters. We desire Your Will, O God. Come forth like a mighty current, Holy Spirit. We submit and surrender ourselves to You, asking that Your Divine Flame would enlighten our minds, purify our souls, and illuminate our spirits to be sanctified vessels, holy and righteous by You and for You, as we walk amongst men. May we find favor amongst You and men, Lord God, for being those who are not of this world, but living for You, the only Eternal Sovereign, Righteous King, Just Ruler, and Beautiful God. In Jesus' name, Amen.

Omniclairvoyant
All-Foreknowing — Can Perceive All Events that Will Happen in the Future

"*Your eyes saw my substance, being yet unformed. And in Your book they all were written, The days fashioned for me, When as yet there were none of them.*"
— ***Psalm 139:16 NKJV***

God is Timeless and Eternal. Therefore, He foreknows all that is to occur and happen.

Before we were formed in the womb, God saw us. Before we lived out any days in the future, God knew us. "Before I formed you in the womb I knew you; Before you were born I sanctified you; I ordained you a prophet to the nations" (Jeremiah 1:5 NKJV).

God foreknows what we are to look like before we are born. God perceives how we will be, act, and think in all circumstances that are to come in the future. God alone is Omniclairvoyant and can see all that is to come, since all that is to come resides within Him.

When we think of God as Timeless, we know He is outside time. Time itself dwells within God. Since He exists outside the very dimension we reside in, He knows all that is to occur.

Many may think time is linear, but it is dependent and interwoven based on specific circumstances, events, perceptions, and externals. When we are bored and have nothing to do, time moves much slower. When we are behind our phones scrolling past things that make us happy and excited, time moves much more quickly.

Time in these two scenarios is the same, but our perceptibility and recognition of how fast it moves depend on our mental faculties and our capacity to be aware of what is occurring.

There is a correlation between consciousness and time. If someone does not understand their purpose, time will move much slower. If someone lives on purpose, however, and their purpose is found in God and what He has declared, then time will move faster.

Time and consciousness work in tandem. This is prevalent in our lives, but it is also seen in God's. God's Consciousness and Eternity work together. Since God's Eternity is not bound by time, but time was birthed out of God's Timelessness, then everything is at once for Him. "That which is has already been, And what is to be has already been; And God requires an account of what is past" (Ecclesiastes 3:15 NKJV).

Since God is Eternal, everything is in an Unbounded, Immediate, Absolute Present for Him. With this reality in mind, we see God is Omniclairvoyant and All-Foreknowing. God knows what the next day will bring before we enter that specific day. God knows the human interactions we will have, how we will feel, what will motivate us, and what temptations will come our way. God alone can perceive all future events that are to happen because they *already are* and have *already been* for Him.

"I say then, has God cast away His people? Certainly not! For I also am an Israelite, of the seed of Abraham, *of* the tribe of Benjamin. God has not cast away His people whom He foreknew. Or do you not know what the Scripture says of Elijah, how he pleads with God against Israel, saying, "Lord, they have killed Your prophets and torn down Your altars, and I alone am left, and they seek my life"? But what does the divine response say to him? "I have reserved for Myself seven thousand men who have not bowed the knee to Baal." Even so then, at this present time there is a remnant according to the election of grace. And if by grace, then *it is* no longer of works; otherwise grace is no longer grace. But if *it is* of works, it is no longer grace; otherwise work is no longer work" (Romans 11:1-6 NKJV).

God has always had a people. He loves them all, and even when life gets complicated, we know God has His reasons. For God not only knows what our future will be, He knows what future will come out of our future.

There are many opportunities that present themselves to us. We have the freedom to accept what comes our way or to reject it. Whatever we choose brings forth a different reality.

When God permits something to come our way, we can reject an opportunity and miss out on what God desires to do. This decision will result in a different future. For example, we might fail to ask for mentorship during a conversation with a CEO. This, in turn, could result in a missed opportunity. Maybe we had the chance of joining another sports team while growing up, but we chose to stay with our friends in a lower-level league. This could result in a lack of becoming the best player we could have been.

God knows all future events and the future of every reaction we do in the future within every different event. Of course, God is Sovereign and can make up for our missed opportunities. However, this is not promised for every missed opportunity.

The beautiful orchestra of life features God orchestrating behind the scenes and humanity navigating within the boundaries He establishes. We have the freedom to succumb to temptations or heed God's call. We can send that job application in faith or doubt that it will lead anywhere. We can think and choose outside God's Will or seek Him in all aspects of our lives.

Whatever we choose to do, God foreknows. He is never caught off guard or unsure. God is always in a continual state of knowing. He is Omniclairvoyant and knows the multiple streams that could result from one decision we make. His foreknowing is not just about what *will* happen but also about what *should* be (For more on the different forms of God's Knowledge, see my book Maximum Mind).

God doesn't just know what *will* happen; He knows what *should* have happened. He knows what we should have done and how we should have responded to create a better future. Nonetheless, God's

Ultimate Will shall prevail (that which He has declared will happen), even though His Perfect Will remains undone (God wants everything to work perfectly, but due to human freedom, this does not occur).

For us who are born-again, we know that we are the "Elect according to the foreknowledge of God the Father, in sanctification of the Spirit, for obedience and sprinkling of the blood of Jesus Christ: Grace to you and peace be multiplied" (1 Peter 1:2 NKJV). Romans 8:29 (NKJV) declares, "For whom He foreknew, He also predestined to be conformed to the image of His Son, that He might be the firstborn among many brethren."

There is this battle within certain denominations that we don't have freedom, but we, in fact, do have freedom. We will unpack more on free will in other parts throughout this series (specifically, in Omnifree (All-Free)).

It would be a much different scenario if Romans 9:29 said, "Who God *predestined*, He also *foreknew*", as that would mean God stamps "Heaven" and "Hell" on people's backs before they are born, and therefore He foreknows – but that is NOT the case. Romans 9:29 specifically reveals that "whom He FOREKNEW, He also PREDESTINED."

God foreknows all libertarian free-will actions of human beings. He knows those who will choose to respond to His call. Of course, He has the Final Say in discerning their authenticity in wanting to know Him for the right reasons. Then, God has the Ultimate Divine say by sending us His Holy Spirit.

God simply *predestines* those He *foreknows* are going to respond to His call and who He will make His elect, based on their authentic profession of Jesus Christ as Lord and Savior and their genuine repentance of their sins.

God's foreknowledge, then, is not simply what *will* be because God declared it to be so; it is also what He knows will occur without Him *making* it happen. An example of this is sin.

God will never force us to do what His Word says is sin. God will never make us do what is contrary to His Nature. He will never tempt us (1 Corinthians 10:13, James 1:13). God foreknows what we will do that is wrong, without Himself making that occur.

We as humans are responsible for wrong, sinful, selfish, evil conduct. God is responsible for the good, love, purity, and perfection that occurs. God alone is Perfect, and His Ultimate Divine Will shall be fulfilled, even when we have tainted His original design by the Fall.

"For there is not a word on my tongue, But behold, O Lord, You know it altogether" (Psalm 139:4 NKJV). All that is to be said in the future, God foreknows. He knows it before it happens, He knows the result of it happening, and He knows what would have been different had it not been said. This is true not just of words but of conduct, character, how we feel on a particular day, what a day will bring, all events, whether we go or stay, what time we get up, what effects lead to how we feel, and the like.

God foreknows what occurs before it happens. God foreknows what will happen due to a particular event or circumstance happening. This is what happened in the Garden of Eden.

When man fell, God knew that man would not listen. God knew that eventually Adam and Eve would eat from the tree of the Knowledge of Good and Evil (Genesis 2-3). However, due to knowing this future event, God already had planned to provide salvation for His creation (Acts 2:22-23). Though we failed, God already foreknew what He would *not have* to do but would *desire* to do out of pure love.

Let us give praise to the Holy One of Israel Who sees all. Truly, He alone is Omniclairvoyant. Though Hebrews 7:3 (NKJV) discusses Melchizedek; and though we are not entirely sure if Melchizedek is Christ, what is described of Melchizedek most certainly resembles the attributes of Christ. May we praise God that He is "without father, without mother, without genealogy, having neither beginning of days nor end of life, but made like the Son of God, remains a priest continually" (Hebrews 7:3 NKJV).

"Remember the former things of old, For I am God, and there is no other; I am God, and there is none like Me, Declaring the end from the beginning, And from ancient times things that are not yet done, Saying, 'My counsel shall stand, And I will do all My pleasure'" (Isaiah 46:9-10 NKJV). What God declares will come to pass. Eventually, the Book of Revelation will come to full fruition.

God is Omniclairvoyant, and what He has declared will happen. For all things have already been for Him Who alone rules and reigns Omnipotent and Sovereign.

"And if you call on the Father, Who without partiality judges according to each one's work, conduct yourselves throughout the time of your stay *here* in fear; knowing that you were not redeemed with corruptible things, *like* silver or gold, from your aimless conduct *received* by tradition from your fathers, but with the precious blood of Christ, as of a lamb without blemish and without spot. He indeed was foreordained before the foundation of the world, but was manifest in these last times for you who through Him believe in God, who raised Him from the dead and gave Him glory, so that your faith and hope are in God" (1 Peter 1:17-21 NKJV).

May all come to know Him Who is Omniclairvoyant and rest in the knowledge that nothing escapes the sight of God. He is Omnipresent (Everywhere at all times). He is Omnivoyant (All-Seeing).

Let us rest in peace, knowing God holds our future and all our tomorrows. "But as for me, I trust in You, O Lord; I say, "You *are* my God." My times *are* in Your hand" (Psalm 31:14-15 NKJV).

O Great and Mighty God, Who alone is above all that can be conceived and known, Who ascends beyond the Heavens, Who shines brighter than the stars, Who brings forth all elements, Who knows knowledge that cannot be known by man, Who can never be consumed or overthrown, Who has forever existed and remains as Almighty, You alone are Omniclairvoyant. O God, help us not to be anxious about anything, but in everything, come before You in thanksgiving and prayer. God, we need You each day, and You are the God of all days. Nothing surprises You. You have everything planned even before it is a reality for us! How great You are, Magnificent and Mighty One! We worship Thee, the Holy Trinity! Holy Spirit, help us not to worry about tomorrow but seek You today. Teach us something new about Thee. Move in ways that can only be done by Your Sovereign Hand. We trust in You, the only Wise God, Who alone is true. Be magnified, O God of the Heavens and Earth. We rest in You, the Omniclairvoyant One. In Jesus' name, Amen.

Omniaudient
All-Hearing – Hears All Things

"*He Who planted the ear, shall He not hear? He Who formed the eye, shall He not see? He Who instructs the nations, shall He not correct, He Who teaches man knowledge? The Lord knows the thoughts of man, That they are futile.*"
— ***Psalm 94:9-11 NKJV***

God hears everything said in this life. He acknowledges every cry, scream, heartache, pain, and suffering. Not only does He recognize these, but He also feels them.

God is not Impassible (the doctrine that God cannot feel). God does feel, and this is revealed all throughout Scripture.

What we feel, God feels. What we speak out, He listens to. What we say, He hears.

No place exists where God is not. There are no words exchanged that He does not hear. God is Omniaudient, and He alone can hear all things.

"Evening and morning and at noon I will pray, and cry aloud, And He shall hear my voice" (Psalm 55:17 NKJV). When we pray, God hears our prayers. God technically hears all prayers insofar as the words that are uttered. However, there is a difference between God *hearing* and *listening* to something.

Many people say their prayers, but they don't actually pray. Many people pray, but they don't pray to the One True God. Many people pray to the One True God, but they are not born-again.

Being born-again is the differentiation between God *hearing* our prayers and God *listening* to our prayers. When we are born-again, God *listens* to every one of our prayers. Why? We are covered by the Blood of Christ and, therefore, have privileged access to the Father. He *listens* to us because we are found in Christ and seen as if we were Christ ourselves.

Only the Blood of Christ brings us into a living relationship with our Heavenly Father. When we are covered by the Blood, the Holy Spirit descends on us like a dove. We are no longer just being *heard* by God; we are being *listened* to and cared for.

When life becomes difficult, we must not get discouraged. When our hearts ache and it seems as if God has abandoned us or does not care, we must endure. We must trust that God is answering our prayers, hearing us, and loving us!

Though we are promised suffering in this life, we know we are not called to suffer alone. Christ declared, "lo, I am with you always, *even* to the end of the age" (Matthew 28:20 NKJV). God tells us, "Fear not, for I *am* with you; Be not dismayed, for I *am* your God. I will strengthen you, Yes, I will help you, I will uphold you with My righteous right hand'" (Isaiah 41:10 NKJV).

God is with us, and He hears us. God listens to our prayers when we pray. He is on the move, either in how we have prayed or in a better way. God's alternative way to how we want Him to move is always better than how we pray.

God is Omnibenevolent (All-Good) and will do only what is Good. Since He is the standard of goodness, we can trust that how He responds to our prayers will always be good.

"You number my wanderings; Put my tears into Your bottle; *Are they* not in Your book? When I cry out *to You*, Then my enemies will turn back; This I know, because God *is* for me. In God (I will praise *His* word), In the LORD (I will praise *His* word), In God I have put my trust; I will not be afraid. What can man do to me?" (Psalm 56:8-11 NKJV).

Every tear from a prayer or due to life is bottled by the Lord when we are born-again. God hears when we cry. God sheds a tear when we shed a tear. God feels when we feel. God is the most empathetic Being. He cares so much, and He hears us, always.

"I have called upon You, for You will hear me, O God; Incline Your ear to me, and hear my speech. Show Your marvelous lovingkindness by Your right hand, O You Who save those who trust *in You* From those who rise up *against them*. Keep me as the apple of Your eye; Hide me under the shadow of Your wings, From the wicked who oppress me, *From* my deadly enemies who surround me" (Psalm 17:6-9 NKJV).

God rises up on behalf of the oppressed. His wrath is toward the sons of disobedience and wicked transgressors (Colossians 3:6). He hears the cry of those who suffer and are in pain. Though the Hebrews were enslaved for around 400 years in Egypt, God eventually arose from His Throne and poured out His wrath.

This is the beautiful reality of God that we love when extended to us, but we tend to despise when given to others. God is "longsuffering toward us, not willing that any should perish but that all should come to repentance" (2 Peter 3:9 NKJV). Before God acts in sudden wrath, He prolongs and extends mercy.

When we are in pain, we want God to rise up immediately. Though God is Omniaudient and hears our cry and prayer, He is preparing a swift vengeance upon those who have wronged us. He is prolonging His vengeance so that no one can have an excuse. When God acts, He does so justly.

We from our human senses may believe that the Hebrews being enslaved by Egypt for around 400 years is unjust, but all that time, God was hearing their prayers. Every prayer stored God's wrath for the Egyptians if they did not repent. As we know, there was no repentance but hardening from Pharaoh (Exodus 8:32). The Hebrews most likely believed God was ignoring them during those years, but little did they know that every prayer and cry was being heard; that every prayer and cry was a rising up of God's wrath toward the Egyptians.

This is how God operates. He hears all and prolongs punishment many times to turn people back to Him. God did this with Jonah to Nineveh, and Nineveh listened. Jonah 3:4-10 (NKJV) declares:

> "And Jonah began to enter the city on the first day's walk. Then he cried out and said, "Yet forty days, and Nineveh shall be overthrown!" So the people of Nineveh believed God, proclaimed a fast, and put on sackcloth, from the greatest to the least of them. Then word came to the king of Nineveh; and he arose from his throne and laid aside his robe, covered *himself* with sackcloth and sat in ashes. And he caused *it* to be proclaimed and published throughout Nineveh by the decree of the king and his nobles, saying, Let neither man nor beast, herd nor flock, taste anything; do not let them eat, or drink water. But let man and beast be covered with sackcloth, and cry mightily to God; yes, let every one turn from his evil way and from the violence that is in his hands. Who can tell *if* God will turn and relent, and turn away from His fierce anger, so that we may not perish? Then God saw their works, that they turned from their evil way; and God relented from the disaster that He had said He would bring upon them, and He did not do it."

Other times, people do not listen (such as the Egyptians), and God unleashes His wrath. Whether He relents from His wrath or pours out His wrath, He always desires mercy and sends Prophets to preach a message of repentance. "Or do you despise the riches of His goodness, forbearance, and longsuffering, not knowing that the goodness of God leads you to repentance?" (Romans 2:4 NKJV).

We must not allow prolonged periods of time to discourage us. We must not feel that God does not care because He is "not answering". God does hear, even before we speak it out! "For *there is* not a word on my tongue, *But* behold, O Lord, You know it altogether" (Psalm 139:4 NKJV). God hears immediately and answers in His time. Never is He in a rush. "But, beloved, do not forget this one thing, that with the Lord one day *is* as a thousand years, and a thousand years as one day" (2 Peter 3:8 NKJV).

Truly, "The righteous cry out, and the Lord hears, And delivers them out of all their troubles" (Psalm 34:17 NKJV). Truly, God "will fulfill the desire of those who fear Him; He also will hear their cry and save them" (Psalm 145:19 NKJV).

"Now this is the confidence that we have in Him, that if we ask anything according to His will, He hears us. And if we know that He hears us, whatever we ask, we know that we have the petitions that we have asked of Him" (1 John 5:14-15 NKJV). When we have the Holy Spirit, we are more prone to pray for the Will of God. When we pray the Will of God, God hears it and will act in the very way we prayed!

This is the fabulous reality about God–He is Good, and He is for us. If He sends us His Holy Spirit, then when we allow the Holy Spirit to lead us in our life, speech, and prayers, God will act and hear us. We learn the art of praying what is good, acceptable, noble, just, loving, wise, and in accordance with God's Will.

When we have the Holy Spirit and allow Him to lead, we can rightly declare, "But certainly God has heard me; He has attended to the voice of my prayer" (Psalm 66:19 NKJV).

"The Lord is far from the wicked, But He hears the prayer of the righteous" (Proverbs 15:29 NKJV). Even though the wicked may pray, they are *heard* but not *listened* to. Instead, they are immediately denied. God does not listen to the wicked and is far from them.

"These six *things* the LORD hates, Yes, seven *are* an abomination to Him: A proud look, A lying tongue, Hands that shed innocent blood, A heart that devises wicked plans, Feet that are swift in running to evil, A false witness *who* speaks lies, And one who sows discord among brethren" (Proverbs 6:16-19 NKJV). The wicked perpetually partake in that which God hates, and therefore God does not listen to them.

"For the eyes of the Lord are on the righteous, And His ears are open to their prayers; But the face of the Lord is against those who do evil" (1 Peter 3:12 NKJV). Clearly, God is Omniaudient and hears all things. Though His ears are open to the prayers of the righteous, 1 Peter 3:12 reveals that the Lord is against those who do evil. It does not say, however, that He does not hear them.

God hears the Enemy's plots and schemes as clearly as He hears the praises of thanksgiving from His people! God hears all the gossip and slander that occurs behind other people's backs as much as He hears the kindness declared of others amongst people. God hears everything people say, even the silent words uttered within the mind (Matthew 12:36-37).

Many times, we utter words and phrases to ourselves within our mind. We may think it is private only to us, but God hears it as if we had declared it aloud. The words of the mind are the same as those spoken out through the mouth. Whatever we think, are silent words hidden from others, but not from God. For God does not need to hear speech to hear the hidden words of the heart.

"Therefore judge nothing before the time, until the Lord comes, Who will both bring to light the hidden things of darkness and reveal the counsels of the hearts. Then each one's praise will come from God" (1 Corinthians 4:5 NKJV). Truly, "'there is nothing covered that will not be revealed, nor hidden that will not be known. Therefore whatever you have spoken in the dark will be heard in the light, and what you have spoken in the ear in inner rooms will be proclaimed on the housetops'" (Luke 2:2-3 NKJV).

The sooner we allow the truth that God is Omniaudient to sink deep within us, the more prudent we will be in our words, actions, and thoughts. We will not mindlessly or carelessly do, say, and think what we ought not. We will become wiser, knowing that God hears every word uttered in public or private, in light or darkness, in speech or mind, before others or ourselves in the heart.

Not only does God hear every word uttered from our lips and from within, God literally hears the Enemy's plots, plans, and schemes. God hears every form of contact uttered by Satan and his demons. God knows what they will say before they say it! God knows what they will do, before they do it! Why? Even Satan must go before God before he can do something (Job 1).

God is Omnipolyglot (able to speak in all ways), *Omnilinguarant (able to speak all languages), and is Omnicommunicent (All-Communicative).* Everything that is said, in whatever language it is said, by any means it is said, in whatever dimension it is said, in whichever realm it is said, is heard by God. God hears all and is never caught off guard.

We may believe someone who is deceptive with their words, but God heard their prior thoughts or plans before they spoke. God may permit them to deceive us, but God does not allow them to get away with their deceit! God will work on our behalf and repay and deliver us in His timing.

Let us always remember that God is Omniaudient. Let us never forget that He hears all and He hears us. He hears when we are happy and joyful, and when we are sad and lonely. He is our God, Lord, King, and Friend. God hears every word and, when born-again, accommodates us based on what we utter and convey.

God shows no partiality. He is keeping track of every idle word spoken. "'But I say to you that for every idle word men may speak, they will give account of it in the day of judgment. For by your words you will be justified, and by your words you will be condemned'" (Matthew 12:36-37 NKJV).

We must be mindful of our words and "Do not be rash with your mouth, And let not your heart utter anything hastily before God. For God *is* in heaven, and you on earth; Therefore let your words be few" (Ecclesiastes 5:2 NKJV).

"Let no corrupt word proceed out of your mouth, but what is good for necessary edification, that it may impart grace to the hearers" (Ephesians 4:29 NKJV). "Let all bitterness, wrath, anger, clamor, and evil speaking be put away from you, with all malice" (Ephesians 4:31 NKJV). Instead, let us "be kind to one another, tenderhearted, forgiving one another, even as God in Christ forgave you" (Ephesians 4:32 NKJV).

God loves us, *hears* us, and, when we are born again, listens to us. God is working even before we know what we need. He is always working, and He hears our laughter and sorrow, joy and weeping, gladness and sadness. He is with us in all seasons and will never cease to listen to the born-again believer.

The God of all is Omniaudient, and nothing escapes His All-Present Ear. May we go to Him in all things and with all things because He is a loving Father Who cares.

―――

God in Heaven, Him Who formed the ear and hears all things, Who formed the eye and sees all things, Who brought everything into being by

Thy Holy, Powerful Word and keeps and maintains all by His Sustaining Will, You are to be revered. O God, bless us with the fear of You, that we might obtain a heart of wisdom. God, grow us in the knowledge of You, that we might not sin against You. Holy Spirit, remind us that You are with us who are born-again, and You hear everything. God, You alone are Omniaudient. You hear our hearts and prayers. You listen to our words when we are born-again and know the Enemy's schemes. God, we are so grateful that You are Sovereign and entirely in control of everything. We give You all that we are that we might receive all that You desire to give. Bless us, that we might bless others. Control our mouths. Guide our hearts. Fill our minds with Your Truth and Word. We love You, God, and we thank You that You truly are for us and not against us. In Jesus' name, Amen.

OMNICONSCIENT
All-Aware – Aware of Everything at Any & Every Moment

"O Lord, You have searched me and known me. You know my sitting down and my rising up; You understand my thought afar off. You comprehend my path and my lying down, And are acquainted with all my ways. For there is not a word on my tongue, But behold, O Lord, You know it altogether."
— **Psalm 139:1-4 NKJV**

God is Omniconscient. He alone is aware of everything at any and every moment.

When we consider how much we are aware of at any given moment, we will see how little we are aware.

Take where we are right now. Consider reading this book. We are not necessarily aware of its weight or how our hands feel holding it. We are not thinking about our thoughts, meditating on what we have to do tomorrow, feeling the muscles in our left leg, or aware of how our body is resting against the furniture.

Greater still, we are unaware of how our eyes see the words on this page, how many words we have read, or how we might have a subtle itch somewhere. We are not perceiving how our heart is beating, the number of times we have breathed while reading, how much our belly is expanding out when we breathe, how long ago we adjusted to a more comfortable reading position... When it comes right down to the facts, we are not aware of much at all at any given moment. God, however, is aware of everything at all moments.

When God is aware of something, we can be sure He is aware of what *was*, just as much as *what is present*. God is always aware of our comings and goings, feelings and emotions, days and nights, good times and bad times, triggers and times of dopamine rush, and words and actions. God is constantly monitoring and aware of who we are, why we are the way we are, and anything and everything we can think of about ourselves.

When we look at everything we are – our body, soul, spirit, and mind; when we look at everything we have – our emotions, environment, parents, upbringing, friends, extended family, shelter, clothing, food, and water; when we look at all other factors about our makeup – our DNA, genes, heritage, ethnicity, nationality, skin color, hair length, eyebrows, size of our lips, the level of symmetry of our face, our height, weight, the amount of surgeries we have had, our brain functionality and capacities, neurological pathways that are strengthened, our personality, what we find humorous, our hobbies, interests, shoe size, what we find joy and satisfaction in, our dreams, goals, aspirations, what we think, what motives us and compels us to do what we do, our intentions, the way we reason... when we unpack all of these things, we see that God is simultaneously and equally aware of all of these things as if they were one thing.

God never *becomes* aware of anything. He is *always* aware of everything. When we become mindful of the weather, the temperature outside, the cloud that is going by us, the tree that is swaying in the wind, the moving grass blades, the bee that is pollinating, the dog barking in the distance, and the feeling of the ground beneath our feet, we find that we are only aware of a few things at any given time.

"The eyes of the Lord *are* in every place, Keeping watch on the evil and the good" (Proverbs 15:3 NKJV). Even in the realm of morality, God is aware of all that is occurring. For God is Omniconscient. He is not only aware of everything about us, but everything about others; not just about others, but about everyone throughout all generations; not just everyone throughout all generations, but the external world and how each person was treated, what shaped them to become who they are, and the good and evil they both did and received. God is equally aware of all these little aspects, which is why He is truly a Righteous and Just Judge (Psalm 7:11).

"Shall not the Judge of all the earth do right?" (Genesis 18:25 NKJV). Truly, God is aware of all that is and shall be instantly. That is why it is impossible for God to be surprised. God is never surprised, for a Being Who knows all and is aware of every single one of our movements, even before we move, speak, or act, cannot be shocked by our conduct, ways, and how we choose to proceed.

When we "have sinned against the LORD", we can "be sure your sin will find you out" (Numbers 32:23 NKJV). God is not merely aware of everything in a passive state. Instead, His awareness dictates His level of judgment and intervention. If something gets too serious and outside His Ultimate Divine Will, He will correct and redirect us through a series of chastisements, disciplines, and convictions. Of course, He does this all out of love. "For whom the LORD loves He chastens" (Hebrews 12:6 NKJV).

"My son, do not despise the chastening of the LORD, Nor detest His correction; For whom the LORD loves He corrects, Just as a father the son *in whom* he delights" (Proverbs 3:11-12 NKJV). When God acts, and it is not the most enjoyable, we can trust He is doing it out of love and for the greater Good. For God is not a dictator nor a lousy father who punishes us out of anger and wrath. No, God disciplines us in this life, but it is always meant to lead us (once again) down the path of Everlasting Life; namely, the Way of the Lord Christ Jesus.

"But He knows the way that I take; *When* He has tested me, I shall come forth as gold" (Job 23:10 NKJV). God's discipline and even testing are meant to refine us, mold us, shape us, and change us more into the image of His Son, the Lord Jesus Christ. We will not fight the momentary discomfort when we see God acting as such. Instead, we will praise Him for His lovingkindness and tender mercies to be longsuffering with sinners such as us.

Therefore, God always acts based on His awareness and what is perceived. He will take action if what is seen and recognized does not lead toward the greater good. If what we think, do, and speak goes beyond the parameters God has allowed our free will to participate in, then God will speak to us and bring what is necessary to get us out of our sinful, selfish state.

Of course, we can reject His discipline and conviction, which only leads to greater misery and pain. Since we can grieve and quench the Holy Spirit (Ephesians 4:30-32, 1 Thessalonians 5:19-22), we can be sure that we can prolong our suffering and even disrupt what God is doing – so much to the point that we either miss out on much, or we remain the same and enslaved to the very thing we are allowing to rule us.

Truly, God declares: "I form the light and create darkness, I make peace and create calamity; I, the LORD, do all these *things*'" (Isaiah 45:7 NKJV). God is not the Creator of evil since evil is just a privation of good. God, however, will bring forth *calamity* when disobedience is perpetually done. This is what we know to be *consequences*, which come from our sinfulness and disobedience to God and His Word.

God's Omniconscience makes Him aware of how He should proceed and act but also reveals His Love for us and His creation. "Are not two sparrows sold for a copper coin? And not one of them falls to the ground apart from your Father's will. But the very hairs of your head are all numbered" (Matthew 10:29-30 NKJV). Even the most minute things we do not know about ourselves, God knows, and He cares.

Though our hairs fall out daily and new hairs grow, God is aware of how many hairs are on our head from the moment we are born to the moment we die. He knows the number of hairs we will have when we are five, twenty-five, and fifty. God knows even the littlest details because He loves and cares for us. Truly, "the very hairs of your head are all numbered. Do not fear therefore; you are of more value than many sparrows" (Luke 12:7 NKJV).

Not only is God aware of the tiniest of details about us at all times, but He is aware of when we are aware. When we become aware of something, God knows we are aware of what we see, perceive, discern, or think. God's Awareness goes deep into the mind and the metaphysical realm, and He discerns what we discern. God knows what we know. God sees what we see. God is aware of our awareness.

God will speak, move, and act differently based on our awareness. What we are aware of can be used by God to get our attention. Greater still, maybe our mind is "blank" or drifting into "no-man's land". If this is the case, God can quickly speak by implanting a silent whisper within our minds. We can receive a revelation, innovation, or a random thought to pray for someone or about something.

God can change our awareness when it is "neutral." When we are not thinking about much and are in a place of quiet, we can hear God best. His Voice becomes the loudest when our surroundings are not.

"And when you pray, do not use vain repetitions as the heathen *do*. For they think that they will be heard for their many words. 'Therefore do not be like them. For your Father knows the things you have need of before you ask Him'" (Matthew 6:7-8 NKJV). God is aware of what we will pray before we pray it. Nonetheless, we should continue to pray.

We must pray for anything and everything, over anything and everything! God wants to hear from us. When our awareness channels us to prayer, God will hear our prayers, so long as we are born again.

God wants us to be constantly aware of Him. Though we are often unaware of His speaking, moving, guiding, and directing, God is aware of everything at all times. God is All-Aware because everything that *is*, resides within Him. Nothing can escape Him or go outside Him, and His Inexhaustible Mind is forever discerning, knowing, perceiving, and aware of all our movements; not just ours, but everyone's; not just everyone's, but the whole of creation and the connective web of how one aspect of life, whether micro or macro, affects the next element of life. Whether rippling through time, generations, or leading toward smaller or bigger situations, creations, or developments later on, God is aware of everything, its coming and going, and He lovingly and Sovereignly rules from His Throne.

"The Lord looks from heaven; He sees all the sons of men. From the place of His dwelling He looks On all the inhabitants of the earth; He fashions their hearts individually; He considers all their works" (Psalm 33:13-15 NKJV).

Glory be to *The Infinite Omni*, Him Who is Omniconscient.

———

Almighty God, Him Who is Omniconscient, You alone are aware of all things as one thing, at all moments as if it were one moment. You alone, O God, are the Instant All Who has always Been and will always Be. You alone, Lord Jesus, are King, Lord, and the Godman Who has provided the way for us to know You. May all come to know You, Lord Jesus. May all come to know Your Love, Grace, Mercy, Truth, and Holiness. God, help us be aware of the reality that You are always aware of. You know our coming and going. You monitor our standing up and lying down. You know what we are to say, think, and do before we even say, think, or do it! Truly, You alone are Omniconscient and Omniscient. God, help us to be aware of everything about You and related to You. May we always be mindful of Your Word, Spirit, and Voice. God, grow us in You that we may glow for You wherever we go. In Jesus' name, Amen.

Omniresponderent
All-Answering – Answers All Things

" *Call to Me, and I will answer you, and show you great and mighty things, which you do not know."*
— ***Jeremiah 33:3 NKJV***

God is Omniresponderent, and He can answer any question we pose to Him.

In our lives, we meet people of varying professions and skill sets. Some may be athletes, whereas others may be readers. Whatever the case, people can answer specific questions on a particular topic. With God, however, there is no limitation to what He can answer.

We can ask God any question geographically, mathematically, historically, psychologically, spiritually, or the like, and He is ready and able to answer. God does not need to think of the answer because He Himself is the Answer.

When God answers, He does not take time to reflect or meditate on how He is coming across. He does not worry about varying aspects that tend to plague our minds within conversations. God does not sit there when asked a question and say, "Mmm...well... let's see, I know this is a tougher Truth to be said. Maybe I should say it more gently? I don't want to offend anyone with My answer. Let's see how I can strategically say this with them still liking Me...".

God knows exactly what to say and how to say it before He says it. He does not worry about our feelings when it comes to tougher truths that we need to hear. God is Omnicurant (All-Caring). He truly cares for us, but Truth does not dissipate or become watered down because of how someone feels.

Therefore, God always answers in the right tone and with the appropriate level of conviction and firmness. When we call to God, He is sure to answer. He will reveal things that we have not known. Only He can always provide an answer because all answers are derived from Him since He has set them up.

When we look at 2+2=4, God created the answer within that equation. We think that the answer has always been and that God merely knows the answer. No, God not only is Omniresponderent; He is the One Who literally created the answer. Since He is the Omniformator (All-Maker), He therefore is Omniresponderent. Whatever has an answer at the end, God has both made it and declared it to be.

Answers do not exist *outside* of God. Instead, answers exist *because* of God. There is no answer that God must reach out and grab. There is no answer where He must go on the search for and gather additional information. No, all information is collected from within Him. All answers are readily available to Him Who is Omniscient and knows all.

When we learn to go to God for the answer, and trust that He will answer, He will, in fact, answer. Our questions, however, must be by way of wisdom and not feeling; they must be led by truth and not complaining.

When life gets difficult, we tend to shy away from God sometimes. We believe He does not love us (based on the moment we currently find ourselves) or that He does not care. We begin to question His Nature and therefore start to see with lenses that taint our sight. Rather than seeing God as Good, Loving, Pure, and Perfect, we start questioning His Nature.

As this occurs, we tell God of all the good we have done and how we "don't deserve what is happening." This is what happened to Job. In much of the early parts of Job, we see him complaining and justifying that he has been righteous. ""So these three men ceased answering Job, because he *was* righteous in his own eyes" (Job 32:1 NKJV).

Eventually, the young man, Elihu, rebukes Job and his three friends who were not speaking right about God. In Job 32:2-5 (NKJV), it says:

> "Then the wrath of Elihu, the son of Barachel the Buzite, of the family of Ram, was aroused against Job; his wrath was aroused because he justified himself rather than God. Also against his three friends his wrath was aroused, because they had found no answer, and *yet* had condemned Job. Now because they *were* years older than he, Elihu had waited to speak to Job. When Elihu saw that *there was* no answer in the mouth of these three men, his wrath was aroused."

As we read on, we see that Elihu rebukes Job and says, ""Look, *in* this you are not righteous. I will answer you, For God is greater than man. Why do you contend with Him? For He does not give an accounting of any of His words" (Job 33:12-13 NKJV). There is counsel to be had in Elihu's statement.

We often forget that God has all the answers, but sometimes, He keeps them from us because we cannot bear them, we are not ready to hear them, or our faith is being tested. In these times, we mustn't go beyond what is appropriate in our questioning. It is not wrong to question God, but it is a sin to dwell on the questioning.

Eventually, God has enough and rebukes Job. "Then the LORD answered Job out of the whirlwind, and said: 'Who *is* this who darkens counsel By words without knowledge? Now prepare yourself like a man; I will question you, and you shall answer Me'" (Job 38:1-3 NKJV). For the following four Chapters (Job 38-41) God rebukes Job and answers him by a series of questions that would humble even the proudest in this life.

It is in the difficult moments we may find ourselves inquiring of God, but He does not answer us. Sometimes, the *lack* of the answer *is* the answer.

When we do not receive the desire we seek, it is because God is creating something unique within us. God is equipping us not to be those who walk by sight but by faith (2 Corinthians 5:7). We can acquire and receive answers to our questions, but the "sight" of our answers is not what keeps us moving forward. Trusting in the One Who is Omniresponderent and Sovereign keeps us pressing forward toward the mark. It is believing that His Goodness will either give us the answer or refrain, which are to our benefit.

God decides when to give answers, what answer to give, and if the answer should be given at all, based on where we are, what season we are in, and where God is taking us. In Job, he never received an answer to his questioning, but God gave him double for what was taken. "And the LORD restored Job's losses when he prayed for his friends. Indeed the LORD gave Job twice as much as he had before" (Job 42:10 NKJV).

God always makes up for what is lost. During the difficult times, we need not become defeated. Instead, we need to trust that *no* answer, *is* the answer, until God says otherwise. The fruits that will come from this will equip us, mold us, and shape us more like Christ. Even in the Garden of Gethsemane, Christ "fell on His face, and prayed, saying, 'O My Father, if it is possible, let this cup pass from Me; nevertheless, not as I will, but as You *will*'" (Matthew 26:39 NKJV).

The Father never gave Christ an answer. He did not say, "No, we must proceed." No, the Father was silent.

There is a Haunting Holiness involved in no answer. God is to be revered, and His answer found by Him not speaking at all is a sure sign that something powerful in the spiritual is occurring. For Job, it was to be part of the 66 Canons of Scripture and to teach us all that God is always in control and is Faithful and True. For Christ, it was for the salvation of mankind.

Therefore, God's Omnireponderence is meant to do something far more potent than our comfort. Nonetheless, during these moments, God will be with us through them. "The righteous cry out, and the Lord hears, And delivers them out of all their troubles" (Psalm 34:17 NKJV). This delivering is not *immediately*, but *ultimately*. It is not in our timing, but God's timing.

"The Lord is near to all who call upon Him, To all who call upon Him in truth" (Psalm 145:18 NKJV). Let us call upon God in Truth so that we may receive help in a present time of need. Let us believe that "whatever things you ask in prayer, believing, you will receive" (Matthew 21:22 NKJV).

Did we pray to be more like Christ? Then we all must have a Judas, be persecuted, go through hardships, mocking and ridicule, and endure suffering. Do we desire to be godly? We must endure the chastisement, discipline, and conviction of God the Father and His Holy Spirit. Do we want God to have His way in us and to save souls through our lives? We must be willing to go into the wilderness and allow those that have been with us all along, who are not meant to be with us long-term, to leave, for many have been hindered by being attached to the wrong people.

Whatever we desire, we must be willing to endure the difficult times as much as the good times. God does not want to make everything easy. If that were the case, then what is faith? The worthiest lives are those that are tested and come out of the fire unscathed and cleansed.

We must know that "this is the confidence that we have in Him, that if we ask anything according to His will, He hears us. And if we know that He hears us, whatever we ask, we know that we have the petitions that we have asked of Him" (1 John 5:14-15 NKJV). May we begin to pray for God's Will to be done, not ours. May we understand that God has the answer to all things.

God will speak. He will answer. He is Omnilinguarant (able to speak all languages). He can speak to us by way of His Word, His Spirit, His Voice, an implantation of a "random" thought in our mind, through a person, a billboard, a friend, a book, a prayer, a dream, a vision... God can and will answer in how He sees fit and in his chosen timing.

Let us have faith in Him Who is the Omniresponderent One. God is truly All-Answering, and He will make sense of what we have yet to understand. May we stop trusting in man for all the answers, for man may master one thing, but God masters that very thing infinitely and perfectly. Not only does God do this for one category or skillset, but for all things. God can answer and do all things because He knows everything and created everything.

"Ask, and it will be given to you; seek, and you will find; knock, and it will be opened to you. For everyone who asks receives, and he who seeks finds, and to him who knocks it will be opened" (Matthew 7:7-8

NKJV). Let us trust in the Transcendent One Who is far Greater than any man considered wise, intelligent, or skilled in this life.

God has all the answers because He created them. May we turn to Him at all times and in everything, for He is a loving God Who will be with us who are born-again to the very end.

———

God in Heaven, Him Who oversees all and is both the Giver and Creator of answers, You are Omniresponderent. You alone, O God, possess the answers to anything and everything. You know all truths because You are Truth. You give wisdom to those who ask because You are Wisdom. O God, infuse in us the simplicity of trusting in You and believing You will answer. Equip us, Lord God, on this path down the Righteous Road. God, we desire to live for Thee all the days of our lives. We want to please Thee every hour of every day. God, give us the strength to fight the Enemy and not succumb to seeking man's approval. God, keep us from going our own way and desiring to have answers given in our time. God, may we know that one day is as a thousand years and a thousand years is as one day for You. Give us the confidence and assurance that You can answer all we need and provide the way within a single day. We don't need a ten-year plan. We don't need to seek the masters of our day. God, we only need to seek You, and everything will make sense and come to be as it should and as You desire it to be. O God, we love You and thank You for being longsuffering and patient with sinners such as us. In Jesus' name, Amen.

Omnijustificus
All-Right — Always Right & Incapable of Being Wrong

"*Moreover the* Lord *answered Job, and said: 'Shall the one who contends with the Almighty correct Him? He who rebukes God, let him answer it.'"*
— *Job 40:1 NKJV*

No one has ever proven God wrong or been in the right when wrongfully proclaiming "God is in the wrong". God can't lie (Hebrews 6:18-19), and it is impossible for Him to wrong, since all Truth resides in Him.

Who has rebuked God and been in the right? Who has questioned God and been found to be correct? Who has been proven just in the presence of Him Who *is* Just? There is not a single person who has questioned God and been found to be in the right.

Now, it is not a sin to question God, but it is a sin to dwell in the questioning. As Job, we can ask and wonder why God would allow something to happen to us. However, when we perpetually ask, we will find ourselves being rebuked by God in one way or another.

In Job 40-42, we see God appearing to Job and continually rebuking him. Why? Job kept questioning and presenting himself as a righteous man. Job thought he didn't deserve what came to him, when in reality, none of us deserve anything but Hell. It is only Jesus Christ Who saves and transforms, and what He Wills is the best for us. What He allows to happen is meant for the greater good.

God is Omnijustificus and always in the right. Not once has He been wrong, in error, or unsure of why He did something. He does not "test" something to see if it will work out. No, God always creates out of His Nature. His plans, ways, and creating are perfect, but we, as sinful creatures, pervert what God intended for good.

"What shall we say then? Is there unrighteousness with God? Certainly not!" (Romans 9:14 NKJV). "The Lord is righteous in all His ways, Gracious in all His works" (Psalm 145:17 NKJV). Everything God does is correct. We may not understand it, but God has never been proven to do something wrong.

When God created libertarian freewill creatures, He did so out of love. Since true love is freely given and freely offered, there was no other way than to place the Tree of the Knowledge of Good and Evil. "And the LORD God commanded the man, saying, "Of every tree of the garden you may freely eat; but of the tree of the knowledge of good and evil you shall not eat, for in the day that you eat of it you shall surely die'" (Genesis 2:16-17 NKJV).

God allowed Adam and Eve to freely disobey, even though they did not know the ramifications of what would happen if they did. God was not wrong with placing the Tree of the Knowledge of Good and Evil there; in the same way, we are not wrong to warn our children not to do certain acts, lest they hurt themselves. Nevertheless, we cannot monitor our children 24/7. Eventually we must allow them to become their own person who takes responsibility for their actions.

We as the parents may raise a child well, but in the end, we are not responsible for every act they do or every word they say. Each of us has our own identity in God and it is essential to know that love allows people to embrace themselves as they have been created. True love does not continually force one to do something, nor does it force one to begin with. True love provides the opportunity and opens the door for one to love back, even though that does not always happen.

God was entirely justified in placing the Tree of the Knowledge of

Good and Evil in the Garden because He wanted His creation to love Him back freely. When they disobeyed, they were entirely responsible, not God. God is always in the right, even when His creation is in the wrong.

"He is the Rock, His work is perfect; For all His ways are justice, A God of truth and without injustice; Righteous and upright is He" (Deuteronomy 32:4 NKJV). When God's Nature is revealed to man, He not only brings forth that very thing but He Is that very thing in its Absolute, Ultimate, Infinite sense. When we are told God is Truth, we see that all truth comes from Him, and He Himself is the Absolute, Ultimate, Infinite Source of Truth. He Himself is Truth.

When a Being is Himself Truth, Who we know is God alone, we can be sure He is never wrong. When we pray to God, we know that all His ways are just, and He cannot be wrong. If He cannot be in the wrong, then His guidance is secure.

What He declares, reveals, and guides us toward or leads us in is the right way. It does not mean it is the most exciting, appealing, or enjoyable way. Nevertheless, it is the right way.

God is Omnijustificus, and He will never be capable of being wrong. For to be wrong is against His very Nature. Knowing this, we should run to God in prayer. We should contemplate Him and "Be anxious for nothing, but in everything by prayer and supplication, with thanksgiving, let your requests be made known to God" knowing that "the peace of God, which surpasses all understanding, will guard your hearts and minds through Christ Jesus" (Philippians 4:6-7 NKJV).

When we ask God if we should marry such and such a person, He will not give a wrong answer. When we ask God what His Will is for our lives, He will not lie. When we are unsure if we should let a friend go, God will not make us wonder. When life becomes unclear about our purpose, God will not deceive us.

In everything, God is Truthful. In any question, God brings a correct answer.

God is Omniresponderent (All-Answering). As there is no question He cannot answer, we find that the answers He provides are always correct.

We may believe there are "gray areas" in life, but there are no gray areas for God. When God speaks, it is the path that leads to everlasting life, the way that leads us down the Righteous Road, and the revealment of what is, despite our original thoughts, viewpoints, or uncertainties.

We can trust that God's answers are always correct. God cannot be wrong, and although we may not understand what He declares, we should move forward in striving to fulfill it. If God tells us to do something contrary to our original beliefs or different from what our parents told us, we can be sure we are on the right track when we follow Him.

"'For My thoughts *are* not your thoughts, Nor *are* your ways My ways,' says the LORD. 'For *as* the heavens are higher than the earth, So are My ways higher than your ways, And My thoughts than your thoughts'" (Isaiah 55:8-9 NKJV).

If what God reveals, declares, or answers is not in line with our thoughts or ways, we can be sure we are wrong. Of course, Him Who ascends beyond the Heavens and the Earth has more excellent thoughts than ours. Of course, Him Who is Timeless knows what should be done for the best outcome. Do we, finite and bound by temporal bodies and limited in many ways, honestly believe our way is always right? Do we truly think we know better than Him Who is *The Infinite Omni*?

Truly, "The statutes of the Lord are right, rejoicing the heart; The commandment of the Lord is pure, enlightening the eyes" (Psalm 19:8 NKJV). Our flesh may not agree with what God has declared, but it never was supposed to agree to begin with – our flesh is to die! Our carnality is to be dismissed! We are not to give into temptation, but to seek God to deliver us from all evil, sin, temptation, and error!

When God gives a command, He does so to protect us. Too many times we don't listen to God, and we wonder why we are being abused in a relationship, why a family dynamic is unhealthy, why we haven't grown or progressed, and why we are down and depressed. If we actually listened to God and believed He was Omnijustificus and acted upon what He commands, we would be much more at peace. Not peaceful always, externally, but peaceful, internally. This is the most incredible peace one can have: No matter what happens in the world around us, we have the Holy Spirit alive and active within us!

"Tell and bring forth your case; Yes, let them take counsel together. Who has declared this from ancient time? Who has told it from that time? Have not I, the Lord? And there is no other God besides Me, A just God and a Savior; There is none besides Me" (Isaiah 45:21 NKJV). What is and comes to be has been declared by God from ancient times past.

We often want to go with our opinions, our viewpoints, what others have to say, an internet search, answers from our parents, extended family, mentors, or friends. Little do we realize that those who can communicate and voice an answer have been created by Him Who is The Answer and Who possesses all answers! Seldomly, do we go to the Source of all Truth Who is incapable of being wrong and is always right in all He does and declares!

If we learn to go to God first and wait upon Him, we will quickly find that all the right answers are within Him. "Shall not the Judge of all the earth do right?" (Genesis 18:25 NKJV).

God is always right not only in what He declares, speaks, or commands, but in what He does. When God brings forth judgment, it is always correct and just. There is no time when God acts that one can say, "God, You are in the wrong! You are being unfair! You don't know what You are doing!" No one has proven this reality, no matter how hard they try.

That is why the continual debate among Atheists is, "If God is good, why does He allow evil?" That question presupposes that God already exists. One does not ask why something would allow something else to happen unless, either directly through the conscious mind or indirectly through the subconscious mind, they believe that something could well exist.

We don't ask questions that presuppose something isn't real. We don't ask, "How big is Big Foot's foot?" or "How fast does Santa's sleigh go?"

Since this is the case, to ask, "Why does God allow evil?" automatically presupposes God. The very question gives evidence that God exists. The question is not about the Existence of God but a question about His Nature. Just as we ask, "How could that father allow his child to act 'such and such' a way?", so too is it with us questioning why God allows evil.

Knowing this, we come to find that He Who created all knows what must happen *to* all, what must be permitted *by* all, and knows when to intervene, bring forth justice, prolong justice, and when to show grace and mercy. All that God does is exercised by His Perfect Nature, and beings of imperfection cannot question Him Who Is Perfection.

When we think we have the correct answer and seek to instruct God how to do something, can we see what has been done in days prior by all aspects, angles, and perspectives? Do we know the thoughts and intentions of people's hearts? Do we see that allowing a particular evil will actually bring out a greater good; and if that evil were taken away, a greater good would not come about? Look at what happened to Christ!

We all could conclude that what He went through and endured was unfair and unjust. We all would seem in the right by telling God, "How could You allow Your Perfect Son to go through this? Do you not love Him? What Father would allow something so horrendous and so horrifying to occur to His Own?" We would think we were in the right, when we would be in the wrong.

Little would we know if we saw all that unfolding in the present, that Christ would be the Way for salvation. That by the Father forsaking Him was actually opening up the opportunity for salvation to be offered to all mankind!

"Whom God set forth as a propitiation by His blood, through faith, to demonstrate His righteousness, because in His forbearance God had passed over the sins that were previously committed, to demonstrate at the present time His righteousness, that He might be just and the justifier of the one who has faith in Jesus" (Romans 3:25-26 NKJV).

When we think God is doing something wrong, we can be sure that *we* are in the wrong. A simple meditation that we are in time, not Timeless; finite, not Infinite; imperfect, not Perfect; prone to sin and fall, and not the Ruler and Creator of all, will give us clarity to never question God, Who is Perfect and Omnijustificus. "Righteous are You, O Lord, And upright are Your judgments" (Psalm 119:137 NKJV).

God sees the whole scope of all that is. His vantage point is entirely differentiated from ours. Everything we are and participate in is localized and bound by the laws around us. Everything about God is Unrestricted, Unbounded, and Unlimited.

Let us never deceptively believe we know better than God, for He

Who is Uncreated created us. We operate based upon the laws He has declared. Our very identity and being cannot be understood or upheld without Him sustaining us moment by moment.

Let us declare as David, "I will extol You, my God, O King; And I will bless Your name forever and ever. Every day I will bless You, And I will praise Your name forever and ever. Great *is* the LORD, and greatly to be praised; And His greatness *is* unsearchable" (Psalm 145:1-3 NKJV).

Praise be to Him, Who is Omnijustificus.

―――

God in Heaven, Unbounded and Unlimited, Who cannot error and is incapable of being wrong, Who alone is Truth and every man a liar, Who is the Invisible Bedrock and Foundation behind all things, You alone are Omnijustificus. You alone, O God, speak what is true, do what is right, and create out of Your Perfection. You alone are Almighty, Creator of the Heavens and the Earth. Who can deceive You, O God? Who can question Your ways? Is not man feeble, finite, and flawed? O God, keep us humble before You and bless us with child-like faith. May we not lean on the arms of the flesh, but upon You. Even when we do not understand, remind us of Your Nature and Faithfulness. You are Just and will never lead us into temptation. You always provide a way of escape. God On High, encourage, strengthen, and guide us into all that is of You. We want to do what is right. We depend on You and believe in You, O Lord, Who alone is Omnijustificus. In Jesus' name, Amen.

Omnirespondent
All-Responding – Always Knows How to Respond

"*The Lord is near to all who call upon Him, To all who call upon Him in truth."*
— ***Psalm 145:18 NKJV***

God always responds to a multitude of requests, prayers, and needs in various ways.

Since God is Omnifacultas (All-Possible – God brings about anything that is possible) and Omnicommunicent (All-Communicative – able to communicate in all ways), He therefore is All-Responding. In whatever possible way it can be that a response can be done, God does so, effortlessly.

The way that God chooses to respond comes from a plethora of ways He could otherwise respond.

Whenever something occurs to us, we are responsible for how we respond. We can either speak or not answer, become upset or discouraged, be joyful or strive to see the good. Whatever happens to us, we have a multitude of responses that unfold according to what is going on within us.

When we have childhood trauma, environmental issues, certain habits, particular family members and friends, and associations to specific groups, all of this can affect how we respond to individual matters. This is important to understand, as we are not perfect in every response we give.

Many times, we become angry when we should have been patient. Other times, we assume rather than seek to understand. There are moments when we are sad when we should rejoice. There are moments when we are happy when we should mourn.

In every situation and moment, we give responses. Our responses, however, do not always match the response that *should* be provided. This is due to many reasons, which we have already mentioned, such as being too focused on the present, too caught up in the past, or not having the ability to look toward the future.

When it comes to God, His responses are always perfect, and He chooses how He might respond from many ways.

When we draw near to God in *Truth*, God draws near to us. What does drawing near to God look like? Of course, we know there is a response, but what is that response? What does it mean? Yes, we know God draws near, but *how* does He draw near? Is it the same way each time? Is there any difference with how He draws near to us instead of others?

God is Omnirespondent. How He responds is based on His Perfect Nature and His willingness and desire to meet us where we are and guide us to where we must be. God wants to be our All-in-All because He is our All-in-All (whether we care to know this truth or not).

We can do nothing apart from Him but the very thing we have mentioned: nothing. We can do absolutely nothing apart from God's permitting, allowing, jurisdiction, and Sovereignty. Without God's Power, Will, and Spirit, we would be nothing. It is only because of God that we are who we are, have what we have, and can live and exist.

Of course, the only thing we can do apart from God (though God *sustains* us to do it but *does not cause* us to do it) is sin.

When we sin against God, we damage ourselves. We distance our outreach to God in truth. In exchange, He lessens His drawing near to us in a way that we can perceive and sensibly understand.

What causes us to once again have a closeness with God and have

Him draw near is repentance. When we repent of our sin, we reveal to God that we desire to live and draw near to Him in Truth. For truth is convicting, but it is also liberating. "Then Jesus said to those Jews who believed Him, 'If you abide in My word, you are My disciples indeed. And you shall know the truth, and the truth shall make you free'" (John 8:31-32 NKJV).

To abide in God's Word and with Him is to obey and follow what His Word declares and reveals. Of course, this is not in our own strength that we can follow in the Way of the Word, but only by the Holy Spirit. It is "'Not by might nor by power, but by My Spirit,' Says the Lord of hosts" (Zechariah 4:6 NKJV).

As we begin to understand this process of drawing near to God in Truth, we will find that God will draw near to us.

All of us have different walks with God. It is all based on the same Truth, namely, Him Who is Truth. The difference is as well-perceived as the difference and uniqueness of how we have been made.

None of us are the same, nor is our walk with God. This is because God can handle an incredible number of differentiations and effortlessly filter through numerous possibilities and variables. His very ability to do this exalts Him to new levels, heights, and realms which we know not.

Since not one thing is the same made by God, He therefore knows exactly how to respond to each aspect of reality that He has created.

Some of us may say, "If God just gave us (fill in the blank), then I would be happy". By God not responding to give us that very thing (either at all or not in the current state of time we find ourselves), He does so out of His Perfection. He does not do what we think because His response does not seek to meet instant gratification or spontaneous desires. Instead, God does what is most profitable for His Kingdom, His Glory, and having others draw close to Him.

"'And whatever you ask in My name, that I will do, that the Father may be glorified in the Son'" (John 14:13 NKJV). God does not respond to everything we pray for because, if He did, we would become narcissistic gluttons. We would feed off our wants, seeing God as a means to our own end, rather than seeing God as the Beginningless End.

When God responds to our prayers when we are born-again and pray in Jesus' name with all faith and not doubting, it is because we are praying out of a pure spirit. Our prayers which God answers are not of the flesh, but of the Spirit. This, of course, does not mean that praying for a new car is always of the flesh. What it means is that when we pray, God analyzes instantaneously and knows that which rules our heart and dominates our thoughts. He knows the motives of why we are praying for that very thing and what the intentions are once we receive that very thing that we are currently asking Him to give.

This is important to understand, as God does not always respond in the way we think or respond at all sometimes. This unperceived response, however, is the response. God will not respond to that which we pray for with selfish, carnal ambitions. He will not answer the heart that pretends to love Him, but secretly wants to use Him for selfish gain. God despises hypocrites and He will not answer that which would further destroy us.

That is why when God does not answer every prayer of the born-again believer, He responds in the way He sees fit. By not giving us what we pray for, He sanctifies us. He reveals to us that we would be destroyed if He responded in the way we desired for what we requested of Him.

"You lust and do not have. You murder and covet and cannot obtain. You fight and war. Yet you do not have because you do not ask. You ask and do not receive, because you ask amiss, that you may spend *it* on your pleasures. Adulterers and adulteresses! Do you not know that friendship with the world is enmity with God? Whoever therefore wants to be a friend of the world makes himself an enemy of God" (James 4:2-4 NKJV).

God's response is always for our betterment. The way He responds by not responding is a blessing, and we should not instantly come to the false conclusion or assumption that "God does not love me" or "God does not care what I think and want." No, God does care and wants to purify us from within. Only then will we ask what is in accordance with His Will, believe that He *Is*, and know that He can do far more than we could ever ask or think.

"'Therefore I say to you, whatever things you ask when you pray, believe that you receive them, and you will have them'" (Mark 11:24 NKJV). As God responds, He prepares us for how we will react, when

He responds. As He gives what we desire, we have desired in purity. As God grants our request, we will respond in thanksgiving and praise. We will not succumb to pride and indulgence. We will be grateful and see that God was more concerned about preparing us for His response than responding to our request. Preparation gives us the ability to hold well the gift that is given.

"And it shall come to pass that before they call, I will answer; And while they are still speaking, I will hear" (Isaiah 65:24 NKJV). Since God is Omnitemporal (Relating/pertaining to all times), He therefore answers from His Vantage Point before we speak and pray. His response is always ahead of our request, for He is not bound by that which He creates. He just at times operates in and through that which He has brought about and made.

As this truth is meditated on, we come to truly find that "That which is has already been, And what is to be has already been" (Ecclesiastes 3:15 NKJV). Everything has already been for God, which means that His responses and actions are already done, even though we have not perceived it to be done.

Prayer is answered before we pray. God hears us before we speak. The future is done before it arrives. What will happen is known and declared by God before it unravels. Everything that has yet to be for us, has already been for God.

This is a miraculous wonder, as the points in the frame of our prayers are bound only by us in time. For God, prayer from a born-again believer in someone's life is a linear line that resides within the sculpted dimension and realm we know as the space-time continuum.

God is All-Responding and His responses work backwards the same way ours work forward. God answers and prepares the way before we request Him to show us the way. God brings forth and sets up the appropriate circumstances and events before we pray for those particular circumstances and events to unravel.

Though God responds to us in time, His response is completed and done outside time. It is final, for that which He Sees is the Reality that will be. Anything else that could have been is God's Knowledge that never turned into His Sight. For what He Sees is reality. How God responds and what He responds to is what has already been made known or will be made known; what will be manifested and done or what has been manifested and done.

"For I know the thoughts that I think toward you, says the Lord, thoughts of peace and not of evil, to give you a future and a hope. Then you will call upon Me and go and pray to Me, and I will listen to you. And you will seek Me and find *Me,* when you search for Me with all your heart" (Jeremiah 29:11-13 NKJV). Though this promise was made and response given to a particular people in a specific point in time, this promise and response is also for us.

When we study the Attributes, Characteristics, and Nature of God, we find He truly has thoughts of peace toward us. He truly wants to give us a purposeful future. As we hope in Christ, we cling to the Ultimate Hope of God! When we call upon God and pray to Him wholeheartedly, He will hear us and respond.

This response will be different for each individual. How God responds is influenced by many external factors. He may respond to a similar circumstance in two different ways with two different people. Why? Everyone has experiences and been through different aspects of life. Each person may have responded to similar events differently. God knows this and knows exactly how each person will respond best to how He Himself chooses to respond.

The same way that God provides the appropriate, necessary amount of Truth for people to come to know Him, in the best way they would receive, so God responds to us in the greatest, most understandable way that we would relate and know it is God responding; not happenstance, luck, or coincidence.

God's responses vary based on many different situations. Still, He will respond by a Holy Ghost whisper, an intrusive thought, a feeling, touching our emotions, compelling us to research or go to a specific location, motivating us to write a book or build a business, the desire to connect with a long lost friend, an encouragement through Scripture, a peace in knowing He heard our prayer and is working, sending someone with the gift of prophecy to speak in our lives... God's responses vary from within Himself, as well as how He operates through His creation.

We must strive to "Ask" knowing "'it will be given to you; seek, and you will find; knock, and it will be opened to you'" (Matthew 7:7

NKJV). Let us understand that "this is the confidence that we have in Him, that if we ask anything according to His will, He hears us" (1 John 5:14 NKJV).

God does not simply hear, He responds. When it is in His Will, He will move Heaven and Earth effortlessly to bring forth that which has been birthed within us by His Holy Spirit. For just as we are vessels, we are temples. Though they be the same, our vessels exercise the faith, while our temples are sanctified by Him Who is Our Faith: The Lord Jesus Christ.

"'And when you pray, do not use vain repetitions as the heathen do. For they think that they will be heard for their many words'" (Matthew 6:7 NKJV). Let us never pray in vain but come to God as holy and righteous slaves. "And having been set free from sin, you became slaves of righteousness" (Romans 6:18 NKJV).

"But now having been set free from sin, and having become slaves of God, you have your fruit to holiness, and the end, everlasting life. For the wages of sin *is* death, but the gift of God *is* eternal life in Christ Jesus our Lord" (Romans 6:22-23 NKJV).

When we know God and God's Holy Spirit lives in us, we can listen to the Voice of God and believe Him in all confidence: "'My Presence will go with you, and I will give you rest'" (Exodus 33:14 NKJV).

God knows how to respond based on whatever we need to hear at that very moment. Whether we need a correcting, encouraging, or convicting word, or we need to be chastised, disciplined, sanctified, or saved, God knows how to speak, act, and move in a way that will bring about the best outcome, opportunity, and chance for us to respond appropriately.

Even when God responds in more painful and unpleasant ways, it is for our good. How He responds based on our actions is out of His Love and Perfection. His Knowledge and Discernment work out the best method and approach for bringing forth the appropriate response from within ourselves.

Let us trust God in how He responds, for He desires us to press into His Love and walk in the fear of Him. God is Omnirespondent, and He will only do what is in our best interest and will grow us in righteousness, godliness, and holiness.

Praise God alone Who is All-Responding and is for His people and desires all to be saved.

God in Heaven, Who responds to prayers before they are prayed, Who speaks before we speak, Who paves the way before we request the way to be paved, Who creates before we can think of something new to be made, Who brings forth inventions and innovation before it can be thought of, You alone are the Immortal One Who cannot die and the Perfect One Who speaks in Love, Strength, Honor, and Glory. God, Your Voice is like a multitude of waters, a manifold of angels, a countless number of storms. In Your Voice is Power, Authority, and Heavenly Holiness that goes beyond any sound that one or many can conjure up. Truly, the Heavens and the Earth quake at Your Presence. A simple step from You can destroy all enemies and shatter realms. A single thought from You can exercise all Good and Justice. A stroke of Your Hand can cast Hell into the Lake of Fire. A spoken Word from Thy Holy Mouth can roll up the Heavens like a scroll. There is nothing like You, O God. You alone are All-Responding. You know and understand all, instantaneously. You created everything that man has come to know and see, effortlessly. Truly, You exist outside even the thought of You. For mind cannot grasp what You are, for mind has been made by You, and ours are bound by the properties of how You created them. O God, You are Preeminent and Superior to all. None can escape You, nor can any revolt against You and succeed. Thank You, Lord God, for how You have responded to us, our conduct, our prayers, and how we go about life. You keep him in perfect peace whose mind stays upon You because he trusts in You. God, we place our confidence in You and we come boldly to Your Throne, giving thanksgiving and praise amid our requests. Respond in the manner that will grow us in You and will bless us with receiving that which You give in all humility. We seek You and trust You for all things, O Him Who alone is Omnirespondent. In Jesus' name, Amen.

Omnicomprehendent
All-Comprehending – God Comprehends All Things

"*Have you comprehended the breadth of the earth? Tell Me, if you know all this.*"
—*Job 38:18 NKJV*

There is no human being on the face of this earth that can comprehend everything; not even Satan, though he was great before his fall when he was in Heaven.

God doesn't just understand *why* things are, but He comprehends *how* things are, since all things have come from Him.

God comprehends all things and their relation to everything else. He comprehends both physical and spiritual things. He knows how the spiritual interacts with the material, and He understands why He has set everything up the way it has been.

God comprehends what is in men's hearts. He knows their ways, their steps, and the reason for their actions. God comprehends all things as one thing and all times as one time.

Only God can grasp, take in, and see all things as they are within less than a moment. Moments are derived from God, and not even moments fill the whole space for comprehension.

We use moments to take in and comprehend certain aspects of reality and what we come to know and understand, but God has brought forth moments themselves. Moments do not confine Him. Instead, they are derived by Him to encapsulate successions and intervals of comprehending.

Of course, our comprehension is different from God's. Ours begins by learning, growing, adapting, molding, shaping, developing, and moving forward into the future. Compared to God, however, His comprehension is immediate.

God does not comprehend things because He has had time to learn them. God does not understand and know just because He has always been. Instead, He knows simply because He *Is*. God Is Knowledge, Understanding, and Comprehension. All that He comprehends is at once because even the ability to comprehend came from Him.

This is difficult for the mind to grasp, as we cannot comprehend all there is to God. We have portions of knowing Him. We understand Him in part, but not *entirely*. We can comprehend how He thinks and what He does, but what we come to understand is just a touch. We do not have the whole picture, nor will we ever. However, we can come to know the Artist, Who is the Lord Jesus Christ.

The Artist is the One Who paints the portrait. Since Christ spoke all things into existence (John 1:3) as the Logos, we know He is the One Who can speak and reveal hidden secrets and mysteries. It is because of Him that we can enter fellowship with God in Heaven, Thee Almighty, Everlasting Sovereign Who alone is Potent.

"Would not God search this out? For He knows the secrets of the heart" (Psalm 44:21 NKJV). God comprehends the heart as if He were looking at a simple math equation. He takes in what is in the heart and knows it immediately. Even before something can be comprehended, God comprehends it altogether.

Before God creates, He knows what He will create, what it will look like, what it will do, how it will bring Him Glory, if it will be given free will, when He will have to intervene, what the beginning and end should be, how long it is permitted to be, when it will be derived, how it will be differentiated from other aspects, what its impact will be for the rest of the future, what role it played to bring forth other beautiful realities, how it aided in a greater good... God grasps what is before it comes to be!

This is the revealment of Thee Ultimate Inventor. For God alone knows with 100% certainty what will be and how it will be done before it is done and becomes!

It is an incredible understanding to take in once fully grasped. As God looks at the heart, He knows what dwells there and comprehends it entirely and instantly before we even come to be!

This is another marvelous, wonderful reality to God. He is Omnicomprehendent and can comprehend things as they *are* before they *become*, but He also can differentiate what is in different intervals within time while holding the ultimate, complete revelatory understanding within a moment. How can He do this? "For He looks to the ends of the earth, And sees under the whole heavens" (Job 28:24 NKJV).

When God searches and seeks, He does not *literally* search and seek. He sees all that is, as it is, even before it is. When God looks to the ends of the earth and under the whole heaven, He sees from multiple perspectives (we will review this more in the Chapter on Omniperspectival, where God sees all perspectives simultaneously).

God looks from both His and our vantage points, both inside and outside time. Therefore, when He looks at the heart of man, He knows it and grasps it in full. He sees the full layout of our desires and passions and how our hearts are and will be. He knows it instantaneously—the good, the bad, the sin, the genuineness, the mischievousness, the desires, the intentions, the motives, the wants, the needs... God sees it all instantly.

As God instantly views all of the heart throughout time, He can also instantly separate the simultaneity and view it in time intervals. This may be a confusing statement, but it simply means that just as God is outside time and in time at the same time, so it is with His comprehension.

"For His eyes are on the ways of man, And He sees all his steps" (Job 34:21 NKJV). God sees all our ways instantly, while simultaneously separating each step from the other. This is a tremendous ability of God that is found only from within Himself.

When we comprehend something, we do so through linear reasoning. We take what we know, compile it, ask questions, read books, learn, pray, and ask God, and eventually, things become known and understood. We can look back months and years later and grasp why certain things happened to us. Of course, the greatest comprehension we can possess is understanding what God was doing all along throughout our lives.

When we realize that the times of uncertainty, when we went through adversity, are now brought to light and God gives us Divine insight into why that occurred, we comprehend and become at peace.

The beauty of peace is that many times, it comes through understanding. When we can understand and comprehend, turmoil has a greater potential to end. Of course, what we comprehend may not be enjoyable. Nonetheless, when we perceive and apprehend why aspects of life occur and why they are, we can move forward in greater peace.

Of course, God is forever in a state of continual peace. Never, does His entire Being go outside the balanced peace that comes from within Himself alone. He is always in a continual state of peace. This peace is found in God's *knowledge*, while His *emotions* may waiver due to different circumstances of evil and sin that take place in the world.

Now, there is a difference between *feelings* and *emotions* (more has been written on this in my book *The Metaphysical Trichotomy of Persons*), but the fundamental principle is that God does not have *feelings*, but *emotions*. Instead of feelings, God has knowledge. God does not feel anything, He only knows it. However, His emotions vary based on what He knows.

The point we want to make is that because God knows, understands, and comprehends all things, even before they come to be, it places Him in a continual state of peace. His Perfect Knowledge gives Him Perfect Peace. When He comprehends all things simultaneously, He remains in Peace continually.

When we don't know or understand something, we feel distress and discouragement. When we are unable to comprehend certain events, people, tasks, or schoolwork, we become perturbed and anxious. "Anxiety in the heart of man causes depression, But a good word makes it glad" (Proverbs 12:25 NKJV).

We *feel* anxious because we do not *know* what is happening, why it happened, how to do something, or how to proceed or move forward. We *feel* anxious which then brings forth an *emotional* state of sadness. This sadness eventually has us *feeling* depressed.

No such cycle happens to God because, again, God has *Knowledge* and *Emotions*, not *feelings*. We cannot hurt God's *feelings*, only arouse in Him an *emotional* state of righteous anger. We cannot make God *feel* bad about Himself, only give Him Glory which makes Him have an *emotion* of joy. We cannot make God *feel* depressed, only bring about an *emotion* of sadness when we reject Him.

This is all important to know when viewing God's Omnicomprehendence. God comprehends all things and is therefore forever in a state of peace. He has emotions due to what He sees at different points in time while remaining entirely tranquil outside of time.

God's emotions range and are displayed to us within time, but from God's Vantage Point His Justice and Love are intertwined into one Godlike State that only He experiences. From within Him all things are known and experienced, comprehended and understood, exercised and done, thought and brought about, but they are differentiated from us. For we are in time, and God is Timeless.

"'Let your heart retain my words; Keep my commands, and live. Get wisdom! Get understanding!'" (Proverbs 4:4-5 NKJV). We are called to press into God and request of Him His Divine Counsel and Wisdom.

When we fail to go to God, we fail to comprehend what could otherwise be known. The only reason *Infinite Omni* was written is because I sought God continually to know more about Him. I was less concerned with the things of this world and wanted a deeper revelation of Him that no one had known before. I was tired of people using the same lingo, remaining stuck on the same revelations, stealing from others in their sermons, and not having anything new.

Of course, this was not the case for everyone, but it was most undoubtedly widespread and the majority. Men talking about other men's quotes and what they found, but not having anything that came directly from the Throne of God! They would listen to sermon after sermon but became numb to the direct Counsel and Voice of the Holy Spirit!

Infinite Omni is a direct testimony of God's Faithfulness and willingness to bless those with greater comprehension of Him, when the desire is to know Him more. When we seek revelation of God from God, God will bless us with minds to know, comprehend, and receive greater understanding of Him.

Let us never drift into comprehending things in our own strength. Many times, for example, what we thought we comprehended about a person, we did not actually know. The times we thought we knew, we were mistaken. We had only part of the story. We only saw things for what they were on the surface, but did not know intentions. Even if we discerned motives, we did not perceive that spiritual implications and childhood traumas affected certain states of individuals. Greater still, we may have understood these realities but lacked the ability to know which was coming forth at which time.

"Let your eyes look straight ahead, And your eyelids look right before you. Ponder the path of your feet, And let all your ways be established. Do not turn to the right or the left; Remove your foot from evil" (Proverbs 4:25-27 NKJV). Our comprehension of aspects, situations, people, and realities will be known when we go to Him Who is All-Knowing. Our ways will be right and secure when we go to Him Who is Our Security.

We can trust in God that when we go to Him, He will answer. "'Call to Me, and I will answer you, and show you great and mighty things, which you do not know'" (Jeremiah 33:3 NKJV). "The secret *things belong* to the Lord our God" (Deuteronomy 29:29 NKJV).

Let us seek to increase our comprehension from Him Who is All-Comprehending. Let us request of God to comprehend Him more, for from Him flows the Rivers of Life. In Him, all things make sense.

When we start with God, we experience peace in our steps, joy in our hearts, understanding in our minds, wisdom in our words, generosity in our hands, and purity in our intentions. When we comprehend God more, we will trust in ourselves less and put to rest the lusts of the flesh. We will see the beauty of Him Who is the Heavenly Vision, the Divine Architect, the Infinite Revelation.

We will set aside every evil thing and desire holiness and righteousness. We will place our faith, belief, trust, and hope in Christ, knowing that we comprehend but little when compared to the

Unending Ascension of Him Who cannot be fully grasped, known, or seen.

Glory be to the Only Omnicomprehenedent, Who alone is God Almighty.

———

God in Heaven, Him Who transcends the Heavens and cannot be fully known or comprehended, Who knows all things in a moment, Who does not waiver and is never uncertain, Who cannot do wrong and forever remains Perfect and Pure, You alone are All-Comprehending and see all things in their entirety and in successive intervals and moments, instantaneously. You do not grow weary and tired of what You know, but Knowledge is of You and all things have been created by You. The only reason You comprehend is because You are Comprehension and You created that which can be comprehended. Before anything was, You already knew it altogether. Truly, Your Ways are Impeccable and Your Word is Immutable. Only You, the Great Sovereign King and Ruler of Heaven and Earth are not bound by anything, but forever exist outside that which You create. Truly, no amount of light can overcome You Who are the Light and dwell in Unapproachable Light. Only You can comprehend the past, present, and future instantly. Only You know what is in time and eternity, eternally. Truly, Your Sight, Vision, Knowledge, and Comprehension is unparalleled, unmatched, and cannot be duplicated. Thank You, Heavenly Father, Lord Jesus Christ, and Holy Spirit for desiring fellowship with us and preparing the Way of salvation. May all come to know You, the only One True God Who alone stands Immortal, Invisible, and was not created by hands nor needs anything from man. Praise You, God alone, that no amount of darkness can come against You. For light and darkness are both light to you, and the darkness shines as the day to Thee. Blessed be Thy Holy Name, O God of Omnicomprehendence. In Jesus' name, Amen.

Omnisapient
All-Wise

"To the knowledge of the mystery of God, both of the Father and of Christ, in Whom are hidden all the treasures of wisdom and knowledge."
— *Colossians 2:3 NKJV*

God alone is Omnisapient. He has all wisdom because He Himself is Wisdom.

Nothing that is *of* God can be derived by another; it can only be given by God. What God is, He must give, and what He gives can only be in part.

When we have wisdom, we possess wisdom because of God. We ourselves, of course, do not possess wisdom at all times and in all ways. However, we can ask God for wisdom at any time, and He will answer. "If any of you lacks wisdom, let him ask of God, Who gives to all liberally and without reproach, and it will be given to him" (James 1:5 NKJV).

Wisdom comes by way of God. There is the gift of wisdom, "for to one is given the word of wisdom through the Spirit, to another the word of knowledge through the same Spirit" (1 Corinthians 12:8 NKJV), and there is also wisdom received when we make our request to God and pray.

All of us who are born-again can receive wisdom and can request God for the gift of wisdom. Nothing in Scripture says we are limited to our current gifts (and for those who know my testimony, other gifts such as tongues and discerning of spirits were given to me by God once I was married). God has His reasons for the immediate gifts He gives, but nothing says we cannot pray for more spiritual gifts. "Pursue love, and desire spiritual *gifts,* but especially that you may prophesy" (1 Corinthians 14:1 NKJV).

We all should pray for more wisdom, but we should always remember that God holds and *Is* the Ultimate Wisdom. He will guide and lead us, but it is important to understand that we must not allow the gift of wisdom to override Him Who is Wisdom.

Some of us want wisdom for a particular situation or relationship or an understanding of what to do in the present or future. This, of course, is a good request, but not at the expense of forsaking God. Many times, we allow the gifts of the Spirit to override God Himself. We can begin to rely on the gifts and God's immediate answers while forsaking Him in the process of understanding.

It is a battle every hour of every day to allow no idols before Him Who is the Sovereign Lord and Ruler of all. Though it is a battle, it is one worth fighting. The desire to seek God for wisdom must excite us, but the answer must not take His place.

"With Him are wisdom and strength, He has counsel and understanding" (Job 12:13 NKJV). Truly, in God is wisdom. God knows what must be done at any and all times. He is never frantic or wondering. He is never pondering or wishing. God is Omnisapient, and He knows exactly how to apply the knowledge He has, wields, and *Is*.

Many people know certain aspects about a career field, textbook, random facts, mathematical equations, how to run a farm, aircraft, technology, raising a child, and caring for a pregnant wife. Many people know many things, but they don't know everything. To know many things does not automatically mean that the known knowledge is wielded well. It takes wisdom to hold knowledge and apply it to how it must be used.

God knows exactly how to approach any and all situations through His Wisdom. God knows what someone needs to hear, when they need to hear it, and how they need to hear it.

The same message to a teenager may not sink in with a parent, but with a mentor, it will. God knows how each of us will reply to any given circumstance, and His Wisdom leads us upon still waters and fertile ground, so long as we listen to the wisdom He gives.

God's Wisdom is not just given and applied, it is done in such a way where it can be recognized and then we have the libertarian free will to listen to God or to disobey.

In our disobedience, we cannot blame God, for He already warned us of the repercussions that would occur if we went the way our flesh was leading us to go. God already told us not to give in or go in the way of sin.

By God's Wisdom, He instructs us through His Word. When we listen to His Word, we will not suffer from our own hand. When we listen to the Wisdom of God, we will be amongst those who walk not only *with* the wise but *as* the wise.

"'Who has put wisdom in the mind? Or who has given understanding to the heart?'" (Job 38:36 NKJV). When man is deemed wise, we automatically give man the credit. Those who are truly wise understand that all wisdom comes from God. Without God, there is no wisdom. With God, there is wisdom.

God is the One Who blesses man with the ability to think, reason, understand, know, and apply. God is the Giver of Wisdom because He is the Wielder of Wisdom. When we recognize someone gives us wise advice, we must thank God for giving that person the wisdom we needed to hear.

Many times, God speaks through other people. He shares Who He is through the mouths of others. Other times, God speaks to us directly. Of course, God speaks through His Word, but when His Spirit is active within us, we have the Spirit of Wisdom Who will guide and lead us. We don't have to depend on man; we only recognize that when man says something wise, it is actually from God.

God's Wisdom is applied throughout all His creation. "When I consider Your heavens, the work of Your fingers, The moon and the stars, which You have ordained, What is man that You are mindful of him, And the son of man that You visit him? For You have made him a little lower than the angels, And You have crowned him with glory and honor" (Psalm 8:3-5 NKJV).

By God's Wisdom, He not only made us as man, but made us in His image. God could have made us in the image of something else, but we would have looked differently than we actually are in body, soul, spirit, and mind; we may not have been made up of body, soul, spirit, and mind.

God's Wisdom knew where to place each star and the reason for placing every star where He did. We might look at the universe at night and be amazed. It is a beautiful, magnificent sight to look upon the stars. When we know God not only created the stars but also, by His Wisdom, placed them where He saw fit, we become more in awe.

By God's Wisdom, He placed the stars where to go in the sky and all of creation. By His Wisdom, He "made from one blood every nation of men to dwell on all the face of the earth, and has determined their preappointed times and the boundaries of their dwellings, so that they should seek the Lord, in the hope that they might grope for Him and find Him, though He is not far from each one of us" (Acts 17:26-27 NKJV).

God's Omnisapience placed us at a determined point within time and space for a specific reason that He knew would fulfill His Ultimate Divine Will. Not only this, but God had the wisdom to place the desire to know His Creator within each man.

Never does someone not think at some point in their life on the more profound questions: "Who am I?", "Why am I here?", "What is Truth?", "Does God exist?", "What is my purpose?", and "What happens after I die?". Everyone has the wisdom to ask such questions because God, by His Wisdom, made it to be so within us.

We are beings who create, who have been made by our Creator. We have the privilege of knowing because the Knowing God allows us to learn, grow, and understand. We have wisdom because the Omnisapient One saw fit for us to be those who could apply wisdom given by Him.

What is the wisdom of God? James 3:17 (NKJV) declares, "But the wisdom that is from above is first pure, then peaceable, gentle, willing to yield, full of mercy and good fruits, without partiality and without hypocrisy."

God's Wisdom corresponds to His Nature. His Nature is the Eternal Foundation by which His Wisdom is applied and known.

All that God does is out of purity, and it is done through perfection. Though perfect things can fade (such as Adam and Eve being made perfect and then disobeying God and causing sin to enter the world), this does not make God imperfect. God is perfect, regardless of whether free will is used in the wrong manner by God's creation.

God's Wisdom brings forth clarity and insight. He alone is All-Wise and never unsure of how to proceed. God is always certain since he has created all things.

God has the wisdom to know the perfect time of all events and when He should act. God's Wisdom is forever with Him since He acts out His Wisdom through His Nature. God has the Wisdom to apply the knowledge of the appropriate time for Christ's Second Coming to occur, when to throw Satan in the Lake of Fire, when to call us Home, and how to impress upon the hearts of others to seek after Him and Truth.

Truly, God's Wisdom is in what He does, how He does it, when He does it, and where He does it. By God's Wisdom alone, He unleashes, speaks, designs, develops, reveals, applies, places, brings forth, guides, leads, and instructs.

God alone is the Greatest Teacher because He alone is the Unlearned Learner. He has never been taught and has never been guided. He alone builds, establishes, declares, makes, creates, and wills what is pure, good, upright, and beautiful.

God's Omnisapience is seen within everything, and we must learn to go to Him to receive instruction that we might be wise in our business, dealings, affairs, tasks, relationships, jobs, and the like.

Proverbs 4:1-27 (NKJV) speaks to us about the security and need for wisdom:

> "Hear, *my* children, the instruction of a father,
>   And give attention to know understanding;
>   For I give you good doctrine:

Do not forsake my law.
When I was my father's son,
Tender and the only one in the sight of my mother,
He also taught me, and said to me:
"Let your heart retain my words;
Keep my commands, and live.
Get wisdom! Get understanding!
Do not forget, nor turn away from the words of my mouth.
Do not forsake her, and she will preserve you;
Love her, and she will keep you.
Wisdom *is* the principal thing;
Therefore get wisdom.
And in all your getting, get understanding.
Exalt her, and she will promote you;
She will bring you honor, when you embrace her.
She will place on your head an ornament of grace;
A crown of glory she will deliver to you."
Hear, my son, and receive my sayings,
And the years of your life will be many.
I have taught you in the way of wisdom;
I have led you in right paths.
When you walk, your steps will not be hindered,
And when you run, you will not stumble.
Take firm hold of instruction, do not let go;
Keep her, for she *is* your life.
Do not enter the path of the wicked,
And do not walk in the way of evil.
Avoid it, do not travel on it;
Turn away from it and pass on.
For they do not sleep unless they have done evil;
And their sleep is taken away unless they make *someone* fall.
For they eat the bread of wickedness,
And drink the wine of violence.
But the path of the just *is* like the shining sun,
That shines ever brighter unto the perfect day.
The way of the wicked *is* like darkness;

They do not know what makes them stumble.
My son, give attention to my words;
Incline your ear to my sayings.
Do not let them depart from your eyes;
Keep them in the midst of your heart;
For they *are* life to those who find them,
And health to all their flesh.
Keep your heart with all diligence,
For out of it *spring* the issues of life.
Put away from you a deceitful mouth,
And put perverse lips far from you.
Let your eyes look straight ahead,
And your eyelids look right before you.
Ponder the path of your feet,
And let all your ways be established.
Do not turn to the right or the left;
Remove your foot from evil."

Wisdom advises us to do right, speak right, think right, act right, and have proper and pure intentions. It motivates us in everything we do and pursue. Of course, we cannot self-generate wisdom to do properly and purely, for we are sinners who constantly need God.

Wisdom truly comes from God since Wisdom was with God before the foundations of the world. Proverbs 8:22-31 (NKJV) declares:

"The LORD possessed me at the beginning of His way,
  Before His works of old.
I have been established from everlasting,
  From the beginning, before there was ever an earth.
When *there were* no depths I was brought forth,
When *there were* no fountains abounding with water.
Before the mountains were settled,
Before the hills, I was brought forth;
While as yet He had not made the earth or the fields,
Or the primal dust of the world.
When He prepared the heavens, I *was* there,

> When He drew a circle on the face of the deep,
> When He established the clouds above,
> When He strengthened the fountains of the deep,
> When He assigned to the sea its limit,
> So that the waters would not transgress His command,
> When He marked out the foundations of the earth,
> Then I was beside Him *as* a master craftsman;
> And I was daily *His* delight,
> Rejoicing always before Him,
> Rejoicing in His inhabited world,
> And my delight *was* with the sons of men."

When God Wills to do something, He uses His Wisdom; and His Wisdom is brought forth and creates by His Word. The Heavenly Father Wills what to be. The Holy Spirit gives Wisdom on how it should be, and the Logos (the Lord Jesus Christ) creates what becomes.

What, then, is the blessing that comes from having wisdom? Proverbs 8:32-36 (NKJV) states:

> "Now therefore, listen to me, *my* children,
> For blessed *are those who* keep my ways.
> Hear instruction and be wise,
> And do not disdain *it*.
> Blessed is the man who listens to me,
> Watching daily at my gates,
> Waiting at the posts of my doors.
> For whoever finds me finds life,
> And obtains favor from the LORD;
> But he who sins against me wrongs his own soul;
> All those who hate me love death."

""The fear of the LORD *is* the beginning of wisdom, And the knowledge of the Holy One *is* understanding" (Proverbs 9:10 NKJV). Let us go to God and seek His counsel and wisdom for all things. He alone is Omnisapient, and there is no wisdom apart from Him.

Truly, if we accept wisdom alone comes from God, "Then you will understand the fear of the LORD, And find the knowledge of God" (Proverbs 2:5 NKJV). To *accept* wisdom from God, we must first *seek* wisdom from God. In our seeking, Proverbs 2:1-9 (NKJV) reveals:

> "My son, if you receive my words,
>   And treasure my commands within you,
>   So that you incline your ear to wisdom,
>   *And* apply your heart to understanding;
>   Yes, if you cry out for discernment,
>   *And* lift up your voice for understanding,
>   If you seek her as silver,
>   And search for her as *for* hidden treasures;
>   Then you will understand the fear of the LORD,
>   And find the knowledge of God.
>   For the LORD gives wisdom;
>   From His mouth *come* knowledge and understanding;
>   He stores up sound wisdom for the upright;
>   *He is* a shield to those who walk uprightly;
>   He guards the paths of justice,
>   And preserves the way of His saints.
>   Then you will understand righteousness and justice,
>   Equity *and* every good path."

"Blessed be the name of God forever and ever, For wisdom and might are His. And He changes the times and the seasons; He removes kings and raises up kings; He gives wisdom to the wise And knowledge to those who have understanding" (Daniel 2:20-21 NKJV).

God alone knows when to do what and how it should be done. Whether it be creation – telling the waves how far they may go, how high to create the mountains, what seasons to permit in what regions based upon a certain temperature, the types of food needed to sustain life, what plants and animals are required in order to continue to be to provide food; whatever the wisdom needed to keep the universe as it is, the laws of nature required to sustain a life-permitting universe, the fine-tuning to sustain our earth and make it livable, the wisdom to develop the proper distances, sets, realities, and the like, God's Wisdom can, has, and will continue to dictate forever and create what is needed by His Will and Word.

Let us see Thee Almighty as the Omnisapient One Who loves, cares, and is willing to help us in all matters. "To God, alone wise, be glory through Jesus Christ forever. Amen" (Romans 16:27 NKJV).

———

O Omnisapient One, You are Great and Mighty, You have no limitations and nothing can exist apart from You. You alone know what to do with anything and everything. O God, what we deem unimportant is important to You. What we are not even concerned with, You are concerned and maintaining. O Great God, You sustain all things in existence. You bring forth realities that are known to us and have yet to be known. You truly are All-Wise and possess all wisdom. God, You alone are Wisdom. May we seek You for Your Wisdom to guide and lead us. Keep us, O God, from depending on the wisdom You give and forsaking dependence on You. May we go to You in all things, for You alone care about all things. God, we love You, and we thank You for loving us first. Open our eyes to see what is and what functions as is because You have declared it to do so and be as such. We want to receive deeper revelations of Your Omniscience and Omnisapience. Guide us into all Truth and expand our minds to receive greater insight and depth of You, The Infinite Omni. In Jesus' name, Amen.

OMNIINTELLEGENT
All-Understanding

"*Great is our Lord, and mighty in power; His understanding is infinite.*"
— **Psalm 147:5 NKJV**

God understands more than we know. This may seem obvious, but through meditation, one will find that *understanding* is better than *knowing*.

Knowledge has infiltrated our lives. We have become accustomed to being informed with much knowledge through technological advancements. We have the books, podcasts, videos, articles, and resources needed to find anything we would like to know.

Knowledge is excellent, but it is greater to *understand* than to *know*. God, of course, has the highest level of functioning in both, because He is both. If His understanding is infinite, so is His knowledge, for one cannot understand without knowledge. Likewise, one cannot know unless they have been provided the means and capability to know.

We may look at someone who knows a lot about marriage counseling, but they don't necessarily understand the deeper-rooted levels (or spiritual levels) behind a couple's marital conflicts. We may look at a scientist who spends his life understanding one aspect about science, yet they fail to understand the "why" behind the "how" they sought to know.

To understand is greater than knowledge, and God is infinite in both. He alone is Omniintellegent, and He understands the "why" behind all things.

If we get in an argument or act a certain way, God understands why that is the case. He knows everything around any act, spoken word, hidden motive, or secret thought. He does not ponder, "Now why are they acting this way? How come this person responded in the way they did? I know they said this to their friend, but I don't understand why they would say such a thing?".

We are beings who ponder; God is Thee only Being Who does not ponder. Though some people may not ponder, it is not because they do not have the answer to all things; it is because they are too lazy. God never ponders because God always understands and knows what is occurring. He is never shocked or surprised. He never gets caught off guard or marvels because something occurs. He knows it perfectly and understands it instantly.

"Hell and Destruction are before the Lord; So how much more the hearts of the sons of men" (Proverbs 15:11 NKJV). All of our hearts are exposed before God. All of our motives are clearly seen and perceived by Him. He understands why we currently are the way we are and how we respond to certain aspects of life.

Have we suffered from child-abuse? Did we go through verbal abuse from "friends" at a young age? Did our parents lack empathy in situations that hurt us? Did we grow up in a household where faith was not instilled in us? Did we lack "I'm proud of you" from our father? Did our mother see us as a burden to her extravagant lifestyle?

Maybe we were made fun of for our acne in middle and high school. Perhaps we were continually promised to get playing time on a team and our coach never followed through. Maybe we tried our best on our tests but could never pass. Could it be we have even been cursed and told "I wish you were dead" and "I hate you" from our siblings?

God knows all these aspects. Not only does He know, but He also understands how these have affected us in our lives and how they affect our responses and how we treat people.

God understands why we might have a guard up with everyone we meet. God knows how the abuse of our past has prevented us from thoroughly enjoying the present. Only the Lord Jesus Christ can understand everything about us and why we do what we do, say what we say, and go where we go.

Amid our trying times and need for healing, God understands our need for Him because He created us to need Him! God has never made something that did not need Him. All things depend on Him. All things find their dependency on the only true Independent One. Everything that is must continually be sustained by God's Will (Revelation 4:11). If not, it becomes dead, obsolete, and vain.

"Your eyes saw my substance, being yet unformed. And in Your book they all were written, The days fashioned for me, When as yet there were none of them" (Psalm 139:16 NKJV). Before we were created, God saw, knew, loved, and understood us. Before we were brought into this world, while our substance was unformed, we were precious to Him. God alone is Omniintellegent and understood us before we could understand.

Along our life journey, we find little doses of revelation about us. We begin to self-reflect and it becomes evident why we think the way we do. If we had a parent that continually suppressed us from entrepreneurship, but told us to "get a real job", then is it any wonder why we lack faith in ourselves? For those who only believe in a Roth IRA for saving, is it a surprise why they are not risk takers? A born-again believer who was only trained by Baptists, is it hard to believe why they don't believe in the gifts of the Spirit?

We must take time to understand exactly who we are, why we believe what we believe, why we respond the way we do, and how we think and go about life. When we ponder these deep-rooted questions, we begin to find answers. As we find answers, we start to understand. When we come to understand, we arrive at a point that God already understood – even before we were born! Truly, God's "understanding is unsearchable" (Isaiah 40:28 NKJV).

"*There is* no wisdom or understanding Or counsel against

the LORD" (Proverbs 21:30 NKJV). Since God understands all things, what can be devised against Him that He does not already understand? If God, Who is All-Understanding, created understanding and the capacities to understand, what can rise a standard against Him? What can prevail over Him? What can be thought of that has not already been known by God? What can be done to outwit Him? The answer is, and will always be, NOTHING.

O the Might and Magnificence of God! "He has made the earth by His power; He has established the world by His wisdom, And stretched out the heaven by His understanding" (Jeremiah 51:15 NKJV). God's understanding stretched out the Heavens, yet we deem a man great when he can understand why we feel the way we do. God's wisdom established the world, yet we praise man who has the wisdom to tell us where to place our finances. God made the earth with His power, yet we marvel at a man who can bench 500 pounds.

Meditating on God makes us realize how foolish we have been to praise man. Yes, we can respect them for what they do, but we must not worship or praise them for what they can accomplish. The only reason they can do, think, and speak the way they do, think, and speak is because of God.

Man's understanding is nothing compared to God's. Man's understanding does not even begin in God's eyes. We may understand a particular aspect that is a revelation to us, but from our All-Revelation God, that is one aspect of understanding that can be learned. *How* and *why* we are and exist results from a myriad of understandings. Yet, we pat ourselves on the back when God permits us to receive one aspect or realm of understanding.

If we ever deem ourselves intelligent and understanding in our intellect and might, may we quickly go to Job 38 and allow God Himself to convict, rebuke, and amaze us at just how little we understand.

Job 38:4-24 (NKJV) declares:

> "'Where were you when I laid the foundations of the earth?
>   Tell *Me*, if you have understanding.
>   Who determined its measurements?
>   Surely you know!

Or who stretched the line upon it?
To what were its foundations fastened?
Or who laid its cornerstone,
When the morning stars sang together,
And all the sons of God shouted for joy?
"Or *who* shut in the sea with doors,
When it burst forth *and* issued from the womb;
When I made the clouds its garment,
And thick darkness its swaddling band;
When I fixed My limit for it,
And set bars and doors;
When I said,
'This far you may come, but no farther,
And here your proud waves must stop!'
"Have you commanded the morning since your days *began,*
And caused the dawn to know its place,
That it might take hold of the ends of the earth,
And the wicked be shaken out of it?
It takes on form like clay *under* a seal,
And stands out like a garment.
From the wicked their light is withheld,
And the upraised arm is broken.
"Have you entered the springs of the sea?
Or have you walked in search of the depths?
Have the gates of death been revealed to you?
Or have you seen the doors of the shadow of death?
Have you comprehended the breadth of the earth?
Tell *Me,* if you know all this.
"Where *is* the way *to* the dwelling of light?
And darkness, where *is* its place,
That you may take it to its territory,
That you may know the paths *to* its home?
Do you know *it,* because you were born then,
Or *because* the number of your days *is* great?
"Have you entered the treasury of snow,
Or have you seen the treasury of hail,

Which I have reserved for the time of trouble,
For the day of battle and war?
By what way is light diffused,
Or the east wind scattered over the earth?'"

When we take time to reflect on the deeper realities of life, we will find God. When we begin to ask questions, such as "Who has put wisdom in the mind? Or who has given understanding to the heart?" (Job 38:36 NKJV), we will discern it is the Omniintelligent One alone Who has brought it forth. Why? He is *The Infinite Omni*, and He alone is All-Understanding.

Let us seek to know and understand God as much as we can, that we might know and understand much more about this life, human nature, God's Will for our lives, Who He is, and His Word. For the greatest knowledge, understanding, and wisdom to ever be achieved, is to know Him Who has created all things.

Blessed be the Trinity, the Father, Son, and Holy Spirit. Amen.

God in Heaven, Who alone is All-Understanding and knows all things in an instant, Who understands why things are the way they are and why they operate the way they operate, Who knows why people interact the way they do and think the way they think, You alone cannot be compared. You alone, O God, cannot be fully understood. There is none like You, nor will there ever be. You alone are Alpha and Omega. You alone are Omniscient and Omnisapient. You are God and we are man. O God, bless us with greater understanding of Thee! Guide our steps, direct our emotions, rule our minds, Holy Spirit, that we might know the Will of Him Who made us. God, we want nothing but to know You more each day. We seek You for Divine instruction, Heavenly counsel, and deeper understanding. Reveal to us what You will, and may we steward well all that You give. We love You, O Omniintelligent One. In Jesus' name, Amen.

Omnidiscretent
All-Discerning – God Discerns the Motives, Intentions & Thoughts of the Heart

> "*I, the Lord, search the heart, I test the mind, Even to give every man according to his ways, According to the fruit of his doings.*'"
> — ***Jeremiah 17:10 NKJV***

God alone can give what is due all men because He alone discerns the thoughts and intentions of the heart.

Who has lived to know the thoughts of the heart? Who continually is engaged with and discerns the motives of others? Who knows the true intentions behind all people aside from God? Truly, no one person knows what another man is truly thinking. None have access to the hearts and minds of men but God alone.

God discerns why we do what we do, the reason behind the way we act and what we say, and what our end goal and agenda is behind all that is done.

Many people do and say the right things for self-gain. We all want to reach the end of what lingers within our hearts and minds. We want people to support our way of life and believe in our vision. If people don't agree, we will do everything in our power to convince them.

This world desires peace, but the road to it can be dangerous. Many believe peace is achieved through tolerance of all belief systems and bodily autonomy. There will come a time when men will pronounce "peace peace" (1 Thessalonians 5:3), but destruction is imminent. In reality, peace is only found in one Source: the Prince of Peace, Jesus Christ.

Since the beginning, mankind has strived to become its own "god." It desires that everyone live according to its standards. However, those in leadership and positions of power rarely follow through with their declarations and promises.

Integrity and honesty are lost virtues. Without them, man will continue to hide behind what appears good, only to get what they desire.

"The thoughts of the wicked are an abomination to the Lord, But the words of the pure are pleasant" (Proverbs 15:26 NKJV). Those who are apart from God think thoughts that are ungodly, immoral, and unjust. Though born-again believers may struggle with their thought-life at times, they are continuously being renewed, adopting the mind of Christ. Their mind is being restored to God's original design when He created man in His image.

"'As for you, my son Solomon, know the God of your father, and serve Him with a loyal heart and with a willing mind; for the Lord searches all hearts and understands all the intent of the thoughts. If you seek Him, He will be found by you; but if you forsake Him, He will cast you off forever'" (1 Chronicles 28:9 NKJV).

God knows those who are truly for Him and those against Him. God immediately discerns if someone is preaching for God's Glory alone or vain glory. God discerns the reason behind certain people's messages. God cannot be fooled.

Though the hidden agenda of others deceive many in this life, God is never deceived. He is Omnidiscretent and aware of everything within an instant. He knows deep down what is harboring within man. He sees what is on the surface and what is lingering within. He knows what someone desires to be perceived as and what they are.

No one can defraud Him Who is Omnidiscretent. No one can keep the Omniscient One from distinguishing what lingers within the mind, heart, intention, thought, and will. God eternally knows all, from the visible to the invisible, to the motives of what one desires to display and the reality of what one actually is.

"Hell and Destruction are before the Lord; So how much more the hearts of the sons of men" (Proverbs 15:11 NKJV). If Hell is before the eyes of the Lord; if God knows who dwells there and what occurs there, how much more does He know what lingers within man's heart?

Man is deceitful, sinful, godless, and selfless at the core of his being. Man is not good. The world may believe such a notion, but Scripture declares, "As it is written: 'There is none righteous, no, not one; There is none who understands; There is none who seeks after God. They have all turned aside; They have together become unprofitable; There is none who does good, no, not one'" (Romans 3:10-12 NKJV).

Truly, God declares, "I am He Who searches the minds and hearts. And I will give to each one of you according to your works" (Revelation 2:23 NKJV). God will reward people, not based on external exercise but based on internal intention. God does not give to man based on output, but on the reasoning and spirit behind the output.

We could give everyone in the world one million dollars, but it would mean nothing to God if we are not born-again. Why? It is vanity if it is not done for God's Glory and led by the Spirit. It must be done in the Holy Spirit's power, wisdom, intention, and declaration. If not, it is led by the flesh, and the flesh produces nothing before God. "It is the Spirit Who gives life; the flesh profits nothing" (John 6:63 NKJV).

God is constantly discerning the reason why we do what we do. A single man texts a woman to get an ego boost and to see if he can achieve his goals through sexual advances and empty promises. Although he may be able to deceive the woman, he cannot deceive God.

God knows that the man is insecure and will immediately leave the woman once he has fulfilled his desire. The boss who builds his company 'on the backs of slaves' and motivates those 'slaves' through empty promises will inevitably face the Lord of the harvest, Who administers justice for the oppressed. Unequal weights and false balances are abominations to the Lord, and He will repay (Proverbs 20:23).

Everything that is done by those rich or poor, famous or marginalized, beautiful or unattractive, tall or short, intelligent or unintelligent, wise or foolish, a child of the Light or a child of darkness, God sees. He is not only acquainted with their going in and coming out and how they arrived where they are now, but He is also aware of what they continually think and do toward those made in His image.

We would do well to remember that the intention of our heart, the motive of our movement, and the thoughts of our mind are naked, accessible, perceived, understood, known, and weighed by God within an instant. From the minute we are born to our last dying breath, God sees it all as if it happened in one moment.

Truly, "there is no creature hidden from His sight, but all things *are* naked and open to the eyes of Him to Whom we *must give* account" (Hebrews 4:13 NKJV). Truly, "nothing is secret that will not be revealed, nor *anything* hidden that will not be known and come to light" (Luke 8:17 NKJV).

Let us pray, "O Lord, You have searched me and known me. You know my sitting down and my rising up; You understand my thought afar off" (Psalm 139:1-2 NKJV). Let us meditate on the reality that "the Spirit searches all things, yes, the deep things of God. For what man knows the things of a man except the spirit of the man which is in him? Even so, no one knows the things of God except the Spirit of God" (1 Corinthians 2:10-11 NKJV).

We must seek more of the Holy Spirit to rule us so He may lead our thoughts, lives, and hearts' intentions, for we are terrible leaders by our own wisdom. We cannot do anything for God in our strength. We are naturally far from Him.

It takes God to even come to know God! To live for Him requires His power.

As we walk with the Lord and we fail in our intentions, motives, and thoughts, may we know that He will not leave us in our weaknesses when we belong to Him. Will He convict us, discipline us, and correct us? Yes, but we need not remain in shame and guilt. "For if our heart condemns us, God is greater than our heart, and knows all things" (1 John 3:20 NKJV).

Our Creator knows everything about us, from the number of hairs on our heads (Luke 12:7) to the words on our lips before they enter our minds. He knows us more than we know ourselves. Before the beginning of time, He foreknew our darkest moments and rebellion, yet He still chose to send His Son, the Lord Jesus Christ, to die on the Cross for our sins so that we might be saved from sin and Hell and enter into a living relationship with Him. Hallelujah!

"For the word of God is living and powerful, and sharper than any two-edged sword, piercing even to the division of soul and spirit, and of joints and marrow, and is a discerner of the thoughts and intents of the heart" (Hebrews 4:12 NKJV). Not only is God acquainted with us, but with His written Word! The Holy Scriptures are composed in such a way that man will feel conviction, although God is not directly speaking with an audible voice.

God's Word is the only Book that can divide soul and spirit and discern the thoughts and intents of the heart. His Word alone can bring revelation to man of himself, forcing him to face the truth of his inner state of being.

The Lord may use others to pierce our hearts and bring us to our knees in humble contrition. However, He primarily utilizes His Word to speak truth into the chambers of our hearts, where we were once self-deceived.

Glory be to God that He is Omnidiscretent and that nothing can fool the Creator, Maker, Preserver, and Sustainer of all things.

Heavenly Father, Him Who discerns the thoughts and intentions of the heart, Who sees the invisible as we see the visible, Who knows all within a moment, Who perceives who man is, why he does what he does, and knows the reality and end motive behind all words and actions, You are to be revered. What can be hidden from You, the Omnipresent One? What can be concealed before You, the One Who is Knowledge and Wisdom? Truly, O God, man has but breath in his nostrils until the Spirit comes to ignite a holy, salvific flame within his being! God, we pray for a greater manifestation of You in us and around us. Help us to discern our own thoughts, recognize when we are in the wrong, and be controlled by You. O Great King, rule the throne of our hearts and dwell within the realm of our mind. God, give us the mind of Christ and renew our minds, daily. We want to think what is pure, act in ways that are upright, speak what is truthful and loving, and have motives that are holy and just. O Great Creator, be our all in all, from now into eternity. In Jesus' name, Amen.

Omniprocessent
All-Processing – Can Process All Things

"The Lord looks from heaven; He sees all the sons of men. From the place of His dwelling He looks On all the inhabitants of the earth; He fashions their hearts individually; He considers all their works."
— *Psalm 33:13-15 NKJV*

God is the only One Who is Omniprocessent. He alone can process all things as one thing, all moments as one moment.

When a computer processes specific code, it operates based upon the pre-made codes and constructs it was given. Artificial intelligence, as we know it, can do many things, but it is confounded to only one thing. It is limited by its function. Chat GPT, for example, cannot create a car. Other artificial intelligence may be able to give answers, but they cannot relate on a personal level. All artificial intelligence is limited. God, however, is not restricted.

When God considers all the works of man and Heaven, God considers it all within an instant. There is no moment-by-moment basis with God when viewing Him from His Eternal scope. God, however, can enter into time and be with us and consider what is, what has been, and what will be within each given moment. Simultaneously, He is outside and in time.

As God can be both in and outside time, He can process everything. Within an instant, He hears all prayers. Within a moment, He feels the emotions of all those He created. All that is, is processed and understood by God.

This processing is not limited by moments; for God, it is an All-in-One Moment, though it is conveyed at different moments within time for us.

"I, the Lord, search the heart, I test the mind, Even to give every man according to his ways, According to the fruit of his doings" (Jeremiah 17:10 NKJV). God gives every man what He deserves and can do so at any moment. Of course, there are moments when men do not deserve what they are due within the exact moment.

"I have seen everything in my days of vanity There is a just *man* who perishes in his righteousness, And there is a wicked *man* who prolongs *life* in his wickedness" (Ecclesiastes 7:15 NKJV). At moments, it seems God overlooks a matter. This is a false view of God. Whatever seems to be overlooked by God is merely being postponed until Judgment Day.

Everyone will receive what is owed them as they stand before God Almighty. "For God will bring every work into judgment, Including every secret thing, Whether good or evil" (Ecclesiastes 12:14 NKJV). "Therefore we make it our aim, whether present or absent, to be well pleasing to Him. For we must all appear before the judgment seat of Christ, that each one may receive the things *done* in the body, according to what he has done, whether good or bad" (2 Corinthians 5:9-10 NKJV).

We must never become perturbed by what seems not to be owed. God is Just, and He will do right.

God's Omniprocessence dwells within His Omniscience. As God knows all, He processes all. As He processes, He appropriately moves in the direction that is aimed toward His Ultimate Divine Will. How God moves forward is always based on His Nature, and His Nature always corresponds with His Omniprocessence and Perfection.

When God processes, He processes the paths of all men as if there were only one man. As He processes, He already knows how He is to respond and how He will eventually respond. Sometimes, however, the delay is meant to turn man toward the right course. It is to give them time to repent and turn from their wicked ways so that they might be saved.

God declares, "if My people who are called by My name will humble themselves, and pray and seek My face, and turn from their wicked ways, then I will hear from heaven, and will forgive their sin and heal their land" (2 Chronicles 7:14 NKJV).

We often need time to process what has been done to us. God needs no time to process. We need time to reflect and know how best to move forward. God knows instantly how to move forward. We want to be sure that our subsequent actions and words best convey what must occur for the longevity of a relationship or our future. God is always sure what to do. He is never in a hurry or a rush, and He already knows what to say, do, and speak in any and every situation. He is Omnicommunicent.

God is the One "Who 'will render to each one according to his deeds'" (Romans 2:6 NKJV). When God looks at a person's life, He does not just see the person. Through His Omnivoyance and Omniperspectival scope, He processes all that has led up to a person being the way they are.

God looks at that person's personality, how they have been brought up, what traumas have occurred through their life, what happened within the last year, month, and week, how they look, their weight, height, what language they speak, how many times they have moved, what their hobbies and interests are, how many friends they have had, when they came to know Him or if they have yet to come to know Him, what triggers them, what their strengths and weaknesses are, how their sleep and stress levels have been, their diet, and many other details. God processes all of these things in a moment, and He either knows and/or understands why a person is acting, feeling, or speaking in a certain way.

God's Omniprocessence perfectly knows and understands the current state of someone, where they are, and how they act because God's processing for a single individual is morphed into an Always-Present, Omniscient Moment.

The past is as equally real for God as the future. Within God's Omnivoyant scope and His Omnitemporal mode of existence, He knows and processes all things within an instant. God not only processes all the information about a single individual (such as the number of hairs upon their head (Luke 12:7)) but also what is around the individual (such as the weather). Not only does He process what is *of* the person and *around* the person, but also what is *within* the person.

Greater still, God does not do this for a single individual but for all of mankind at the same time. God's Omniprocessence is not limited or confined by time or a certain amount of people but is all at once. God does not grow tired, for numbers do not equate to an infinite scale. Greater still, the amount of creations and information cannot outweigh an Infinite Mind, even when compared to an eternal time.

Indeed, God does not grow weary or tired (Isaiah 40:28). His Mind never wears thin. His Omniprocessence never needs rest. God processes all things, all the time.

We may process different things at various times, but God processes all things at all times. God processes the same number of things in 2,000 B.C. as He does within our current moment. If it is the future we have yet to arrive at, God already processes what is of the future. For Him, "That which is has already been, And what is to be has already been" (Ecclesiastes 3:15 NKJV).

Let us never forget, "Do not be deceived, God is not mocked; for whatever a man sows, that he will also reap. For he who sows to his flesh will of the flesh reap corruption, but he who sows to the Spirit will of the Spirit reap everlasting life" (Galatians 6:7-8 NKJV).

Whatever we do, God is monitoring and processing. Though we cannot change our past, we can proceed with greater clarity and caution in the future.

The wise take their actions and steps to heart and do not justify wrongdoings when they operate in the flesh. The man who takes responsibility for his actions and humbles himself before God will be exalted (Matthew 23:12).

Let us always remember that "Each one's work will become clear; for the Day will declare it, because it will be revealed by fire; and the fire will test each one's work, of what sort it is. If anyone's work which he has built on it endures, he will receive a reward. If anyone's work is burned, he will suffer loss; but he himself will be saved, yet so as through fire" (1 Corinthians 3:13-15 NKJV).

God's Omniprocessence need not go into the past and attempt to reflect on previous emotions and memories, for all is at once for God alone. He will give what is due each man on that Final Day. May all come to know the Lord Jesus Christ as they humble themselves before Him and repent of their sins. "Every way of a man is right in his own eyes, But the Lord weighs the hearts" (Proverbs 21:2 NKJV).

———

Heavenly Father, You are the Omniprocessent One Who processes everything at all moments. You are Him Who knows us better than we know ourselves. O God, teach us to trust in You. Give us a heart after You. Help us to number our days so that we may gain a heart of wisdom. God, You are truly The Infinite Omni Who knows, processes, and sees all things. Nothing is too hard for You. May we die to self and lay ourselves down as a living sacrifice, holy and acceptable to You. God, give us the strength to take up our cross and follow You. Holy Spirit, may You move more mightily in us than we do in ourselves. God, we love You. Help us to live lives worthy of the call. May we live for You all the days of our life, to the very end. In Jesus' name, Amen.

Omnicogitament
All-Thought — Able To Think All Things

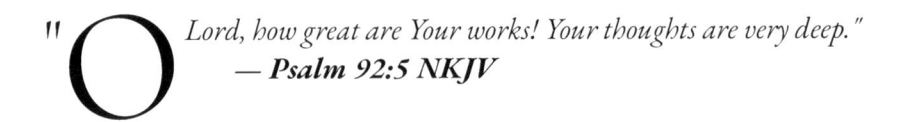

"*O Lord, how great are Your works! Your thoughts are very deep.*"
— ***Psalm 92:5 NKJV***

The capacity to think is derived from God, and all thoughts come from His permitting us to think.

Though our thoughts do not always align with Scripture and God's nature, God sustains our mind so that we can think as we do within any and every given moment. Though we are sinful and God is forever sinless, God has nonetheless made us in His image. Part of being made in His image is being blessed with the ability to have a mind that thinks thoughts.

When we think, we do so using the metaphysical faculties God has given us. Though our thoughts can range from inappropriateness to innovation, creativity, love, goodness, or evil, God's are always appropriate, pure, perfect, holy, creative, and loving. All minds can think because of the Infinite Divine Mind which is Omnicogitament Himself.

When we recognize that our thinking is not due to our power but we have the power to think thoughts outside of the Perfect Will of God, we will more readily go to God to be renewed. "And do not be conformed to this world, but be transformed by the renewing of your mind, that you may prove what *is* that good and acceptable and perfect will of God" (Romans 12:2 NKJV).

We can only think rightly, justly, and purely when the Holy Spirit renews and controls our thought life. Of course, this can only come by way of us submitting all we are to God. Only then, will God come forth and control all that we are. Using our free will in a manner controlled by the Holy Spirit's Will is the ultimate use of our will.

As we become more entuned with the Holy Spirit and are renewed daily, we will begin to see that God is All-Thought. Anything that can be thought in accordance with the Word, Ways, Will, and Nature of God is from God.

"For God is not *the author* of confusion but of peace, as in all the churches of the saints" (1 Corinthians 14:33 NKJV). We know "that by two immutable things, in which it *is* impossible for God to lie, we might have strong consolation, who have fled for refuge to lay hold of the hope set before *us*" (Hebrews 6:18 NKJV). "Let no one say when he is tempted, "I am tempted by God"; for God cannot be tempted by evil, nor does He Himself tempt anyone" (James 1:13 NKJV). "God is light and in Him is no darkness at all" (1 John 1:5 NKJV).

Anything that does not bring pure creativity, appropriate actions, good thoughts, and a holy imagination is not of God. According to the verses above, God is not a God of confusion; He cannot lie; He does not tempt, and He has no darkness in Him. Therefore, whatever thoughts include such aspects are not from Him but from our fallen nature or the Enemy.

As we proceed with this knowledge, we realize how deep, true, and boundless God's thoughts are – for whatever can be thought, has already been thought by God. All-Thought is God, and God is All-Thought. Truly, He is Omnicogitament and has an infinite number of thoughts.

All of creation was once a thought to God. As God thought, so He created. Therefore, all that *is* was thought by God.

God thought of Who He would create and when He would create them. God thought of the laws He wanted to set up for a fine-tuning universe. God thought of what circumstances and events He would allow and permit. God deciphered how many stars He wanted to create in our universe. God thought how many blades of grass He would have grown in our front yard.

God's thoughts range everywhere from the micro to the macro, from the finite to the infinite.

All thoughts are found in God, and properties, faculties, laws, how nature has been created, and creation itself were all thoughts. For God does not act until He thinks, and from His vantage point, His thoughts are simultaneous with His act of creation. God's Supra-Eternality has no beginning or end; it is simply a Pure Instant. This is only in relation to God, as He is the only One with this mode of Existence.

Therefore, when God thinks, He creates. What God creates is a former thought. Even greater, God's thoughts continue to unravel themselves to us within our universe.

Think of all the future babies to be born. Meditate on the deeper truths of life, why you have been created, what you are here for, and what the future holds. Look around and see how technology is being made and how our earth changes daily. Take time to see animals you had not known before. Think about what has been visualized and what is perceived before you. When you look at a person, you don't just see a face, but a body; not just a body, but a personality; not just a personality, but a soul. All that a person is was a thought to God before they were created.

"For You formed my inward parts; You covered me in my mother's womb. I will praise You, for I am fearfully *and* wonderfully made; Marvelous are Your works, And *that* my soul knows very well. My frame was not hidden from You, When I was made in secret, *And* skillfully wrought in the lowest parts of the earth. Your eyes saw my substance, being yet unformed. And in Your book they all were written, The days fashioned for me, When *as yet there were* none of them" (Psalm 139:13-16 NKJV).

All that we are comes from Him Who is Omnicogitament. We are beings created and made to live and exist within God and reality. We came into existence because of God's Decree, which proceeded from His Thought. O "How precious also are Your thoughts to me, O God! How great is the sum of them!" (Psalm 139:17 NKJV).

Not only is all that is a former thought within God, but because God is All-Thought, there are realities that have yet to be for us that God will bring forth. When we look at someone who is creative and innovative, we applaud them. We become amazed when rare men bring something forth into the world that never was. Though men have been known to do amazing things, their thoughts are not their own but from God.

God, many times, is the One Who plants innovation within the minds of men. Men believe they come up with something on their own, when it actually was derived, permitted, and given by God. For God is the Uncreated Creator and the Ultimate Innovator. God is the Ineffable Inventor, bringing forth everything, even through secondary causes.

God not only thinks by Himself, but He blesses man with thoughts that come from Him, directly. When someone finds a new attribute about God, that does not come from that person – it is given by God. For whatever God is, is given to man by Him. Man cannot think or grasp something about God that God does not give, for nothing is found out by man on his own, only imparted and given by God. God is the First behind all things and, therefore, the Giver of all things.

When we begin to see that God blesses man with creativity, innovation, and the ability to imagine and think beyond what has always been, we will start to praise God all the more. For all thoughts come from Him Who is All-Thought.

The fantastic reality that comes forth from understanding these truths is that God will forever be revealing what He is thinking. Though there are things that God will keep forever concealed, there are realities, creations, experiences, understanding, knowledge, and comprehension to be gained on that which has yet to come for us. Within an Infinite Mind, there is no maximum reach of Him Who is Divine.

Truly, God is forever thinking and always creating. "'For My thoughts are not your thoughts, Nor are your ways My ways,' says the

Lord. 'For as the heavens are higher than the earth, So are My ways higher than your ways, And My thoughts than your thoughts'" (Isaiah 55:8-9 NKJV). Not only are there thoughts of God to be understood, perceived, and made known in the future, but there are thoughts that will never be known.

Is everything we see truly what had to be? Did everything we experienced have to happen? The answers to these questions are no, yet God sought fit to create and permit what He permitted. Everything that happens did not have to happen. God could have thought of a world where there would be no bears or zebras. That was a possibility within God's Mind. Though He thought of this possibility, He did not act on it for Divine reasons we do not understand.

Take this understanding and multiply it to everything that is and everything we see. Though everything is a thought by God that He spoke into existence, it is not a thought that necessarily had to be. Based on other thoughts He had, God could have done things differently. There are possibilities within His Infinite Mind that could have led toward a different universe or world, but one with the same Ultimate Divine Willed outcome.

God is not limited by what is, for He is Omnifacultas. He produces all that is possible, and what He brings forth comes from within Himself, since He is Omnicogitament.

As we continue to meditate on how God is All-Thought, we see that every thought He has cannot be revealed to man. Just as in Heaven we will go through eternity and have infinite new experiences and revelations of God, eternity still cannot grasp all that God is. God will forever conceal more than He reveals. His thoughts are a realm of their own, for their realm is God, and God is His Thoughts.

God will forever keep an infinite amount of thoughts, knowledge, and revelation from us. None of these can be fully obtained from an Infinite Being Who is *The Infinite Omni*. We will never get bored in eternity, for we will always learn, grow, know, and understand more about God. However, eternity is not enough time to unravel what resides within God's Infinite Divine Mind.

God shall forever be the Revealed One Who gives revelation but continues to remain Thee Unlimited Mystery. All that God is transcends all that we know about God. All that God reveals is not all that is harbored within His Divine Mind. Indeed, this is the excellent, magisterial truth about God – He will never be fully grasped, understood, and comprehended.

Every step forward truly is like a step back. We have gained more about what lingers within God's Thoughts, but our beginning is as if we never began. For infinity has no end, and our pursuits will forever be as if we never started the quest.

Glory be to Him Who is the Omnicogitament One Who gives and reveals thoughts, Who implants creativity and innovation within our minds, Who blesses us with more knowledge and understanding about Him, and Who allows us to think, perceive, and reason. For nothing comes out of our own doing; it is directly given and permitted by God.

May our thoughts always glorify God. May we always pray and strive to know God better, for what we have learned is only the beginning.

"'For I know the thoughts that I think toward you,' says the Lord, 'thoughts of peace and not of evil, to give you a future and a hope'" (Jeremiah 29:11 NKJV). Truly, God's thoughts toward us are filled with Goodness, Love, and a desire to have fellowship with us. May all come to know *The Infinite Omni*, Who alone is the Infinite Divine Mind that is Omnicogitament.

O Mighty Omnicogitament One, Who thinks all thoughts and all thoughts are derived from Him, Who brings about what He thinks but does not reveal all the thoughts He thinks, You truly are above and beyond all that exists. God, in You is an unending amount of revelation and understanding. God, the Knowledge of You, the Holy One of Israel, is what we seek. Grow us in You and stretch our minds beyond their finite thinking. Bring us into Thy Divine Presence and fill our minds with Your Truth. You are Alpha and Omega. You have no beginning and no end. God, You alone can do all things, for all things come from You. Your thoughts toward us are Good, Lord God, and we desire to live righteously and holy before You. Help us, Holy Spirit, to live the Christian life in the fear of the Lord. May we work out our salvation in fear and trembling, revering You and giving You all the glory. For Who can think and be beyond You Who rules the Heavens and the Earth? Blessed Art Thou, O Omnicogitament One, Who is All-Thought and blesses us to think and know Thee. O God, may all come to know You and be promised eternity by believing in You and repenting of their sins. In Jesus' name, Amen.

Omnicertus
All-Certain — Always Sure of What, When & How to Do Something

"*God is not a man, that He should lie, Nor a son of man, that He should repent. Has He said, and will He not do? Or has He spoken, and will He not make it good?"*
— ***Numbers 23:19 NKJV***

God is All-True and All-Certain. Everything He does and Is, is that which He knows He will do and that which He Is.

Many of us go about life uncertain of what is to come. We don't always know what will happen next, and we often don't know who is truly for us. We are unsure of the path God has for us and what His Will is for our lives. Even on a day-to-day basis, we don't know what tomorrow will bring.

"Come now, you who say, "Today or tomorrow we will go to such and such a city, spend a year there, buy and sell, and make a profit"; whereas you do not know what *will happen* tomorrow. For what *is* your life? It is even a vapor that appears for a little time and then vanishes away" (James 4:13-14 NKJV). What then should we do, knowing we are unsure of what will occur tomorrow? "Instead you *ought* to say, 'If the Lord wills, we shall live and do this or that'" (James 4:15 NKJV).

Everything comes down to God. We should seek what He wills and speak what His Word says. His Wisdom should be the Light within us to guide us in our daily outings. God is the One Who knows what is best at all times, knows what to do at any time, and knows how to do what He will do.

When we read Scripture, we think that God just did something, and how He did it was the only option. Little do we realize that God could have done many things in different ways, but He was certain of the best way. He was sure what He would do would fulfill His Ultimate Divine Will.

In Exodus 3, God speaks to Moses through a burning bush. Did God have to do this? Was He obligated to speak to Moses in such a way? What about at that specific time? Did all that need to happen? Couldn't God have done it another way?

Instead of speaking to Moses in a burning bush, God could have talked to Him on the mountain or through the air. God could have never chosen to have him be led to the mountain. Instead, God could have spoken to Moses periodically each night for a week through dreams. God could have spread open the sky and appeared and talked to Him. Of course, God had many alternatives of what He *could* have done, but God was sure of what, when, and how to reach Moses for the best outcome.

Everything God reveals in Scripture is meant to bring forth deeper truths and revelations. If God would have spoken in dreams to Moses, Moses may have never asked the question ""Indeed, *when* I come to the children of Israel and say to them, 'The God of your fathers has sent me to you,' and they say to me, 'What *is* His name?' what shall I say to them?"" (Exodus 3:13 NKJV).

Moses may have just said "the God Who appeared to me in my dreams told me to tell you, Pharaoh." This would have brought a different understanding to God in Scripture that would have been in line with one of the many ways God communicates with His creation (through dreams, such as He did with Joseph). Still, we would miss out on hearing God declare to Moses' question, "I AM WHO I AM" (Exodus 3:14 NKJV).

We think that Scripture is precisely how it is because God has declared It, but little do we realize God declared It to be as such because He filtered through and knew instantaneously what He wanted included within His Word.

Everything in Scripture is not how it had to be, as God is not bound by His Holy Scriptures. Instead, His Holy Scriptures are bound to Him. What God reveals and declares comes from God. What has been declared and revealed did not have to be as such, but God was sure of what He wanted to reveal and speak.

When an author creates a story or writes a book, are they bound by the finished product of the book? Or does the finished product of the book become as such because the author wrote it? Likewise, is it with God.

God was, is, and will forever be certain in all He declares and reveals. Aside from the Only Way of salvation through Christ, What God chooses to do is one of many alternatives.

When we see that Scripture could have been different (insofar as God revealing different parts about each person's life in the Scriptures, how He presents Himself to them, what He speaks and presents before them, etc.), we see that God alone is Omnicertus.

When we deal with variables and different ways of doing something, we tend to test or go with our "gut feeling". We often don't get something done or accomplish what we desired on the first go. Why? We are finite and not as wise as we think we are. God, however, is different.

Though God has an innumerable number of variables on what He *could* do, He nonetheless is always and forever instantly certain. God knows all aspects of every situation. God is the God of possibility and knows all hypothesis, variables, and differentiations and continuations of different circumstances, causes, and effects. God knows that by putting certain verses in Scripture, He would present and reveal a new attribute about Himself to me as I write this, for example, and to the public at the time of you reading this Chapter.

"The Lord of hosts has sworn, saying, 'Surely, as I have thought, so it shall come to pass, And as I have purposed, so it shall stand'" (Isaiah 14:24 NKJV). What God purposes will come to pass. He is never a day late or a day early. He is never rushed or in a hurry. He is Omnicertus on what to do and how what He does will unfold throughout time.

We think that we were randomly placed within the family we were, but God had it done for a purpose. We may think aspects of life are "luck" and "coincidences", not knowing that God is behind the scenes the whole time.

Does not He Who created life, meaning, and purpose know what is always best? Does He Who designed us, knit us in our mother's womb (Psalms 139:13-14), and knows the number of hairs on our head (Luke 12:7), know what is best for us and when we are to grow, mature, receive, and endure adversity? Does not He Who created all things know when and how all things should be brought into existence? Or when they should be permitted to do something? Only God is All-Certain and never questions, ponders, or wonders.

In life, we tend to question the world around us. We ask, "How could God allow (such and such) to happen?" When alone, we ponder, "Why am I here? What is life really about?". When we see something new, we wonder, "How does that work?". We are beings who, if we possess any wisdom, ask questions. We want to know the truth behind things.

As we ask, we don't always know what answer we will find or receive. Sometimes, the answers we receive from others are unreliable and should not be taken as the Gospel Truth. Not so with God. When God answers, He is certain in His answer, and we can be certain His answer is based upon His Nature: Truth.

"The counsel of the Lord stands forever, The plans of His heart to all generations" (Psalm 33:11 NKJV). When God gives His counsel, it stands throughout time. He does not finish speaking to us and think, "Did I really say the right thing? Maybe I should have tested this first." No, God is the only Being Who does not need to test something to know the end outcome. He is the Ultimate, Unending End, and He knows the end of everything, even before they have a beginning!

Before God creates, He knows exactly how He will create, what will be the result of creating, where He will need to intervene and do what must be done, how He will speak and do what can only happen from Him, and the perfect timing of when it should take place. God is certain of all of this in an instant. He is Omnicertus and never waivers in His Word, wonders in His Mind, is unsure about what He created, or uncertain about the future. God is Certain because certainty is derived from within Himself.

Can anything be certain apart from God? Can we be certain of anything without God's declaration, power, and creation? Can we truly say, "This is the way" or "This is the truth" without God? All certainty comes from Him Who is All-Truth. All truths come from Him Who is Truth: The Lord Jesus Christ (John 14:6).

"Heaven and earth will pass away, but My words will by no means pass away" (Matthew 24:35 NKJV). When people give us their word, we often take it as certainty. After some time living in the real world (not the world we believe or create in our mind), we will find that many people do not keep their word. God, however, always keeps His Word.

When God declares something, it remains. Forever. God does not revert or go back on His Word. He does not think, "Well, I said that, but now I'm going to go back on My Word." No, God's Word is based on His Nature. When we see times in Scripture that it looks like He reverts from His Word, it is to show us the power of intercessory prayer.

God's Sovereignty is not an excuse to be lazy. Many people think that because God has everything under control, they don't need to do anything. They think prayer is unimportant because "God's Will is going to be accomplished regardless." This comes from a slothful spirit that stunts Christians from the fullness of what God desires to do in them and through them. When this occurs, they are those who will miss out on much.

When it seems God is changing His Mind in Scripture, He always knew what He would do. He is showing us and teaching us what can happen when we pray (and what will happen if we do not pray).

"Jesus Christ is the same yesterday, today, and forever" (Hebrews 13:8 NKJV). Seasons may change, but God never changes. He is certain and sure of what He has done, what He will do, what He has already said, what He will continue to say, and what He will speak.

From God's perspective, the future is fixed, even though we have freedom entering it (for more on seeing things from God's perspective compared to man's, see my book *Shadowed Realities: God's Vantage Point vs. Man's Vantage Point*). God is certain of what will happen because He has either created it or permitted it to happen. He already sees and knows the future, for the future resides within His Eternal Being.

Let us never forget that "all the promises of God in Him are Yes, and in Him Amen, to the glory of God through us" (2 Corinthians 1:20 NKJV). God's promises are for us. He is certain of the promises He has declared to us who are born-again, and He will bring forth His promises at different moments in time. We can rest assured that if God has spoken it, He will fulfill it. He is certain of the time since He discerns our hearts. He knows when we are "ready" to receive. He knows when He will unleash His blessing.

In the intermediate state of our waiting, may we remain faithful. May we depend on Him Who can do all things and never doubt the Omnicertus One Who possesses Perfect, Unlimited, Hidden Knowledge.

We can be certain of Christ's Word in Luke 21:12-19 (NKJV) that if we follow Him, "You will be brought before kings and rulers for My name's sake. But it will turn out for you as an occasion for testimony. Therefore settle *it* in your hearts not to meditate beforehand on what you will answer; for I will give you a mouth and wisdom which all your adversaries will not be able to contradict or resist. You will be betrayed even by parents and brothers, relatives and friends; and they will put *some* of you to death. And you will be hated by all for My name's sake. But not a hair of your head shall be lost. By your patience possess your souls."

Living life for God is better than living for this world. Shining bright for Christ is more excellent than living in darkness all our lives.

Let us never forget "when God made a promise to Abraham, because He could swear by no one greater, He swore by Himself, saying, "Surely blessing I will bless you, and multiplying I will multiply you." And so, after he had patiently endured, he obtained the promise. For men indeed swear by the greater, and an oath for confirmation *is* for them an end of all dispute. Thus God, determining to show more abundantly to the heirs of promise the immutability of His counsel, confirmed *it* by an oath, that by two immutable things, in which it *is* impossible for God to lie, we might have strong consolation, who have fled for refuge to lay hold of the hope set before *us*" (Hebrews 6:13-18 NKJV).

Truly, "This *hope* we have as an anchor of the soul, both sure and steadfast, and which enters the *Presence* behind the veil, where the forerunner has entered for us, *even* Jesus, having become High Priest forever according to the order of Melchizedek" (Hebrews 6:19-20 NKJV).

Glory be to Him Who is Omnicertus and always sure of what, when, and how to do anything and everything.

———

Heavenly Father, Great I AM, Him Who dwells in Unapproachable Light and Revealed Himself through Christ, Who stays true to His Word and declares what Is, Who by His Word brought forth all things, Who is Immutable and cannot lie, You are worthy of all worship, honor, and praise! You alone, O God of the Heavens, are Omnicertus. God, Who is like You? Who is sure of what must be done and when? Who keeps their word at all times? Who is never in a rush but always certain of what must be done, declared, and revealed? Only You, O God of Israel, know what is best. God, draw us into Thy Presence and help us to trust in Thee. May we not succumb to the flesh and what we believe is right. Keep us reliant and dependent on You, the only Independent and Sovereign Source behind all that is and will ever be. In Jesus' name, Amen.

Omniconfident
All-Confident – Confident in Who He Is, What He Can Do & What He Has Declared

"*Behold, I am the Lord, the God of all flesh. Is there anything too hard for Me?*"
—*Jeremiah 32:27 NKJV*

Since God is Omnicertus and *certain* in all things, He therefore is *confident* in all things.

When one is certain about something, they are confident. If a person knows who will win the game before it is played, they will confidently declare that team will win. If a pro team is going against an amateur team and plays at full capacity, one can confidently assert that the professional team will beat the amateur team.

In all walks of life, there is a range of confidence. Some are more confident in themselves and what they can accomplish than others. Others are more confident in how they look than others. Sometimes, confidence is not even derived from within, but without – due to clothing, makeup, money, the car one drives, the house one lives in, etc.

Confidence is an interesting aspect to ponder because many people may be confident in a particular area but lack confidence elsewhere. Others are so filled with pride that they have a false sense of confidence and believe themselves to be the most important person. Of course, narcissists may appear confident when, in actuality, they are very insecure.

When one is insecure, there is no confidence, only a façade of wanting others to believe that they are confident.

There is no security in insecurity. Therefore, one does not base one's life, views, or beliefs on anything concrete. Instead, those who are insecure continually fluctuate and change like chameleons. They don't know who they are yet desire to manipulate how others are.

Narcissists are the most insecure people and lack security in anything. The means of what they try to accomplish is not appropriate, and any confrontation drives them to alternative reactions, and getting defensive and gaslighting. This occurs because they have been exposed and have nothing to balance on. Therefore, they overreact and seek to distract, even though the prudent and wise see right through them.

Suppose one is not firmly grounded in confidence. In that case, they will seek to make much loudness — causing drama and wreaking havoc in an attempt to keep the discerning man or woman distracted and not continuing in the knowledge they know about the insecure narcissist. However, when we look at God, He knows not of insecurity or a lack of confidence.

God is Omniconfident. He is All-Confident in Who He is and what He can perform. He knows precisely what is to happen, what must be done, and what will occur. God is never confused or unsure on what to do and what will happen. Instead, He remains forever confident in all He *Is* and can do.

Nothing is too hard for God; rather, all things are easy. God does not ponder and wonder how He will perform something; He merely does it. God does not dwell within Himself, thinking, "What exactly is going to happen here?" No, before something comes to be, it is already seen by Him Who rules over the foundations of the world and exists outside the Heavens.

"God is not a man, that He should lie, Nor a son of man, that He should repent. Has He said, and will He not do? Or has He spoken, and will He not make it good?" (Numbers 23:19 NKJV). Some of us have been given a multitude of empty words and promises. For me, it happened most of my life (up until the age of me writing this at 29).

At the time, I had a best friend who always flaked out on me and said he couldn't hang out at the last minute. In college I was promised a starting spot multiple years (before getting injured), but my coach did not follow through. My boss at the time, who I worked for free for one year, and in the next two years only made $12,000 (yes, you saw that right), promised me six figures for the next 3-4 years. He spoke all these wonderful things that were in the works. Time and time again, I was promised a salary increase. Even when I followed up, it would be postponed and prolonged. If the raise were to come, it would be very little (mind you, I made less than half of what his son was making).

In the past, I had built roughly 3-5 extra business plans for friends. I gave them the idea, wrote the business plan, and spoke of the following steps we would need to take together. They would not attend meetings or follow up on their part (however, thankfully, I have two friends who have stuck through it by helping me work on startups throughout my 20s).

In my life, I have found many people derive their confidence level from instant bursts of emotions. This, over time, is proven useless. Like paying for motivation, discipline is the only thing that will help one continue in that motivation. You can give an external or go off an external to make yourself confident in how you think, talk, and act, but it lasts a moment. Eventually, time tests what lies within and whether one is truly confident.

With God, we need not worry if He will keep His Word. He always keeps His Word and has revealed that through the Holy Scriptures. When we meditate on God and all He is, we can see He is entirely confident in every regard.

When God makes a declaration, He doesn't "hope for the best". He doesn't see if "things will go according to plan". Whether we follow the path He has paved for our lives or not, He will make all things lead toward His Ultimate End. "I know that You can do everything, And that no purpose of Yours can be withheld from You" (Job 42:2 NKJV).

God allows room for us as humans to make decisions, but even if we make the wrong decision, He will work out that bad decision for a greater good, or He will bring someone else into the equation to bring forth what should have been done.

God deals with infinite variables and possibilities, but none of this frightens Him. He is entirely confident and concrete in Who He is. He is secure because security is derived from Him. There is no security without God first being secure. All security comes from Him, as nothing can become saved apart from accepting Him.

In high school, one kid would always talk a big game but never back it up. It was rather comical. Of course, in high school, we all try to pretend to be somebody, and most of us are uncomfortable with who we are. In exchange, we don't press into who we truly are, and we seek to blend in or partake in certain groups so we feel "at home"; even if we are in crowds that we really don't enjoy, but for the sake of reputation and protection, we stay in those groups. This is due to many reasons, one being not accepted, affirmed, and encouraged at home. However, the root of it all is not finding our identity in Christ.

Continuing with the story about the kid in high school. It was the typical need to speak and brag, but when questioned and put to the test, he could not perform. That is why it is always important to follow up with what someone says. If they say they can do it, put them to the test! With this particular kid, he would say, "Oh yeah, I can dunk. My vertical is 42 inches!". I remember asking him once in gym class, "Well, let's see it!"

As I followed and asked him to dunk, he immediately said, "Well, I don't know if I'll be able to get it right now, I just worked out and I'm sore." I said, "Not a problem, just give it a go." As he attempted to dunk, he could not even touch the rim. He returned and said, "Yeah, I'm just sore and...". He continued with other excuses I don't remember.

What we want to gather from all of this is that some people may appear extremely confident on the surface, but when asked or pressed to support their statements, they crumble and fall. They make excuses. They cannot provide a sound reason for their beliefs. They believe that money, the number of books they read, or even the bloodline relatives they are related to automatically makes them wise and understanding.

When one believes themselves to be as such, they become confident.

However, this *confidence* is quickly revealed as *cockiness*: an underlying condition of those who base what they are by what they can do, what they have, and who they are connected to; not who they are, directly.

God alone is All-Confident. He stands above all. Nothing compares to Him. Nothing is more excellent than Him. Nothing can offset Who He is within Himself. God's Confidence is entirely derived from within Himself, knowing truly, wholly, and fully Who He is. God never questions Himself of what He can do, perform, bring about, direct, declare, create, and *Be*. Nothing will ever come against God or speak wrongly of Him and cause Him to become insecure.

Atheists may mock and call God, "A giant spaghetti monster" (as if this is some hilarious insult). People may use God's name in vain or pursue a religious, man-made pursuit in the name of God (and just because something is done in the "name of God" does not mean it is *of* God). Others may place upon God the evil that is in the world and blame Him. All of this does not in one respect make God insecure and lack confidence. Despite what His creation says about Him, God remains concrete in Who He is.

"But our God is in heaven; He does whatever He pleases" (Psalm 115:3 NKJV). God does whatever He pleases, and it is correct. No matter what spiritual entity or person made in the image of God may say or do against God, it does not affect Him.

God does not question Himself, His identity, if He did the right thing, or what He can do. God means what He says, He knows Himself entirely and has revealed Himself truly through His Son the Lord Jesus Christ. When people go against Him, His confidence does not waver. Instead, man destroys his own potential of coming to know God. In the end, if this is continued, the opportunity to know God begins to dwindle and, ultimately, vanishes, when one is thrown into Hell and the Lake of Fire.

Isaiah 55:11 (NKJV) declares, "'So shall My word be that goes forth from My mouth; It shall not return to Me void, But it shall accomplish what I please, And it shall prosper in the thing for which I sent it.'" When God declares what is to come, it indeed *will* happen. When God reveals Who He is through His Son and Word, it is true. If man does not accept it, that is man's problem.

God's Sovereignty cannot be trumped or abolished, and His power cannot be fully obtained or replicated. God is entirely outside and forever above all He creates. Nothing will make Him question Himself and what He has done.

If we have trouble with God's Word, let us ask Him. Let us not sit there and say, "God, *how* could you allow this to happen?". Instead, let us ask, "God, *why* did you allow this to happen?".

"The counsel of the Lord stands forever, The plans of His heart to all generations" (Psalm 33:11 NKJV). God is *confident* because He is *certain* in all things. God is certain because He alone can bring forth anything He desires. God can bring forth anything He desires that corresponds to His Nature and Word because He alone is God.

"There are many plans in a man's heart, Nevertheless the Lord's counsel—that will stand" (Proverbs 19:21 NKJV). God is not a God Who can lie, nor a God that can, in the fullness of Who He is, die. God never lacks confidence. He never has, and He never will. Confidence comes from Him, and that is why we must put our trust in Him. Only then, can we find our identity in Him.

We don't need to find our confidence in the money we make, the multiple houses we live in, or a big real estate. We don't need to pretend to be confident and hide behind possessions and position. We need not associate with other people and groups for the sole sake of covering up our own insecurities. We need not lie to others and pretend we have it all together, when we do not.

We do not live to please man, nor should we strive to do what man desires. We must live for God and Him alone. We must find our identity in Christ and Christ alone. He is our Rock. He is our Confidence.

"Such *is the* confidence we have toward God through Christ. Not that we are adequate in ourselves *so as* to consider anything as *having come* from ourselves, but our adequacy is from God, Who also made us adequate *as* servants of a new covenant, not of the letter but of the Spirit; for the letter kills, but the Spirit gives life" (2 Corinthians 3:4-6 NASB).

We are not who we are based on externals. We are not who we are by association of others. We are not who we are by what we can produce, do, and what we have. We are who we are because God has made us as such. We need not lack confidence and wish we were taller, stronger, faster, or looked different. We need not lack confidence by what we don't have – for many times, what we don't have is a blessing from God, as it keeps us from adultery and idolatry.

We can have complete confidence in Who we have residing in us and Who has saved us. The world will label us as many things. God declares only one thing when we are covered by the Blood of Christ and led by the Spirit: "This is My child, whom I have predestined for My glory. I have given you a new name, a hope, and a future. I have brought you out of the world and into My loving arms. My Word is Your weapon and your confidence shall be found in Me alone, the Rock of your salvation."

Let us glorify Him Who is Fully, Wholly, and Truly All-Confident. God alone is Omniconfident, and is never insecure, doubtful, indecisive, or unsure. God is Confident in all He is, all He can do, all He knows will come forth, all He brings forth, and the future. It has been declared by God, and will therefore be.

We must find our confidence in Him Who is All-Confident. Only then, will we live in the trueness and fullness of all God desires us to be – both in life and in Him.

God in Heaven, Who created the foundations of the world by wisdom, Who stretched out His arms and created the Heavens, Who does not waiver or doubt, Who cannot lie and cannot die, You alone are Sovereign over all. God, Your Confidence motivates us to press into Thee. You alone are always sure of what to do, certain of how to bring it forth, and confident in Thyself. Never do You waiver in Your decision and Your view of Thyself, for You alone are the Great Vision and Unending Revelation. You alone are Truth and Power. You alone sustain all things by Thy Will, without help. Truly, none can tell You what You cannot do. None has taught You or can keep Your Ultimate Divine Will from occurring. You alone are The Infinite Omni, the God of the Heavens and Earth. You alone, O Mighty King and Perfect Ruler, are our Rock, Deliverer, and Healer. Give us ears to hear Your voice and make us deaf to the voices who doubt us or seek to destroy us. Though man has failed us, You will never fail us. For You are true, and let every man be a liar. We will not place our hope in man, but the God Who created man: the God of Abraham, Isaac, and Jacob. We worship You and ask that Your Truth of us would wash over us. May we see ourselves as You see us. May we see others the way You see them. We love You, O Omniconfident One. In Jesus' name, Amen.

Omniconsiliument
All-Counseling

> *"Counsel is mine, and sound wisdom; I am understanding, I have strength."*
> — ***Proverbs 8:14 NKJV***

God is Omniconsiliument. He alone can give counsel in all aspects and walks of life. At any moment, His advice is readily accessible to the born-again believer. We must simply deny ourselves and go to Him.

Since I wrote this (09/24/2024), much of my life has been spent attempting to do in the flesh what can only be done in the Spirit. Though I walk with God and go to Him in a good amount of things, I don't go to Him in *everything*. Due to my own neglect of doing what I know must be done, I suffer and prolong aspects that could otherwise go smoothly.

I say this upfront because many of us attempt to go on our own counsel and advice. We don't seek help from others but simply follow what we think is best. Other times, we go to others without consulting God. Both aspects are in error and should be avoided. God is All-Counseling, and we must seek Him for His advice in all areas of life, whether big or small.

"There are many plans in a man's heart, Nevertheless the Lord's counsel—that will stand" (Proverbs 19:21 NKJV). We have many plans in our hearts, but they are not guaranteed success. If we take time to review our lives, we will find that many of our plans failed. Of course, we don't want to do this type of reflection. Rather, we only want to meditate on what has progressed us to where we are or what makes us happy and smile.

Rarely do we want to meditate on where we got it wrong. Yet, it is in wisdom that we do this; the fool knows of no such way.

When we plan, we many times plan in our own hearts. We lean on our own devices, methods, and strategies. We go off the finite knowledge we have obtained and understood while God remains Infinite and willing to counsel us.

When we don't go to Him, we remain in the very thing we want to get out of and do not increase or progress further. Even if we do, it is guaranteed that it will be short-lived.

If Scripture reveals that the Lord's counsel will stand above our plans, why do we still neglect to go to God in all things? Why do we attempt to out-plan or out-strategize without God's assistance? Why do we believe that our plans are better than the advice and counsel of the Omniconsiliument One?

God declares, "I will instruct you and teach you in the way you should go; I will guide you with My eye" (Psalm 32:8 NKJV). God's Sight goes beyond space; it filters in and through time. God stands above both space and time and sees the beginning from the end as equally as He sees the end from the beginning. To have His Eye guiding us is to give us advice and counsel based on what He knows will happen.

If we learn to forsake our plans and take up God's purposes, we will endure less and live with less stress. "I will bless the Lord Who has given me counsel; My heart also instructs me in the night seasons. I have set the Lord always before me; Because *He is* at my right hand I shall not be moved" (Psalm 16:7-8 NKJV).

When God is ever at the forefront of our minds and hearts, we will be instructed in the way we should go. This can go from the biggest of decisions in life to the smallest.

I remember that I was recently at the grocery store. I thought in my head about which shopping cart I should take. I heard the Holy Spirit say, "Not that one." I thought, "It doesn't matter". Guess what happened? I spent my whole time in the store with a squeaky wheel! If I had just listened to God, I could have saved myself from the nuisance I put myself under.

We are to go to God in all things and listen to Him in all things. We can't just go to Him and, if He gives us an answer we weren't expecting or don't want to hear, say, "Thank You, God, but I don't think You are in the right here. I'm going to do it my way." Is it any wonder when we suffer? In many cases, it is by our own hands, and it goes against the very answer from God to the question we are seeking!

"Your ears shall hear a word behind you, saying, 'This is the way, walk in it,' Whenever you turn to the right hand or whenever you turn to the left" (Isaiah 30:21 NKJV). As we are born-again and keep in step with the Spirit, He will silently utter what we are to think, do, speak, and where we are to go. He gives us the time and the place, the specific fruit to reach for at the grocery store, the person to speak to about Him when at a theme park, and what clothes to wear for the day.

God can and is willing to counsel us in every area we go to Him about and ask questions. If we lean into Him, He will begin to speak more audibly. Those who lean into someone speaking can silence the noise around them as they reveal to the person through their actions that they want to hear what that person is saying. This is the same with God.

If we go to Him and allow Him to be in every part of our day, He will give us advice and counsel concerning anything. Of course, it takes a full surrender and humility to admit we don't know all things. Greater still, it takes a denying of self to get past the pride of "I'm not going to God about (fill in the blank). That means nothing to Him, and it's such a small thing."

If we go to God concerning what we should wear for the day, maybe what we wear intrigues someone else. They may say, "Where did you get that dress?" or "Where did you get those shoes?". As we answer and they reply they really like them, we can then begin to find a way to share the Gospel.

God can give us counsel in everything, and whatever He gives counsel in is for a greater purpose and cause in the future. We may think it is silly to go to God about what to wear for the day, but God could tell us the very thing that would have someone who is friendly and open speak to us and be ready to hear about the Gospel. Of course, if we wore whatever we thought looked good, we would be going off what we thought was best. The outfit we choose may not intrigue the person who would otherwise reach out. They would just be a passing face on the sidewalk amongst our walk in the city, but nothing more.

The "Lord of hosts, Who is wonderful in counsel and excellent in guidance" (Isaiah 28:29 NKJV), He will always give us a perfect answer and perfect guidance as to what we should do, say, think, act on, refrain from doing, monitor, be aware of, who we should befriend, when to set boundaries, what to have for lunch, and if we should watch a movie in the evening or go on a walk. God is in the details, and if we believe that He is All-Counseling, we will do well to go to Him and follow His every answer.

"For unto us a Child is born, Unto us a Son is given; And the government will be upon His shoulder. And His name will be called Wonderful, Counselor, Mighty God, Everlasting Father, Prince of Peace" (Isaiah 9:6 NKJV). Christ has many names, and one of them is Counselor.

We see that Christ continually counseled the Disciples. So much so that He rebuked the disciples for not heeding His counsel, understanding Who He was, and still not yet knowing that His Words were true. John 14:7-11 (NKJV) is a perfect example:

> ""If you had known Me, you would have known My Father also; and from now on you know Him and have seen Him."
>
> Philip said to Him, "Lord, show us the Father, and it is sufficient for us."
>
> Jesus said to him, "Have I been with you so long, and yet you have not known Me, Philip? He who has seen Me has seen the Father; so how can you say, 'Show us the Father'? Do you not believe that I am in the Father, and the Father in Me? The words that I speak to you I do not speak on My own *authority;* but the Father who dwells in Me does

the works. Believe Me that I *am* in the Father and the Father in Me, or else believe Me for the sake of the works themselves.'"

Philip still did not understand Who Christ was, and Jesus showed frustration! How many times does God get frustrated with us? Of course, He is never surprised, but He most certainly can be disappointed. God can become annoyed when we don't seek Him or obey the answer He gives us.

How many times have we not sought counsel from *The Infinite Omni*? Greater still, how many times have we disobeyed Him? Does this please God? Of course not. Now, multiply this by the number of people within our generation. Even still, times that by the number of generations that have existed. We quickly come to find that the counsel of the Lord is many times neglected. This frustrates, discourages, angers, grieves, and makes God upset.

God is not Impassible (unable to suffer or feel pain). He feels and has emotions; only His are always perfectly balanced. They never go outside the boundaries of His Perfection and Purity. He always acts in accordance with Who He Is, His very Noumena, and Nature.

"The way of a fool *is* right in his own eyes, But he who heeds counsel *is* wise" (Proverbs 12:15 NKJV). "Listen to counsel and receive instruction, That you may be wise in your latter days" (Proverbs 19:20 NKJV). If we desire to walk in wisdom and succeed in all that God has purposed for our lives, we will do well to go to Him Who knows all things, in all things.

God wants us to live for Him. God wants to be intricately involved in every aspect of our lives. With Him, nothing is too small or too big. He desires fellowship, to walk with us, and to guide us in each step we take.

Let us go to Him Who is Omniconsiliument, and Who alone is All-Counseling. For His advice is Timeless, Secure, and Sure. It is never wrong, but always right. It is never recommended but is always what must be heard and done. It is not unsure but stable and concrete.

Life is better lived when we allow Him Who is Life to be involved in our everyday life – from what we eat to when we sleep; from what we watch to what we wear; in how we treat our spouse and friends to how each day ends; whether involved in career and business, or in our hobbies and interests; whether it be in our dreams or how to achieve the end by particular means, God wants to advise, speak, and reveal.

It is good to have counselors, as Proverbs 11:14 (NKJV) declares, "Where *there is* no counsel, the people fall; But in the multitude of counselors *there is* safety." Greater still when we go to Him Who is the Divine Counselor and is willing to bless us with a spirit of wisdom and revelation, we will never lack. God will speak and reveal what He desires, and we will have greater peace as we invite Him into all aspects of our lives. In return, God will make known His Presence in our lives and will show us great, deep, and hidden things we have yet to know.

To walk with God is a practice. To listen to His counsel and advice takes obedience, but it is in obedience that the blessing comes.

Let us run to God and never allow the Enemy to lie and tempt us to believe that it is silly or unnecessary to go to God in all things. Rather, let us draw nigh to Him, knowing He will make our paths straight and will tell us exactly what needs to be done or said within the time it needs to be done and said.

To follow the All-Counseling God is to be blessed with realities that would otherwise not be, had we chosen the lesser path of doing things in our own strength or might. We are weak, but truly, He is Strong.

Blessed be Him Who is Thee Omniconsiliument One.

———

God in Heaven, Who fills Heaven and Earth, Who does not grow weary, Who cannot be deceived, Who alone is Light and has no darkness in Him, You are the Great Divine Mystery Who has Revealed Himself through Christ. You alone, God, are Deity, the Divine Counselor, the Omnipotent Ruler, the Righteous Judge, the Pure God Who desires to save, bless, direct, guide, advise, and lead His people upon still waters. God, help us to go to You in all things. Make known the fruits of going to You. Quicken our soul's to will to know Your Will at all times. May we not go in the way of our flesh or our own devices and plans. Instead, help us to go to You, trusting that You will answer. Give us the strength to obey, no matter the cost. To follow You, Lord, is worth more treasures than all the

Earth can give. For what the Earth produces is what will perish, but what You give to the obedient heart who follows You shall remain forever. Touch us, Heavenly Father, and comfort us. Counsel us and guide our every step. Keep us from the Enemy. Give us the strength to submit to You, resisting the Devil and knowing he will flee from us. May You be exalted forevermore, and may all see the fruits in our lives of going to You, the only One Who is Omniconsiliument, in all things. In Jesus' name, Amen.

Omnipotent
All-Powerful

" *And I heard, as it were, the voice of a great multitude, as the sound of many waters and as the sound of mighty thunderings, saying, 'Alleluia! For the Lord God Omnipotent reigns!'"*
— ***Revelation 19:6 NKJV***

God possesses all power because He Himself is Power. He alone is Omnipotent and He rules and reigns Sovereign over all.

God's Power is Endless. It is a Roaring Sea that never runs out. It is a well that never runs dry. God's Power is exercised and touches that which is outside Him, but His Power comes from within Him.

We become amazed when we recognize what man can do power lift, move objects, and lift heavy things. We think that the strongest man in the world can do so much, but when compared to God, he does very little.

If a man is building a skyscraper, cranes must be considered. There are machines required to do the heavy lifting that man cannot. When looking at God, however, He needs nothing.

God does not need help to lift something, do something, create something, or exert power. His Power comes from within Himself and it flows without.

Whatever is that we see and recognize before our eyes was once nothing. Not everything has existed forever. There has been a beginning point for all things. This beginning came from Him Who is the Unbegotten Omnipotent.

All that we see and all that is came from the Omniscient Mind, Omnipotent Hand, and Sovereign Decree of God Almighty. Nothing has always been, but God alone. All that is, is because of God alone.

When we look at God's Power, we see He truly can do everything. The might and magnificence of God doing all things consists in what He can do, how many times He can do it, the speed at which He does it, what He can do simultaneously alongside it, and what He exerts to do it.

"Ah, Lord God! Behold, You have made the heavens and the earth by Your great power and outstretched arm. There is nothing too hard for You" (Jeremiah 32:17 NKJV). When God creates, He does so with the end in mind. God knows what will be, before He creates. Simulatenously, He is aware of what He will make and how He will create it.

When we seek to create something—whether an invention, house, business, or puzzle—we operate based on what already exists. We use what is available to do what is before us. Even if we choose to be innovative and do something that has never been done, we are still dependent on people, technology, and other resources to supply the need for what we see as possible. God, of course, needs nothing and no one.

When God uses His Power, He uses it in a way that is not dependent or needing anything else. God does not need to be charged like a battery. God does not need to rest before creating. God does not need time to complete what He will do. God can do whatever, whenever He chooses.

When God wanted to create the Heavens and the Earth, He knew how to do it and what amount of power it would take—simply put, it would take "God-power."

God's Power is the same in all that is made and created. The exact amount of power from God to create an atom is the same amount it takes for Him to create our world.

"Have you not known? Have you not heard? The everlasting God, the LORD, The Creator of the ends of the earth, Neither faints nor is weary" (Isaiah 40:28 NKJV). What God does takes no effort on His part. God can create anything as easily as something else.

When God creates a flower, it is the same as creating the sun. There is no differentiation in the exertion of God's Power. What He does from His Omnipotence is not seen as a task to be taken care of. No, God does not see in the same light that we do. He finds nothing complicated, but sees all things as easy.

That is why when we pray to God, all things are small things for Him, no matter how big they are for us. Nothing is too large or too small. When we grasp this reality, we will begin to pray, believe, hope, and endure more. For when God is on the move, nothing can get in the way.

When God creates, He does not extract energy. God is not made up of energy, as He is made up of Himself and needs only Himself. He is Omnisesent (All-Self): self-existent, self-sufficient, and self-dependent (for more on God's Omnisesence, see my book, *In God Alone: Understanding God's Self*). God alone needs Himself to be God and do what He does.

As God creates and does what He does, His Power used is as if He did not use any power. This is a miraculous wonder.

Unlimited is the supply of God's Power, for He Himself is Power. It is by Him that power is something we can use and partake in. We can have power for our lights. We can have power in the position we lead. We can have the power to lift and move objects.

All powers are possible because God is Power. Since we are made in the image of God (Genesis 1:27), we therefore have aspects that we can partake in and do, one of these being power.

All powers come from God, and there is no power without God. As God creates a pebble of sand, it is the same amount of power to create a flower; the same amount of power needed to create a flower is the same to create the world; the same amount of power to create the world, is the same to create our galaxy; the same amount of power to create our galaxy is the same amount to create our universe; the same amount of power it is to create our universe is the same amount to create the Heavens.

The power to create a pebble of sand is the same as creating the entire universe. Both are equally effortless for God, since He does not grow weary, tired, or faint. All things are easy for Him Who can do whatever, at any given time, and in the way He sees fit.

God is in no rush or hurry. When He creates, He does so on His time. "Thus the heavens and the earth, and all the host of them, were finished. And on the seventh day God ended His work which He had done, and He rested on the seventh day from all His work which He had done. Then God blessed the seventh day and sanctified it, because in it He rested from all His work which God had created and made" (Genesis 2:1-3 NKJV).

God's rest was not *literal*. He did not need to rest to regain energy; He chose to *rest* from creating. God was not *tired* from creating; He was just done creating and, therefore, took a rest. His rest signifies to us the need for us to take a Sabbath and rest from our labor once a week. If we do not, we will reach a point of burnout.

It always puzzles me when people spend a lifetime arguing for new earth or old earth; whether God created the heavens, the earth, and everything in them in six literal days or not. God could have made everything in six seconds! Better yet, six milliseconds! Regardless of what one believes about this debate, so long as they hold to the view that God could have done it in less than a second, they are free to believe what Scripture says and seek what science (not corrupt scientists) reveals.

With this in mind, we see that God creates all things without difficulty and can do so at any speed. Whether He takes His time, like a painter taking his time to make a beautiful landscape, or creates something extremely fast, like taking a picture of a beautiful landscape, God is equally powerful in both. He reveals His Sovereignty in both.

Therefore, what seems to take long is not long for God. God is never in a rush. He can do all things quickly or He can take His time. There is beauty in both, and God is the Omniscient (All-Knowing), Omnisapient (All-Wise) One Who knows what is best, since He is Thee Best.

Truly, "beloved, do not forget this one thing, that with the Lord one day *is* as a thousand years, and a thousand years as one day" (2 Peter 3:8

NKJV). Whether God does something throughout one-thousand years, or God does something within a day, He has the Power to do whichever He chooses.

God alone has the Power to prolong certain events and creations because He sees the scope of all time. Everything resides within Him (Acts 17:28), and nothing can go outside His Being.

When God acts, it is the best time for Him to act. He does nothing less than operate based on His Perfection. He alone is Omnipotent and has the power to act immediately or to wait patiently until what He deems is the appropriate time.

As we recognize that God can create anything and that the same amount of power is always used, as we see that God truly can create anything at any given speed, and as we understand that He can create all things within less than a second, we come to find that God has an Unlimited Amount of Power to infinitely create without exhausting any Power and growing weary and fatigued.

This is an amazing reality—God's creation of the Heavens and the Earth in the beginning (Genesis 1:1) could have been done one billion times over. God could create a billion of our universes over the span of one billion years (that is, one universe per year), and He would be just as He is from the creation of the first as He is in the one billionth.

We can push this even further—God could create one billion universes within a second, and it would be just as easy for Him as creating one billion sands upon the shore of a beach!

"Is anything too hard for the Lord?" (Genesis 18:14 NKJV). Truly, God is Omnipotent! It is no wonder that "All the inhabitants of the earth are reputed as nothing; He does according to His will in the army of heaven And among the inhabitants of the earth. No one can restrain His hand Or say to Him, 'What have You done?'" (Daniel 4:35 NKJV).

"For with God nothing will be impossible" (Luke 1:37 NKJV). God truly can do all that is possible! He is not limited by anything. Of course, Atheists may ask, "Can God create a stone so heavy He cannot lift?" This is a logical impossibility. It is the same as asking, "Can God make a married bachelor" or "Can God make a round square"? These are literally nothing but mere word play. They cannot be anything, for the latter words go against the very nature of the first words!

Other logical impossibilities include God recreating Himself, making Himself not exist, allowing something material to come into existence apart from Him (or apart from His permitting), God literally forgetting, or God creating human beings with the ability to understand something that He does not know. All of these are logically impossible and cannot be done because they are not real to begin with—they are contradictory statements!

When we understand these truths, we find that God can do everything! Logical impossibilities are *literally* nothing, which does not mean "God is not able to do such and such" because "such and such" does not exist and cannot be done!

"If God is for us, who can be against us?" (Romans 8:31 NKJV). When we are born-again and understand the power of God, we will more readily and quickly run to Him Who is Omnipotent and can do anything! God is the Creator of the Heavens and the Earth. He is the Creator of the visible and invisible, the physical and metaphysical, realms and dimensions, entities and beings, formations and formulas, sets and numbers. God is the Creator of all, and He alone rules and reigns Omnipotent and Sovereign!

""Remember this, and show yourselves men; Recall to mind, O you transgressors. Remember the former things of old, For I *am* God, and *there is* no other; *I am* God, and *there is* none like Me, Declaring the end from the beginning, And from ancient times *things* that are not *yet* done, Saying, 'My counsel shall stand, And I will do all My pleasure,' Calling a bird of prey from the east, The man who executes My counsel, from a far country. Indeed I have spoken *it;* I will also bring it to pass. I have purposed *it;* I will also do it'" (Isaiah 46:8-11 NKJV).

What God purposes, will be done. Nothing can stop God from doing what He will do. No power is greater than Him Who is Power Himself; not only Power, but All-Powerful. "Then Job answered the LORD and said: 'I know that You can do everything, And that no purpose *of Yours* can be withheld from You'" (Job 42:1-2 NKJV).

God's Omnipotence is in what He does, what He performs, in Who He is, and in His Nature. God has the power to love all people, to save anyone willing to turn to Him and away from their sin, to care for all

His creation, to heal all things, and to bring forth a new Heaven and new earth.

"Now I saw a new heaven and a new earth, for the first heaven and the first earth had passed away. Also there was no more sea. Then I, John, saw the holy city, New Jerusalem, coming down out of heaven from God, prepared as a bride adorned for her husband. And I heard a loud voice from heaven saying, 'Behold, the tabernacle of God *is* with men, and He will dwell with them, and they shall be His people. God Himself will be with them *and be* their God. And God will wipe away every tear from their eyes; there shall be no more death, nor sorrow, nor crying. There shall be no more pain, for the former things have passed away'" (Revelation 21:1-4 NKJV).

God alone has the power to perfect, purify, redeem, restore, make new, and complete what He declares. God alone has the Power to keep His Word because it is by His Word He creates.

God is Omnipotent, and He is worthy of receiving all praise; He alone is to be revered.

"God has spoken once, Twice I have heard this: That power belongs to God" (Psalm 62:11 NKJV).

O Omnipotent One, Who created all things and does so effortlessly, Who does not grow weary or tired, Who can do all things in the smallest amount of time, Who can create an infinite amount of creations an endless amount of times over, Who will never be exhausted of His Power, Authority, and Strength, Glory be to You, Him Who rules and reigns in the Heavens! Truly, You alone, O Lord, raise up kings and bring them down. Truly, You, O All-Powerful God, cannot be overthrown and cannot be defeated. Nothing compares to You, the Sovereign Lord Who uses the Earth as a footstool. God, You are Magnificent and High and Lifted Up! You are to be praised all the days of our lives! O God, grow us in deeper knowledge, revelation, and understanding of Your Might and Power. You alone, O God, are truly The Omnipotent One Who cannot be conquered, compared to, overthrown, or thwarted. Glory be to You, O Just and Righteous God, that You will have justice done on that Final Day. Truly, Lord

Jesus, no weapon formed against us can prosper when we are covered by Your Blood, abide in the Vine, and have the Banner of Your Name upon our foreheads. Is it any wonder that the demons tremble before You, O God? You are Almighty! We love You, God, and we trust in You to be our Protector, Sustainer, and Provider. You alone are our Rock, our Tower, our Strong Fortress. We hide under the Shadow of Your Wing, knowing that we are eternally safe when we are near to Thee. We bless You, Omnipotent God. Thank You for loving, protecting, calling, guiding, and leading in our lives. In Jesus' name, Amen.

Omniperfunctent
All-Performing – God Can Perform & Carry Out Anything

"Ah, Lord God! Behold, You have made the heavens and the earth by Your great power and outstretched arm. There is nothing too hard for You."
—Jeremiah 32:17 NKJV

All of us have limits. There are certain things we cannot do or perform. We may have the mental capacity to think of many different things and what "could be", but what "could be" we cannot always make happen.

For example, if we desire a relationship, we may imagine what it would be like with someone. If that particular person does not like us, we cannot force the relationship to work. Due to people having their own unique will and us not being able to force them to love us, this, many times, is a reality we cannot have occur.

When it comes to relationships, God often protects us. He keeps us from marrying someone who will destroy us and our destiny. Unfortunately, some of us are married to the wrong person. We did not listen to the warnings or heed the signs God revealed. We wanted it our way, and we ended up going against the very revelation God had portrayed. We wanted what we wanted, and in exchange, we suffered for our desires.

This is why it is essential to wait upon God. The very thing we desire can be given to us if we trust God and wait upon Him. We will not have rest if we strive to work it out in the flesh. If we wait upon God, we will be blessed beyond comprehension. We will "taste and see that the Lord *is* good; Blessed *is* the man *who* trusts in Him!" (Psalm 34:8 NKJV).

In this one example, we see the danger of attempting to work out what only God can do. However, when we wait upon God, we trust in His Omniperfunctence. We believe He is All-Performing and can perform and carry out anything He desires.

Our rational minds may like to say, "Well, I'm getting too old. There is no way I am going to meet the person God has for me. I need to go on dating apps. I need to put myself out there", when God is saying, "Spend time in my Presence. Trust me. Watch me perform my wonders and miracles."

Many times, God will refrain from blessing us because we lack faith. "But without faith *it is* impossible to please *Him,* for he who comes to God must believe that He is, and *that* He is a rewarder of those who diligently seek Him" (Hebrews 11:6 NKJV). Some of us request that God do something, but we don't believe He will do it! To our demise, we lack faith, resulting in no results. We prolong the process and delay what He desires to do simply because we are, once again, unwilling to die to self and reason. We lack the simple call to trust God with a child-like faith!

Cannot He Who created the world and everything in it; Who set up the foundations of the Earth, Who commands how far the seas may go, Who raises the mountains to a certain level, Who set into motion the laws of gravity, Who keeps the Earth balanced on nothing, and Who knit us in our mother's womb perform our heart's desires? If they align with His Will, and we believe He will move, nothing can interrupt the flow of the Holy Ghost! God will do it, for nothing can thwart Him and succeed. Nothing can go against Him without punishment. God does what He will do, so that we may honor and revere Him Who conquered Death and Hades.

"The Lord kills and makes alive; He brings down to the grave and brings up. The Lord makes poor and makes rich; He brings low and lifts up" (1 Samuel 2:6-7 NKJV). What God Wills to do, He will do. If something goes against His Perfect Will, His Ultimate Will shall still come forth (we will cover this more in the Chapter on God being Omnivoluntatem (All-Will)).

"Behold, I am the Lord, the God of all flesh. Is there anything too hard for Me?" (Jeremiah 32:27 NKJV). Cannot He Who created all laws, limitations, boundaries, ground, forms, and functions establish and bring forth what He Wills? Cannot Him Who alone creates what *is* from that which is not, and perform that which comes to be simply because of His Expressed Thought and Declarative Word? Truly, "with God nothing will be impossible" (Luke 1:37 NKJV).

We are amazed when a man can perform an act, master a craft, or outdo another in skillset, but we quickly forget all the things he cannot do. He who built a billion-dollar business could not bench 400 pounds. He who can bench 400 pounds cannot refrain from pride in what he can accomplish. Those who cannot refrain from pride in what they can achieve continually lack humility. Those who have the utmost humility cannot constantly do right.

In every procession there is a distinct negation. One may excel and do well in one avenue and realm, but they fail in another. Those who may be known for their conduct and character still cannot do what another can in the power of the Spirit. Those who have spiritual giftings still lack certain gifts. Those who are blessed with all the gifts (which come from continual request to God and believing He will answer) do not have all of them maxed out.

In some particular aspect of life, there is a lack. We are never full, and since we are never full, our proportion to perform is always less than another's. We may be incredibly gifted in one area, but we cannot conquer all areas. Only God is the One Who has the Highest, Unending Capacities and Capabilities to do that which only He can do. For God is that which no other can or will be. He alone stands as All-God, the One and Only Sovereign, The Founder of Life and Giver of every perfect and good gift from above (James 1:17).

When we desire something to occur, we depend on other things to cooperate. When we want to see something come to fruition, we do not do it on our own. Even he who develops a multimillion-dollar company as a Solopreneur is still dependent on technology working and clients coming. Without either, he has nothing.

God alone can perform anything without the cooperation of anything else. God does not need our cooperation for His Ultimate Will to be fulfilled. This is a beautiful revelation for those who struggle with God's Sovereignty and free will.

Though we will unpack it in other Chapters, it is essential to note that God knows when to intervene with something and when to refrain from intervention. From the Highest Realms of Eternity, God looks down and exercises what He will do, based on what He knows, sees, and a variety of other aspects.

God doesn't need us to pray for Him to do what He may. God does not require us to be perfect to perform His Will by His Spirit working through us. God does not need to breathe down our necks for us to cease from sin. God does not need to control every movement we make to have all things arrive at the end which He has already declared.

God can perform whatever He wants. If two people fail to reach someone who has yet to hear the Gospel, God can move upon the third person's heart. If the third person ignores Him, God can visit the fourth in a dream. If the fourth person dismisses the dream, God can lead the fifth man to a particular Scripture. If the fifth person does not go based on the direct word God is giving them, He can set up the sixth person's day to cross paths with the person who has yet to understand Christ. If that person does not follow through, God can use the seventh person He brought to the same spot to speak to the unbeliever. If that person heeds the call, God performed that which He could have controlled and intervened with the first person, but instead did so with the seventh. Why? Because it is a greater Power and Mightier act of Sovereignty to allow libertarian free-will creatures to move and operate without controlling their every move and operation.

God's Sovereignty is most greatly displayed by setting up the boundaries for free will creatures to operate within those boundaries. God "has made from one blood every nation of men to dwell on all the face of the earth, and has determined their preappointed times and the boundaries of their dwellings" (Acts 17:26 NKJV). If we go outside those boundaries, God will intervene. He allows room for maneuver in how we go about our day-to-day lives. He does not need to control every movement, for those who must control others' every movement are insecure, controlling, and manipulative.

Just because God is in *control* does not make Him *controlling*. The Devil is controlling, and that is what unclean spirits of Jezebel (and other unclean spirits) do. They seek to control and manipulate others. Why? Because they don't have the Ultimate, Divine, Sovereign Power that God does. He alone remains in control despite giving others freedom of the will.

When one truly understands this, the world opens up. God *sustains* every movement, but it does not mean it is *performed* by God. Acts 17:28 (NKJV) declares, "in Him we live and move and have our being", but that does not mean God controls every aspect of how we live, every move we make, and how we grow and develop our being. We can sin and distance ourselves from Him. We can attempt to go our own way, though this path leads to the grave. We can desire enlightenment, though it only comes through humility and walking in the fear of Him.

As human beings, we can do whatever is contrary to God and His Word. We are free to do so, and God is not responsible. Though we do wrong, God remains in control, and can have us draw our last breath at any moment. Thanks be to God, however, that He is not out to destroy or damn us, for "The Lord is not slack concerning *His* promise, as some count slackness, but is longsuffering toward us, not willing that any should perish but that all should come to repentance" (2 Peter 3:9 NKJV).

God can do anything at any given time. He does not need everything to work perfectly for Him to perform His Will effectively, and He did not need everything lined up for His Sovereign Son to be raised up. It is by God that His Will is fulfilled. If He Wills it, that is the way. If that is not His Will, then it is not the way.

Again, we will review the different "Wills" of God in more depth. For now, it is important to note that whatever God desires in His Ultimate Will shall be fulfilled.

Truly, our "God shall supply all your need according to His riches in glory by Christ Jesus" (Philippians 4:19 NKJV). Do we desire food? He will provide. Do we need clothing? He will bring it forth. Do we lack confidence in who we are in Christ? The Holy Spirit will reveal what that means. Are we unsure what a passage of Scripture means? God will give discernment. Are we afraid to enter the next season of life? God will be with us who are born-again. Do we need a financial miracle? God will have it manifested.

Whatever we fear and are stressed about is something we believe must be worked out with what we see and what we currently have as accessible. If we would learn to turn to Him Who is Omniperfunctent, we would quickly realize God can perform it! We must not worry about how things will be done, the timing of when they will occur, and what is needed. We need only trust and lean on Him Who can perform anything in a moment and raise up an individual within a second.

What shall we fear if the world spins on the finger of God and the Universe is His garment? "If even the moon does not shine, And the stars are not pure in His sight" (Job 25:5 NKJV), shall any amount of darkness overthrow Him? Deep within God are mysteries untold. In the "Nucleus" of His existence are unbounded, unknown realities of revelation and wisdom that far exceed the mental capacities of men and angels.

Since this is true, why do we suffer want? Why do we neglect the simplicity of what God demands? Why do we drift so far from seeing He can perform anything when He Wills and by His Own discretion?

"Behold, God is exalted by His power; Who teaches like Him? Who has assigned Him His way, Or who has said, 'You have done wrong'?" (Job 36:22-23 NKJV). Nothing that God does is proven wrong. Man may attempt to overthrow Him Who looks down upon us as the dust of the Earth, but their efforts are folly. To go against Him Who is All-Performing is to lack understanding that God's Way is only One Way. Though He performs in many ways and is already prepared for our mistakes, and can make up for wasted time and efforts, there is only One Way to know Him; and that is through the Lord Jesus Christ.

If demons believe and tremble at the Almighty (James 2:19), if angels cry, "Holy, Holy, Holy" (Revelation 4:8), and if God commands the righteous to stand courageously and boldly (Psalm 31:24, Proverbs 28:1), shall we not bend our knee before the Maker of Heaven and

Earth? Shall we not believe in Him Who simultaneously *does* before He *declares*, and *declares* before He *performs*?

We must "know that all things work together for good to those who love God, to those who are the called according to His purpose" (Romans 8:28 NKJV). No amount of time robbed can disassemble the Ultimate Will of God. Though we may have sacrificed much in years prior and suffered from our wrongdoings and failings, new beginnings remain on the horizon. God will perform and bring forth all that He Wills. He waits, looking down, wanting to comfort and help us amid our struggles and sufferings.

"For *it is* better, if it is the will of God, to suffer for doing good than for doing evil" (1 Peter 3:17 NKJV). "But Jesus looked at them and said to them, 'With men this is impossible, but with God all things are possible'" (Matthew 19:26 NKJV). We will never perform the Will of God apart from God. We will never receive what He wills to give and do if we lack faith and trust in Him.

We must open the capacities of our hearts and not allow the Enemy or the world to taint or destroy the true knowledge and revelation of *The Infinite Omni*. We must declare and prophecy that God will perform what He shall, not using what is seen or what we believe, but by His Own Discretion and Decree.

May we all bend our knees to the Sovereign Lord, Who is the Most High. He alone will carry out and actualize the reality that He desires. We need only see who we are before Him and Who He is in light of the Word and what the Holy Spirit reveals.

Let us never doubt, stress, worry, or fear, for Him Who stretched out the Heavens and creates all things out of love, is near: the Everlasting, Never-Ending, All-Performing God of the Holy Scriptures.

Blessed be the Trinity, from the Uncreated Beginning through the Unending Eternity.

God, Who alone is Omniperfunctent, Who thinks and it is done, Who declares and it shall be, Who performs all mysteries, Who reveals the hidden things, Who disperses portions from the wicked to the righteous,

Who never leaves those who are born-again, Whose plans and purposes are greater than ours, Who possesses all knowledge and continually discerns instantly what must be allowed, done, and permitted, there is none like You. God, You alone are Perfect. Never have You been in the wrong. Never have You done wickedly. You are the God Who hates iniquity. You are the Only God Who exists. You alone do not tempt man. You are the Ultimate Judge Who will throw all transgressors and unclean spirits in the Lake of Fire. You are Him Who desires mercy over sacrifice. You are the One Who by Your kindness draws us to repentance. O Magnificent King and Ruler, none is like You nor will ever be. God, You know our situation and our trials. You know our suffering and our desires. God, we offer our praise of thanksgiving up to You. May it be a fresh fragrance in Your nostrils. May we pray the prayers that come from Your Throne and are birthed in our spirit by Your Holy Spirit. O teach us to pray, that we might know Thy Will continually. Redeem the time and restore to us the joy of our salvation. We seek to see You in all that is, for Your Divine Power and Unending Love is seen through all. Keep our eyes off of this world and may we find You in every aspect of our day. We desire that which comes from You and we gaze to the Heavens, desiring that Your Face would shine upon us. Be glorified, Him Who lives forever, performs all things, and can change the course of the future in an instant. We depend on You. We trust in You. We believe in You, O Lord of Heaven and Earth. In Jesus' name, Amen.

OMNICOMPLETUS
All-Completing — Can Complete All Things

"*Being confident of this very thing, that He Who has begun a good work in you will complete it until the day of Jesus Christ;*"
— ***Philippians 1:6 NKJV***

Whatever God starts, He will bring to completion.

In this life, we tend to start many ventures. Our pursuits range from careers to hobbies, businesses to relationships, dreams, ambitions, places to travel, people to meet, building, and creating. Most of what we set our eyes on and operate for is for something greater and "beyond." There is hope in completing something so that we might feel filled and satisfied and move on to the next thing.

All that we do in this life is for something greater. Whether we realize it or not, everything affects the present and how the future unfolds. Although nothing can outdo the Ultimate Sovereign Will of God Almighty, it can most certainly align with what God knows, allows, permits, or does Himself.

In our life, that which we do truly affects the future. Everything that is done, will affect what is to come, what will be done, and ultimately, the Final End. All that we do is being recorded. There is nothing that escapes the Divine Eye of God Almighty and His Omniscient Mind.

God alone is Omnicompletus. He alone completes all things He sets out to do. Of course, His Perfect Will is not fulfilled when not everyone accepts Christ and ends up in Hell. However, what God sets out to do *Himself* is what will be completed. It is not a failure on His part that not everyone goes to Heaven, but ours. He does everything to draw man. We are responsible for how we respond. In the end, God has the Final Say on how He responds to our response.

It is essential to understand the distinction between how God *sets* certain aspects of life up and what He does *directly*. God is not responsible for how everything lives, moves, and has its being in Him (Acts 17:28). God is not to blame when things go wrong, evil is done, or we sin against Him. God is not the author of these things; He has only set up the means and functions that can be used in a perverted, twisted, ungodly manner that brings about that which is against Him. For that which is *from* God can be used *against* God through libertarian human freedom.

That which God sets up can be misused just as we can use a computer program and play a video game. If we stay within the boundaries of how the program and video game was set up, everything will run smoothly. If we go outside the boundaries set, there will be consequences, respawn, and an inability to function appropriately. So it is with evil and sin.

When Adam and Eve disobeyed God in Genesis 2-3, that is when what was *set up* by God was used *against* Him. Instead of obeying, humans got to straying. They went outside the boundaries God set up, and in exchange, they received the penalty of not being able to enter the Garden again.

"Then the Lord God said, "Behold, the man has become like one of Us, to know good and evil. And now, lest he put out his hand and take also of the tree of life, and eat, and live forever"— therefore the Lord God sent him out of the garden of Eden to till the ground from which he was taken. So He drove out the man; and He placed cherubim at the east of the garden of Eden, and a flaming sword which turned every way, to guard the way to the tree of life" (Genesis 3:22-24 NKJV).

Man went against the way things were created and meant to operate and run. Even in the Garden, Adam and Eve had libertarian free will. They could walk where they wanted without God controlling them as robots and telling them where to plant each step. God merely gave a simple command, and Adam and Eve disobeyed. This was mankind's fault; not God's.

When we understand this reality, we can better understand that when God operates, directly, He will bring it to completion. "Ah, Lord God! Behold, You have made the heavens and the earth by Your great power and outstretched arm. There is nothing too hard for You" (Jeremiah 32:17 NKJV). No matter what God sets out to do, it will be done. It is not difficult for Him to complete that which He Himself does.

God does everything easily. There is nothing forced or coerced. God does it whether others agree or not. It doesn't matter whether we want it to happen or not; if God begins something, He will bring it to an end.

This is the pattern of all that God does. God never leaves a project half complete. He always finishes the job. He is faithful to complete it.

Even amid the most testing, trying, impossible situations, God can and will perform the miraculous. "But Jesus looked at them and said to them, 'With men this is impossible, but with God all things are possible'" (Matthew 19:26 NKJV).

After God confronted and rebuked Job in multiple chapters, we see Job answered Him "and said: 'I know that You can do everything, And that no purpose of Yours can be withheld from You'" (Job 42:1-2 NKJV).

Too many times we attempt to do God's Will our way, when God's Will can only be completed God's Way. There is no other alternative. We can try to be good on our own and perform what God has called us to apart from Him, but if He is not in the midst, it will not work. God must be there. If He is, then that is the desire He will bring forth. It is not by our doing but by Him. If God intervenes or moves directly and understands this is what He wants to happen and must happen, God will do it.

If God is doing it directly, nothing can stop His Omnipotent Hand from moving upon man and bringing about miracles within hearts and amongst His creation. Unbelievers cannot deny it. Demons cannot defy it. Human sin cannot prevent it. Satan cannot destroy it.

"Now to Him Who is able to do exceedingly abundantly above all that we ask or think, according to the power that works in us" (Ephesians 3:20 NKJV). Is it any wonder God can do more than we ask or think? Too many times our vision is tainted, and our dreams are limited. We are focused on ourselves and cannot look past our driveway. Even if we can, our dreams and vision for our lives are still bound by state or nation. They may even reach the pinnacle thoughts of being global, but it may be fleshly. Even if it is not fleshly, it focuses on the physical rather than the spiritual.

We don't think and dream as we should. We fail to take up the Vision of God and partake in His thoughts and affairs. As this occurs, we set ourselves up for disappointment and depression. We begin to question God when, all the while, God was not directly associated with our dreams and visions. We didn't go to Him. We didn't speak with Him. We did nothing but go our own way, hoping God would confirm it and join us along in our own self-made and self-created journey.

Is it any wonder why so many things go wrong in our life? We believe we can bring all we desire to completion when it is only God Who is All-Completing. We take pride in ourselves and boast about how we have conquered a particular area of life or sin, while we struggle with fifty others we fail to recognize. In fact, we are so spiritually dry in our pride that if God were to reveal such things we would deny them. Even still, if we had a heart to listen to Him telling all the other sins we need to take care of, we would be overwhelmed.

That is the way of those who think they can complete everything on their own. Sadly, they only focus on what they have accomplished, but fail to see what they could not complete. They want humankind to see their successes and view them as one who can get anything done that "they set their mind to", when that is not the case nor reality for any human being.

Talk to anyone on this Earth and ask them about their successes. They may brag about specific accomplishments financially, relationally, or other aspects of life. Maybe they overcame specific struggles and difficult times. They may even be those who are well-known in this life and willing to be transparent in a particular area. Of course, don't stop at this point. Continue to press with a further question. Ask, "What still lingers that you have not conquered?".

Anyone who says, "Nothing, I've done it all" has revealed the blindness of their sight and how little their vision goes. They believe and see only what they complete, but they are unwilling to address all that they have tried to complete but were unable to; maybe they were able to complete such things, but they allowed present feelings to persuade them into a fading future reality – one that could have been but is no longer; one that might have been, but was disrupted and distorted due to laziness, discouragement, hopelessness, and maybe even trusting in oneself.

All of this reveals the tragic condition of man, and it begs the question, "Why do we esteem man?". This is why we are "not put your trust in princes, *Nor* in a son of man, in whom *there is* no help. His spirit departs, he returns to his earth; In that very day his plans perish" (Psalm 146:3-4 NKJV).

Psalm 146:5-10 (NKJV) goes on to further say:

"Happy *is he* who *has* the God of Jacob for his help,
> Whose hope *is* in the Lord his God,
> Who made heaven and earth,
> The sea, and all that *is* in them;
> Who keeps truth forever,
> Who executes justice for the oppressed,
> Who gives food to the hungry.
> The Lord gives freedom to the prisoners.
> The Lord opens *the eyes of* the blind;
> The Lord raises those who are bowed down;
> The Lord loves the righteous.
> The Lord watches over the strangers;
> He relieves the fatherless and widow;
> But the way of the wicked He turns upside down.
> The Lord shall reign forever—
> Your God, O Zion, to all generations.

Praise the Lord!"

Truly, "'If you can believe, all things are possible to him who believes'" (Mark 9:23 NKJV). Our belief must not be found in ourselves but in God. He alone is Omnicompletus. Every pursuit that He is directly involved with shall come to His desired completion.

Not every desire of His comes to pass, but what He Himself sets out to do, directly, will most certainly be completed. For it is not trusting in man, who uses their freewill in tainted, ungodly, misled ways. Instead, trusting in God is solely believing He will bring forth that which He alone will do.

Time does not dictate the end, but God. Our past and sin do not declare what we are, but God. People may have their perceptions of us. Others may speak ill of us and seek to ruin us, but God alone has the Final Sovereign Say.

Though we have made mistakes, God can make up for our mistakes. God can still bring forth a beautiful reality. It shall be done if we pray that God's Will be done. When we open our being to all that God Wills, His Will will be exercised more rapidly and expansively through us.

What is completed for God is "'Not by might nor by power, but by My Spirit,' Says the Lord of hosts" (Zechariah 4:6 NKJV). God is the Author and Finisher of our faith. Though we have the freedom to do wrong and backslide, in the end, if we find ourselves receiving the invitation into Heaven, it is because God kept us in faith.

Of course, we had freedom to choose along the way, but if we truly desired God, He will bring our faith to completion. He will not let us venture too far to the point where it would cost us our salvation and to commit the unpardonable sin. Instead, if we desire God, and God sees our desire will always be for Him throughout our life, He will do everything in His Power to bring us back. He will convict, send angels, visit us in a dream, prophecy through a friend... He will do whatever is necessary.

God always completes what He is directly involved with and will do. Truly, Christ is "the Alpha and the Omega, the Beginning and the End, the First and the Last" (Revelation 22:13 NKJV).

Let us cease from attempting life and completing pursuits in our strength. Let us first go to God, knowing He will complete all that is directly from Him.

We know we are guilty of starting up specific intended pursuits, only to flake out, dismiss them, quit and give up. We know we often had good intentions initially, but lacked patience and endurance as we strived for the ending. We are not beings who complete everything we attempt, only God.

"For You formed my inward parts; You covered me in my mother's womb. I will praise You, for I am fearfully and wonderfully made; Marvelous are Your works, And that my soul knows very well" (Psalm 139:13-14 NKJV). God's works are stupendous and marvelous. He always brings to completion what He is directly involved in and Ultimately Wills to do, personally.

We can trust in the Omnicompletus One to fulfill His call on our lives. Even if we stray, as long as we see God is the Way and repent when we sin, God will accept us like the Prodigal Son.

Let us go to God and request that He enlarge our vision and directly involve Himself in fulfilling and completing His Will and Vision for our lives. If we do so continually, we will not be disappointed but overcome with humility, awe, and wonder at Him Who is the Glory of Days.

Truly, 'The things which are impossible with men are possible with God'" (Luke 18:27 NKJV). "For with God nothing will be impossible" (Luke 1:37 NKJV).

God in Heaven, Great I AM, Him Who brings to completion all that You are directly involved with, Whose Sovereign Decree within Thy Holy Word has come to fruition and continually unfolds into the manifold of what is to come through the declaration in Thy Word, You are Mighty and Awesome, Unconquerable and Immoveable, You alone are Him Who created the foundations of the world, mathematical truths, and laws of nature. You alone, O God, are the Absolute Moral Perfection of Goodness and cannot do evil. Far be it from You, the Almighty, to commit iniquity. God, what You have declared You will bring to pass. Teach us to go to You in all things. Keep us from pursuing that which You never called us to, O

God. Keep us from finding out the hard way, getting disappointed, and blaming You for something You never intended us to do and follow. God in Heaven, Him Who alone is Omnicompletus, You will bring to completion everything You reveal to us will happen. When You are in it, it cannot go wrong. By Your Will, things exist, and by Your Power and Spirit, that which You declare is completed. O God, may we rest on Your Sovereign Shoulder, hearing Your commands and instructions and receiving rest. Bless us with deeper revelation and greater illumination that nothing is too impossible for You. Truly, You alone do great and marvelous things without number. Help us, Holy Spirit, to always go to Thee and depend on Thee for all things. In Jesus' name, Amen.

OMNIVIRES
All-Strength

"If *it is a matter* of strength, indeed *He is* strong; And if of justice, who will appoint my day *in court?*"
— ***Job 9:19 NKJV***

God is the Strongest Being to exist.

There is nothing that goes beyond God in Strength. More remarkable still, nothing goes beyond God in all that God *Is*. Forever, He Is Above.

God's Strength is greater than any man or woman's strength. People may be well versed in their strength of lifting weights. Some may be stronger than others at bearing bad news. Some are strong when working on farmland, and some are strong in mind when hearing terrible news. There are many strengths in life, and God remains infinite in each one.

Since God never grows or learns, He remains strong in the wisdom and knowledge He already possesses and knows. Since God is Power Himself, there is no amount of power for or against Him that can either go past Him or overthrow Him. God is All-Strength, and He forever is the Mightiest Being. Nothing will ever be greater than Him in everything that is *of* Him.

"The Lord is my strength and my shield; My heart trusted in Him, and I am helped; Therefore my heart greatly rejoices, And with my song I will praise Him" (Psalm 28:7 NKJV). The Bible is a Book of Infinite Revelation, and one common theme we see is God's saints being led into situations where they must trust God.

Many times throughout Scripture, we see that those who are faithful and remain in the belief of God, placing their trust in Christ, experience incredible moves from God. Those who trust Who He is will be led toward jubilation and rejoicing! For the God of Israel, the Alpha and Omega, Him Who rules every piece of existence throughout all generations and realms is our Strength! He loves and cares for us and has the strength to complete what we cannot on our own.

God is willing and gracious to give. His Strength is derived from within Himself, and He alone is Omnivires.

God has the Strength to love us when we fail Him. God has the Strength to resist unleashing His wrath immediately when people grieve Him and anger Him with their sin and wicked ways. God has the Strength to bear all thoughts, ideas, understanding, and knowledge. Whatever it is in this life, God has the Strength to do the opposite of what we otherwise would do.

This, in turn, simply put, is receiving understanding that God has the Strength to do the right thing at all times. He never ceases from possessing the strength to do what is right. Continually, He gives the correct answers, does the right actions, and is willing, desirous, and wanting to save all.

"Trust in the Lord forever, For in Yah, the Lord, *is* everlasting strength. For He brings down those who dwell on high, The lofty city; He lays it low, He lays it low to the ground, He brings it down to the dust. The foot shall tread it down— The feet of the poor *And* the steps of the needy'" (Isaiah 26:4-6 NKJV). God has the strength to bring down the proud. In this life, many people can recognize that someone is proud, but very few have the strength to bring them down.

Yes, man can confront the prideful, but where the prideful are positioned we, many times, do not have the strength to bring them down.

Only God can bring them down, for it is God alone Who "removes kings and raises up kings" (Daniel 2:21 NKJV).

No amount of humility can bring down the prideful. Humility can confront and convict pride, but it is the Strength of the Omnipotent (All-Powerful) and Omnihumilitas (All-Humility) One Who can bring the prideful down. "God resists the proud, But gives grace to the humble" (James 4:6 NKJV).

God alone has the strength to resist sinning. Even in a state of perfection, we fell. Angels who dwelled with God in perfection in Heaven fell, too. God, however, has always been Perfect and has the Strength to remain Perfect.

Even when surrounded by evil, wickedness, and sin, the Lord Jesus Christ had the Strength to resist the Devil, worldliness, carnality, and the flesh. "Seeing then that we have a great High Priest Who has passed through the heavens, Jesus the Son of God, let us hold fast *our* confession. For we do not have a High Priest Who cannot sympathize with our weaknesses, but was in all *points* tempted as *we are, yet* without sin. Let us therefore come boldly to the throne of grace, that we may obtain mercy and find grace to help in time of need" (Hebrews 4:14-16 NKJV).

Christ's Strength must compel us to go to Him and receive grace, help, and strength. Without going to Christ, we do not have the strength to receive newness of life. Without the Holy Spirit, we do not have the strength to be holy. Only *by* God and *with* God can we fulfill the *call* of God and walk by the Holy Scriptures and in His Will.

"God is our refuge and strength, A very present help in trouble" (Psalm 46:1 NKJV). Since God "Neither faints nor is weary" (Isaiah 40:28 NKJV), He can help us and strengthen us amid trying and difficult times. God's Omnivires (All-Strength) allows Him to reach out to us at any moment, as well as others, without reducing strength.

The Strength of *The Infinite Omni* is never-ending, overflowing, and continually in a state of completeness, while simultaneously being infinite. When billions of people need strength, God can meet the needs of everyone who humbles themselves and calls upon the Lord. God can do so immediately, since He is Omnivires and His Strength does not run out.

When we feel like giving up, God has the Strength to reach out and sustain us, while simultaneously reaching out and encouraging others.

When someone is in a state of sadness or discouragement, it can be daunting. We can become tired after hearing about a few people's problems, let alone a single person going through a difficult season. Many times, we don't have the strength to listen, provide feedback, pray outside of meeting with the person, or encourage them. We cannot do this continually, nor were we made to, because we are not a person's Savior! Only Jesus Christ is Lord and Savior.

When writing this (October 8, 2024), my wife currently meets with multiple women daily. By the end of the day, on top of having her own things she is going through (and we are going through with many externals around us), she is tired. Her strength decreases substantially, and it is difficult for her to hear of all these stories. Women being raped, husbands abusing their children, suicide, murder... it is a lot. Though the coaching will be coming to a close, due to incredible events beginning to unfold in our lives by God's Sovereign hand, I am proud that she is so willing to be there for others – even to the point of neglecting to care for herself. She truly has a heart for the lost, hurting, and broken.

All this to say, it is essential to know that God sees everything that occurs, hears everything that happens at all moments throughout the day in everyone's lives, and He does not become affected in Strength. His Omnivires allows Him not to let externals offset Him to the point where God has "an off day" or "a bad day". No, God is the Creator of "days" themselves, and He has the strength to see, hear, give, and understand all realms of life and not become stressed and overwhelmed.

This is why God alone can give "power to the weak, And to those who have no might He increases strength" (Isaiah 40:29 NKJV). Truly, "those who wait on the Lord Shall renew their strength; They shall mount up with wings like eagles, They shall run and not be weary, They shall walk and not faint" (Isaiah 40:31 NKJV).

When we know God and walk with Christ, we can declare, "You are the glory of their strength, And in Your favor our horn is exalted" (Psalm 89:17 NKJV). "The Lord is my rock and my fortress and my deliverer; My God, my strength, in Whom I will trust; My shield and the horn of my salvation, my stronghold" (Psalm 18:2 NKJV).

"The Lord is my strength and song, And He has become my salvation; He is my God, and I will praise Him; My father's God, and I will exalt Him" (Exodus 15:2 NKJV).

We can hold to the bedrock truth of God's Omnivires and declare, "I can do all things through Christ Who strengthens me" (Philippians 4:13 NKJV). We can know that through Christ, all things are possible. Why? "All things were made through Him, and without Him nothing was made that was made" (John 1:3 NKJV).

Knowing that we can do all things in Christ should compel us to "be strong in the Lord and in the power of His might" (Ephesians 6:10 NKJV). For "The Lord God is my strength; He will make my feet like deer's feet, And He will make me walk on my high hills" (Habakkuk 3:19 NKJV).

"For You have armed me with strength for the battle; You have subdued under me those who rose against me" (Psalm 18:39 NKJV). No matter what comes our way in life, God's Strength will be our supply, sustenance, and strength. God Himself will give us the strength for every battle against sin and temptation. If we submit and surrender to God in every moment that trying times and temptation come, we will have victory! Not in our strength, but because of His!

Though we are bound to fall in this imperfect life, we should not make excuses. We are to fight and continue to fight against that which would seek to destroy us. In so doing, we will hear the still small voice of the Holy Spirit whispering to the hearts of us who fight against sin, "'My grace is sufficient for you, for My strength is made perfect in weakness'" (2 Corinthians 12:9 NKJV).

"And my soul shall be joyful in the Lord; It shall rejoice in His salvation. All my bones shall say, 'Lord, Who is like You, Delivering the poor from him who is too strong for him, Yes, the poor and the needy from him who plunders him?'" (Psalm 35:9-10 NKJV). God is our Confidence and Strength, and He is worthy of all praise.

Let us never attempt anything in our strength and might, which is limited and bound to fail. Instead, let us go to Him Whose Well never runs dry and is always overflowing. For in God, are all things, and from Him, all things came to be. "For of Him and through Him and to

Him *are* all things, to Whom *be* glory forever. Amen" (Romans 11:36 NKJV).

"But the Lord stood with me and strengthened me, so that the message might be preached fully through me, and *that* all the Gentiles might hear. Also I was delivered out of the mouth of the lion. And the Lord will deliver me from every evil work and preserve *me* for His heavenly kingdom. To Him *be* glory forever and ever. Amen!" (2 Timothy 4:17-18 NKJV). When we know God is Omnivires, what can occur that He cannot deliver us out of or keep us from? Truly, we can be as Isaiah and know that no weapon formed against us will prosper (Isaiah 54:17).

We can know that God has the Strength to deliver us! If He did so with the Israelites and delivered them out from captivity of the Egyptians; if He kept Daniel from the lion and strengthened him, and even allowed Paul to continue to live when he almost died many times, He can help us.

Paul declares, "From the Jews five times received forty *stripes* minus one. Three times I was beaten with rods; once I was stoned; three times I was shipwrecked; a night and a day I have been in the deep; *in* journeys often, *in* perils of waters, *in* perils of robbers, *in* perils of *my own* countrymen, *in* perils of the Gentiles, *in* perils in the city, *in* perils in the wilderness, *in* perils in the sea, *in* perils among false brethren; in weariness and toil, in sleeplessness often, in hunger and thirst, in fastings often, in cold and nakedness" (2 Corinthians 11:24-27 NKJV). In all this, God gave him the strength to endure to the very end.

"For I am already being poured out as a drink offering, and the time of my departure is at hand. I have fought the good fight, I have finished the race, I have kept the faith. Finally, there is laid up for me the crown of righteousness, which the Lord, the righteous Judge, will give to me on that Day, and not to me only but also to all who have loved His appearing" (2 Timothy 4:6-8 NKJV).

This is the promise to all those who do not lean on their own strength, but on God's strength to see them through and bear their burdens. Christ declares, "'Come to Me, all *you* who labor and are heavy laden, and I will give you rest. Take My yoke upon you and learn from Me, for I am gentle and lowly in heart, and you will find rest for your souls. For My yoke *is* easy and My burden is light'" (Matthew 11:28-30 NKJV).

Let us seek Him for His Strength to do and be like Christ in any and all situations.

———

God of All-Strength, Who never grows tired or weary, Who is never concerned or confused, You alone are All-Wise, Powerful, Magnificent and Majestic. You alone are greater and mightier than any foe or entity. Truly, only You can bear the burdens of man. You alone, Lord Jesus, had the strength to bear mankind's sin and the full blow of the Heavenly Father's wrath toward sin. Thank You for taking on our punishment and saving us from our sins. May all accept what You did by placing their faith and trust in You as Lord and Savior, and repenting of their sins. God, may You move mountains in our lives. Give us the strength to endure to the very end. Help us to be Christlike in all situations. We exalt You, for You alone are Omnivires. In Jesus' name, Amen.

OMNIDEFENDENT
All-Defending – Capable of Defending & Protecting All Things

"*The Lord will fight for you, and you shall hold your peace."*
— Exodus 14:14 NKJV

God alone has all Power and Might. Strength is His, and He alone can defend and protect all things.

When we examine our lives or the lives of others, we can clearly see God's Sovereign hand at work. We can see how God intervened at times and worked things out that should not have occurred.

Many people may call happy results that were unexpected as "fate", "luck", or "destiny", but we know Him Who is behind the scenes, working all things "together for good to those who love God, to those who are the called according to *His* purpose" (Romans 8:28 NKJV).

God alone is the Great Defender. He alone can defend anyone from anything. Whether that be evil, sin, suffering, adversity, or temptation, God *can* defend us at His Own discretion.

As we reflect on this, we may quickly ask, "If God can defend us from these things, then why doesn't He?". The answer is, HE DOES!

How many things could have occurred to us if God had not intervened? If we are mature in the faith, we may say "many times". However, what about for "baby Christians" or those who are unbelievers? They may believe God is not defending them, but He is actually.

God only allows evil to occur if it will work out for a greater good (Genesis 50:20). God also allows us to use our free will in a wrong manifestation and sin, which ultimately brings forth consequences and suffering. Of course, if we look at a born-again believer, we see that our wrongs and sins further validate God's Grace, Mercy, and willingness to save such wretched sinners as us!

An unbeliever cannot deny these truths, when the truths of our sin reveal the Greatness of Him Who is ready and willing to forgive!

"The Lord is my rock and my fortress and my deliverer; My God, my strength, in whom I will trust; My shield and the horn of my salvation, my stronghold" (Psalm 18:2 NKJV). There are many attacks toward our lives that we know not, but that God has protected us from. When Scripture says, "God *is* faithful, who will not allow you to be tempted beyond what you are able, but with the temptation will also make the way of escape, that you may be able to bear *it*" (1 Corinthians 10:13 NKJV), this shows God's Sovereignty.

God is Omnidefendent, and He protects us from temptations that would have otherwise occurred, had He not intervened.

The common phrase typically uttered is "God won't give you more than you can handle", but we clearly know He gives us more than we can handle to point us to Him and allow Him to be our Strength amid our weakness. God will give us much, which should lead us to Him for the ability to fulfill what He has brought forth. God also prevents temptations from occurring that would have otherwise occurred, and He does this as a means of defending us from the inevitable.

A man may be strong in one area of temptation, but weak in another. If we look at a different man, their strength and weakness may flip-flop from the first man regarding temptation. God allows us to be tempted to provide a way of escape. He provides a way of escape to train us. When we build that habit and fight against temptation, we will be more readily prepared in the future when bigger temptations come.

A man who is offered the opportunity to swindle others and be rewarded one million dollars cannot say "no" to that temptation until he has gone through times prior. A man who is offered to have sex with a curvy woman who is not his wife cannot have the strength to say no unless he has first learned to conquer the temptations of prior lust.

Every little temptation God *allows* to come our way is meant to train us, grow us, and have the self-control, discipline, and willingness to run to God. "Therefore submit to God. Resist the devil and he will flee from you" (James 4:7 NKJV). When we learn to submit to Him Who is our Defender, He will defend us from the temptation He has permitted to come our way.

Therefore, when we are tempted, we can rationally understand that many other temptations could have happened, but God did not allow them to occur. He was already defending us behind the scenes without us even realizing it!

If God permits temptation to come our way, we are fully responsible when we give way to that temptation. If God says we can bear the burden of a particular temptation, we can equally walk away from it. If we give in, it is from our own doing, not God's. "Let no one say when he is tempted, "I am tempted by God"; for God cannot be tempted by evil, nor does He Himself tempt anyone" (James 1:13 NKJV).

What happens when we don't run to Him Who is our Defender against temptation? "But each one is tempted when he is drawn away by his own desires and enticed. Then, when desire has conceived, it gives birth to sin; and sin, when it is full-grown, brings forth death" (James 1:14-15 NKJV).

"'He will guard the feet of His saints, But the wicked shall be silent in darkness. For by strength no man shall prevail'" (1 Samuel 2:9 NKJV). God promises to guard our feet. He will warn and convict when temptation is prevalent. If we fall, we must "come boldly to the throne of grace, that we may obtain mercy and find grace to help in time of need" (Hebrews 4:16 NKJV). "For a righteous *man* may fall seven times And rise again, But the wicked shall fall by calamity" (Proverbs 24:16 NKJV).

If we fall when born-again, we repent and rise up, knowing we have been forgiven. We press on in the strength of Thee Almighty. We do not continue in our iniquity.

"For the Lord will be your confidence, And will keep your foot from being caught" (Proverbs 3:26 NKJV). A sensitivity to God's speaking comes from drawing near to Him and spending time in His Word. If we are not present with Him Who is Omnipresent (everywhere at all times) and Omnipraesent (present at every moment – readily available to speak and be with us), we will not be sensitive to the movement or speaking of the Holy Spirit.

Therefore, we must grow in the knowledge of The Infinite Omni and desire to spend time with Him Who is above all and over all.

"The Lord is on my side; I will not fear. What can man do to me?" (Psalm 118:6 NKJV). "Though I walk in the midst of trouble, You will revive me; You will stretch out Your hand Against the wrath of my enemies, And Your right hand will save me" (Psalm 138:7 NKJV).

God is our Defender not just against temptation, but against the Evil One, his legion of angels, and witchcraft.

There is much witchcraft being done in our day and age, and it is an abomination to the Lord. Deuteronomy 18:9-14 (NKJV) declares:

> "'When you come into the land which the LORD your God is giving you, you shall not learn to follow the abominations of those nations. There shall not be found among you *anyone* who makes his son or his daughter pass through the fire, *or one* who practices witchcraft, *or* a soothsayer, or one who interprets omens, or a sorcerer, or one who conjures spells, or a medium, or a spiritist, or one who calls up the dead. For all who do these things *are* an abomination to the LORD, and because of these abominations the LORD your God drives them out from before you. You shall be blameless before the LORD your God. For these nations which you will dispossess listened to soothsayers and diviners; but as for you, the LORD your God has not appointed such for you.'"

Before marrying my wife, I used to believe that witchcraft was all fantasy. Of course, this is what I thought when I spent most of my life in the United States in a quiet, secluded area. Overseas, especially in certain places in a continent like Africa, witchcraft is very prevalent.

In the United States, it is also prevalent, just dressed up nicely.

"What's your Zodiac sign?", "New age", and other words lighten the debauchery of witchcraft in our eyes. Of course, this is "no wonder! For Satan himself transforms himself into an angel of light" (2 Corinthians 11:14 NKJV).

What God hates in the Old Testament, He hates in the New Testament. He never changes His mind regarding what He hates because it is forever contrary to His Nature.

Anyone skeptical of witchcraft today need look no further than ex-witch testimonies from those who have become born again. If we know our battle is not against flesh and blood, we should understand that some spiritual hindrances and attacks occur to our spiritual man that we are unaware of with our natural senses.

I digress the matter, but may Ephesians 6:10-13 (NKJV) be our starting point to fight against the powers of darkness:

> "Finally, my brethren, be strong in the Lord and in the power of His might. Put on the whole armor of God, that you may be able to stand against the wiles of the devil. For we do not wrestle against flesh and blood, but against principalities, against powers, against the rulers of the darkness of this age, against spiritual *hosts* of wickedness in the heavenly *places*. Therefore take up the whole armor of God, that you may be able to withstand in the evil day, and having done all, to stand."

When we are strong in the Lord, having placed on the entirety of God's Armor each day, we may declare Psalm 91:1-6 (NKJV):

> "He who dwells in the secret place of the Most High
>   Shall abide under the shadow of the Almighty.
>   I will say of the LORD, "*He is* my refuge and my fortress;
>   My God, in Him I will trust."
>   Surely He shall deliver you from the snare of the fowler
>   *And* from the perilous pestilence.
>   He shall cover you with His feathers,
>   And under His wings you shall take refuge;
>   His truth *shall be your* shield and buckler.
>   You shall not be afraid of the terror by night,

Nor of the arrow *that* flies by day,
Nor of the pestilence *that* walks in darkness,
Nor of the destruction *that* lays waste at noonday."

God is our Defender and He will keep us from the Evil One. God loves those made in His *image*, but He primarily defends those who are His *children*.

"For this cause everyone who is godly shall pray to You In a time when You may be found; Surely in a flood of great waters They shall not come near him. You *are* my hiding place; You shall preserve me from trouble; You shall surround me with songs of deliverance. *Selah*" (Psalm 32:6-7 NKJV).

God Defends us from many dangers. He keeps us on the straight and narrow. Truly, "The Lord of hosts is with us; The God of Jacob is our refuge. Selah" (Psalm 46:7 NKJV).

God defends us against our enemies. "You will keep *him* in perfect peace, *Whose* mind *is* stayed *on You*, Because he trusts in You" (Isaiah 26:3 NKJV). "When a man's ways please the Lord, He makes even his enemies to be at peace with him" (Proverbs 16:7 NKJV).

God will rise up and defend His people, even when it seems He is not All-Defending. Everything is in His time, and He knows the perfect time to rise from His Holy Throne and tear down the schemes of man and the plots of darkness.

God alone speaks against the darkness and the Light of His Word breaks it. He is the One Who exposes, and He will expose all One Day.

Let us give praise to the One Who is Omnidefendent and is capable of defending and protecting us against temptation, our enemies, witchcraft, demons, and Satan himself.

Is it any wonder that "Even the demons believe—and tremble!" (James 2:19 NKJV)? Truly, God rules and reigns above all and can defend and protect us from anything and everything. What He permits, is for Divine reasons. We are to thank Him for protecting and defending us from what we do not know. For He always wants the best for us.

Truly, we must "Fear not, for I am with you; Be not dismayed, for I am your God. I will strengthen you, Yes, I will help you, I will uphold you with My righteous right hand" (Isaiah 41:10 NKJV).

"But You, O Lord, are a shield for me, My glory and the One Who lifts up my head" (Psalm 3:3 NKJV).

Let us rest in the knowledge of Isaiah 59:18-19 (NKJV):

"According to *their* deeds, accordingly He will repay,
> Fury to His adversaries,
> Recompense to His enemies;
> The coastlands He will fully repay.
> So shall they fear
> The name of the LORD from the west,
> And His glory from the rising of the sun;
> When the enemy comes in like a flood,
> The Spirit of the LORD will lift up a standard against him."

Triune God, Who alone is Omnidefendent, Who knows the plots and schemes of man, Who ascends beyond any principality and power, Who is greater than any darkness or deception, Who stands as the Way, the Truth, and the Life, You are our Defender. Great and Mighty are You, O God, our Protector. Without You, we can do nothing. We are helpless before the Enemy. We cannot defend ourselves against spiritual attacks. O God, we thank You for Your Holy Spirit Who is greater in us than him who is in the world. God, Your Light can cast away any amount of darkness. You are Beauty and Majesty. You deserve all honor and praise. You equip us for battle and train us. You place Your Armor upon us when we abide in Thee. O God, truly You are All-Defending and willing to fight our battles for us. We need only be still. We bless You, O Infinite Omni. In Jesus' name, Amen.

Omniratio

All-Reason – Reason For All Things

"*Yet for us there is one God, the Father, of Whom are all things, and we for Him; and one Lord Jesus Christ, through Whom are all things, and through Whom we live.*"
— *1 Corinthians 8:6 NKJV*

All things are *from* God and are meant to be *for* God. No one thing in its initially intended state exists outside of God. Everything is the way it is, because God has declared it as such.

God is Omniratio and is the reason for all things. He Himself is the reason why there is life, the functions behind lifeforms, the reason there is variety and range of personality, and the 'why' behind all things.

We may look at a specific creation and say, "What good was making something like that?". We might look at a person and wrongfully judge and be critical and say, "Well, that person isn't going anywhere." Whatever viewpoints we have, God's original reason for creating trumps what we think or believe, for our beliefs are formed on limited understanding and sight, whereas God's reason for creating is Perfect, since He alone is God, Creator, Omnivoyant (All-Seeing), Omniscient (All-Knowing), and Omnificent (All-Creative – unlimited in creative power).

"You alone are the Lord; You have made heaven, The heaven of heavens, with all their host, The earth and everything on it, The seas and all that is in them, And You preserve them all. The host of heaven worships You" (Nehemiah 9:6 NKJV). God is the Maker of the Heavens and the earth and everything in them and therefore is the reason why there is anything at all.

The greatest minds will not ask whether or not *something* came from *nothing*, but "How come there is something rather than nothing?".

When we look around, we must see there is a reason for all that is. Certain events that occur through history are not random or happenstance. There is a reason for every event that occurs. In our lives, we cannot think everything is predetermined and holds no weight. We cannot fall into the false view that "it is what it is" and there is nothing more to what we go through, come across, or endure. All events and situations about the world, a particular nation, a state, city, or our lives have a reason.

God permits what He permits for Divine reasons that move all things toward His Ultimate Divine Will. If something falls outside His Ultimate Divine Will, God intervenes, redirects, or takes action. He is not a passive God Who created and now remains unmoved by what occurs. No, God is the God of detail. He cares about everything related to us—even the number of hairs upon our heads (Luke 12:7).

Truly, God is Omniratio. He is All-Reason and the reason for all things. There is a reason why you have been made to look the way you do. There is a reason you were placed in the particular family you were put in. There is a reason for the people who have come into your life (for better or worse). There is a reason why you have been given what you have been given. There is a reason for the delay of your desires and why God is making you wait for something particular about your life... there is a reason!

We don't have to sit around and wonder why things are the way they are. We don't have to spend time dwelling on why such and such has not happened yet, why God didn't make us look like another person. We don't need to waste time comparing or competing with others. God has reasons for uniquely creating us and making us different from others.

We must embrace this fact! Let us press into our Creator and know that He is Omniratio. Nothing has been made that was not made through Him (John 1:3)!

When we begin to see that we are exactly who we were made to be, we will start moving forward rather than being weighed down by unnecessary prolongment of questioning. When we cease from allowing what we *don't* have to get in the way and override what we *do* have, we will be more productive for God.

When we stop trying to work something in the flesh that was never meant to occur, we will grow in God and find that He can truly do more in a day than we can do in a thousand years. "But, beloved, do not forget this one thing, that with the Lord one day *is* as a thousand years, and a thousand years as one day" (2 Peter 3:8 NKJV).

"The earth is the Lord's, and all its fullness, The world and those who dwell therein. For He has founded it upon the seas, And established it upon the waters" (Psalm 24:1-2 NKJV). Everything on earth has been created, made, and brought into being at a specific point in time. God is the reason for why things come to be as they are in the timeframe they come to be. There is a reason why a dog with a specific personality was born *where* it was and *when* it was. Had it not been born at that time frame, a family would have gotten a different dog, leading to potentially less happy times and more difficult ones.

We always look with a singular eye on our situations when we need to look with a singular eye toward God! We must pray, "O God, give me a single eye to Thee, that I might focus on things of eternity!" "If then you were raised with Christ, seek those things which are above, where Christ is, sitting at the right hand of God. Set your mind on things above, not on things on the earth" (Colossians 3:1-2 NKJV).

We will find God immediately when we set our minds on things above. We will see He is Omniratio and the reason behind all things. We, who tend to suffer from viewing aspects of life with singular sight, will look to Him Who is Omnivoyant (All-Seeing). When God looks, He does not look merely at what is, but at what led to it and where it will lead if allowed and permitted. God is Omniperspectival (Able to view all things at all different points within time through His Divine sight).

For something good to happen in our world, God must allow a

certain evil to occur. Of course, God works evil out for a greater good (Genesis 50:20). However, sometimes for someone to build that business that will help many, they must go through abuse from a boss. For teenagers to begin becoming adults, they must be trained and permitted to work with tools independently (potentially risking (God-forbid) getting hurt in the process). An athlete meant to be raised up to speak about Christ will have to go through being surrounded by worldly teammates, while holding their ground for the Lord in the process.

God has a reason for allowing everything that comes to be to occur. God is moving all things toward a beautiful end. "The end of a thing *is* better than its beginning" (Ecclesiastes 7:8 NKJV). What God brings to an end is always better than the beginning of something we are going through. Not all beginnings are happy, but in the Lord, all endings are beautiful, redemptive, and restorative.

Beyond looking at our scope, events, and situations, we see that God has reasons for why He chose to create. It is to our benefit that God created. God needed nothing and gained nothing from us. Nonetheless, He made us out of a desire to have fellowship.

God was not lonely when He created us. He did not have an insatiable need that was unfulfilled since He finds His full satisfaction and supply within Himself alone. No, God created us to reveal Himself to us and allow us to have a living relationship with Him. It is entirely to our benefit that God created us. It is to our own demise when we reject Him.

"Every good gift and every perfect gift is from above, and comes down from the Father of lights, with Whom there is no variation or shadow of turning" (James 1:17 NKJV). God is the reason for every good gift. A gift of a spouse, child, job, gift, talent, vacation, toy… all of it is from God! God is the reason for all miracles and blessings! Every good gift truly comes from Him.

Nothing is good without God first being Good. Truly, all good gifts come from Him Who is Good and has offered us the best gifts: Salvation through Christ and sanctification by the Holy Spirit!

Since God has always been and is the Uncaused Cause, He therefore is the reason for why there is something rather than nothing. Something cannot come from nothing. God, however, can speak out of nothing the something that comes to be.

It takes God for all aspects of life to make sense. Ideas, innovation, imagination, and mind did not evolve from the material world. Never, in the history of history, has the material brought forth something immaterial (insofar as referencing our construct and makeup). The material does not create free will. The material did not create mind or soul. The material is not the reason for spirit.

God is the Metaphysical Necessity behind all spiritual realities. Nothing makes sense to be traced back to something that is not Timeless, Metaphysical, Spiritual, Infinite, Eternal, Transcendent and is Spirit and Mind. Truly, God must exist for all else to be.

God is the reason for why all things *are*. He makes sense of why there is something. Without Him, there would be nothing, and we would not be. Thanks to God, however, that He *Is*, has always been, and will always be God!

God is even the reason for reason itself. God is Reason and the Highest, Ultimate, Purest, Infinite form of it! We cannot reason without God first being Reason. We can reason because God has given us a mind to reason. We are beings of rationality, casting our vision for the future, discussing ideas through debates, coming to conclusions, and seeking resolution by interacting and hearing other viewpoints.

Reason is what a rational mind does, which only comes from God and has been given to us who have been made in His image. Truly, in God "we live and move and have our being, as also some of your own poets have said, 'For we are also His offspring'" (Acts 17:28 NKJV).

God is the First behind all firsts. He is the Reason for reason itself. Nothing exists in the physical or metaphysical without Him. Nothing was formed or brought to be without God. All things were brought forth and find their reason for existing, functioning, and participating in creation from Him Who is the Omniratio One!

"Who among all these does not know That the hand of the LORD has done this, In whose hand *is* the life of every living thing, And the breath of all mankind?" (Job 12:9-10 NKJV). God is the reason for life and existence. He Himself is Life and Existence, and all things are as they are and function as they do because God Thought, Willed, and by Wisdom, created by His Word, all that we know and will come to know.

God is the Reason and He is behind all seasons and all times of life. Ecclesiastes 8:1-8 (NKJV) declares:

> "To everything *there is* a season,
>   A time for every purpose under heaven:
>   A time to be born,
>   And a time to die;
>   A time to plant,
>   And a time to pluck *what is* planted;
>   A time to kill,
>   And a time to heal;
>   A time to break down,
>   And a time to build up;
>   A time to weep,
>   And a time to laugh;
>   A time to mourn,
>   And a time to dance;
>   A time to cast away stones,
>   And a time to gather stones;
>   A time to embrace,
>   And a time to refrain from embracing;
>   A time to gain,
>   And a time to lose;
>   A time to keep,
>   And a time to throw away;
>   A time to tear,
>   And a time to sew;
>   A time to keep silence,
>   And a time to speak;
>   A time to love,
>   And a time to hate;
>   A time of war,
>   And a time of peace."

God is not only the Creator and Maker of time itself, but He is the reason for there being a time for everything within time! There is a time when He brings forth and when He sets apart. There is a time when He creates and when He destroys. "I form the light and create darkness, I make peace and create calamity; I, the LORD, do all these *things*'" (Isaiah 45:7 NKJV).

God creates and brings about various things at specific points, based upon His knowledge of knowing when these things should occur. Of course, God's calamity is a form of *judgment*, not *evil*, since God can do no evil. "'Therefore listen to me, you men of understanding: Far be it from God *to do* wickedness, And *from* the Almighty to *commit* iniquity'" (Job 34:10 NKJV). "Surely God will never do wickedly, Nor will the Almighty pervert justice" (Job 34:12 NKJV).

God is the reason for what is and the separation of other aspects. He created light and darkness. He created the sky above and the earth below. He is the Reason for why there is land and why there is water. He is the Reason why there are animals and why there are sea creatures. What *is*, has been brought about at a certain point in time and in a particular season. Whatever God deems should come at a later time is not meant to occur now and will bring forth ruin, destruction, or disruption.

God alone knows *when* must be *what* and *what* must be *when*. He is the Reason for all things, and He is Perfect. His timing, creating, bringing forth, allowing, and intervening are all perfect. God cannot act against His Nature, and since His Nature is Perfection, there truly is a perfect reason behind all things.

"Then the LORD said in His heart, 'I will never again curse the ground for man's sake, although the imagination of man's heart *is* evil from his youth; nor will I again destroy every living thing as I have done. "While the earth remains, Seedtime and harvest, Cold and heat, Winter and summer, And day and night Shall not cease"'" (Genesis 8:21-22 NKJV).

God created the winter and summer, day and night, cold and heat. He is the reason for what is and the reason *why* it is. Truly, "the Lord is the great God, And the great King above all gods. In His hand are the deep places of the earth; The heights of the hills are His also. The sea is

His, for He made it; And His hands formed the dry land" (Psalm 95:3-5 NKJV).

God is Omniratio, and He is the Reason behind all things. Let us trust in the Great and Mighty One, Who is High and Lifted Up. Let us seek Him for understanding, guidance, and counsel. Does not He Who created all know why He made it and what it is for? Does He not know why reality is the way it is?

Reason in part is a desire to seek that which corresponds to reality. We must learn to go to God with clean hands, a pure heart, a thirsty soul, and a teachable spirit to learn what the Omniratio God has to say behind the reality He has created.

May we cease striving in the flesh, and go to God, Who is our rest. He alone is Omniratio, the reason behind all things, and why there is something rather than nothing.

———

Great Omniratio God, Who is the reason for why there is creation, Who formed the seasons and created the landscapes, Who by wisdom formed the waves and the motion of the water, Who places animals in the forest and mountains, Who brought forth different seasons and is the Creator of time itself, we praise Thee and worship Thee! O God, there is no one like You. Who can answer any question posed to them? Who can give the reason behind all circumstances, creations, people, and history? God, You alone are the Timeless One Who holds the book of the past, present, and future. You are the One, O Lord, Who is the Author of the great book of time. O God, help us to seek You and find our meaning and purpose in You alone. Guide us, O Great Writer of time, for You will bring to completion what You start. Write our story, reveal to us the reason behind why we are and why things are the way they are. Help us to understand and press into all You have for us, for Thy Glory alone. Teach us, O Omniratio One, to go to You in all things. You alone are All-Reason, and we seek Thy Infinite Mind for guidance, counsel, instruction, and knowledge. We love Thee, O God. In Jesus' name, Amen.

OMNIULTIMUS
All-Ultimate

"*The Lord shall reign forever and ever.*"
— ***Exodus 15:18 NKJV***

God is the highest level of ultimacy than can be fathomed, achieved, recognized, and reached. There is nothing beyond God, as He is the Unending, Ultimate Reality behind everything.

God is Omniultimus in all realms and all ways. Nothing is outside or beyond Him, and nothing can fully reach or comprehend Him. Forever, God stands alone as the All-Ultimate.

When we say that God is All-Ultimate, we mean He is the Greatest and Highest in any form, field, or feature.

People may love each other, but God Himself is Love (1 John 4:16). We may attempt to be holy, but God alone is Holy (1 Peter 1:15-16). We may be creators in this life, but we are not the Creator of all life (Colossians 1:16).

God alone forever ascends beyond anything that can be reached. God made Himself to be understood, known, and experienced through the Lord Jesus Christ, but God in His collectivity is forever beyond all.

He is the Highest Form, Highest Reality, and Unending Ascension behind everything.

We understand that God is Omnipotent (All-Powerful), Omniscient (All-Knowing), Omnipresent (All-Present), and Omnibenevolent (All-Good). These are the four common attributes discussed about God and "Omni" characteristics. However, when we look at Who God is, being *The Infinite Omni*, we quickly find that He is the Unending All behind all things.

As this Volume Series portrays over 200+ new attributes of God, we find He is Ultimate in All of them, because All of Them *are* Him and *of* Him. God *is* Power, but He also is the Giver of power – allowing humans to exercise it as God sees fit and allows.

God is Omnisapient (All-Wise). He is the Ultimate form of wisdom because He *is* Wisdom. Not only is He Wisdom, but the Giver of Wisdom.

Daniel 2:20-21 (NKJV) reveals the Power and Wisdom of God and how He is both Them and the Giver of them: "Daniel answered and said: 'Blessed be the name of God forever and ever, For wisdom and might are His. And He changes the times and the seasons; He removes kings and raises up kings; He gives wisdom to the wise And knowledge to those who have understanding.'"

Since God is the Ultimate of what He is, He can dictate what is permitted and allowed. God alone can give what He desires because He is the Ultimate manifestation of it. He alone is God and God is that which He is.

"'Heaven and earth will pass away, but My words will by no means pass away'" (Mark 13:31 NKJV). God has the Ultimate, Final say. Whatever He declares, comes to be and is. Nothing can change what He has declared, only revolt against Him.

When people want to change their identity or find it in something else, this is not of God. This is direct rebellion against a Holy God Who is the Omniultimus.

Too many people are trying to become something they are not and going in ways that God warned them to depart from, resulting in consequences, destruction, and damnation. God wants people to find their identity in Christ and return to their Creator. He wants to reveal what

He has to say about them, which trumps any words from man or ourselves. God is Omniultimus in everything He is, including His Word.

If people understood the truth of God's Word and the benefits and blessings of knowing God, they would more quickly go to Him; not out of seeking *something* from God but seeking God Himself. There is no more tremendous blessing than knowing God and having God know us.

God desires a living relationship, which is why He has given us His Word. He wants to reveal Himself in His Word so that we might accept Christ and receive the Holy Spirit. God wants all to repent of their sins so they might become born again (2 Peter 3:9). Truly, God desires fellowship with His creation, for He is the One Who created all things.

When we discuss how God is Omniultimus, we understand all that He is ultimate in. For example, we know that words are powerful. "Death and life *are* in the power of the tongue, And those who love it will eat its fruit" (Proverbs 18:21 NKJV). Words carry weight. They can create or destroy. They also carry Truth or deception.

When we speak the Truth, we are speaking what is of God and comes from God. If we are talking about the Lord Jesus Christ, we are speaking about the Truth Himself. Our words can do much, yet they cannot do the same as God's.

God has given us His Holy Scriptures, the Bible, through His Words. God has declared what is and what He wanted to convey, through men who were led by the Holy Spirit: "knowing this first, that no prophecy of Scripture is of any private interpretation, for prophecy never came by the will of man, but holy men of God spoke *as they were* moved by the Holy Spirit" (2 Peter 1:20-21 NKJV).

God's Word was carried through men, but led by the Holy Spirit. God's Word is Truth and filled with truth in what *It teaches*. When we use words, we tend to have only one meaning behind them (sometimes there is more by decoding phrases or deception). Most times, however, we speak what we want to convey. With God, it is different.

When God gave us His Word, It means what It says. However, since God is Omniultimus in His Word, there is more to learn behind His Words. God has given us the Holy Scriptures, and when we have the

Holy Spirit to interpret the Holy Scriptures, we see a holy reality emerge.

Deeper revelations become known. God begins to speak in certain passages in more than one way. Historical context is good, but spiritual revelations are better. Reading the Word at face value is good, but passages will be illuminated when guided by the Holy Spirit and deeper understanding and findings will be seen in the text.

God's Word, therefore, is not just in an instant, truthful revealment, but a continual, revelatory experience. Greater still, this is not where His Word ends.

We know God is the All-Ultimate behind all things, and His Ultimacy is in words because He is the Word. "In the beginning was the Word, and the Word was with God, and the Word was God" (John 1:1 NKJV).

When we see that Christ is the Word, we see that He is the Living Expression of Continuous Truth and Perpetual Revelation. In Christ, there is never an inconsistency, misunderstanding, deceit, lie, or evil. Christ is Perfect, and His Perfection as the Word reveals that He is always and forever speaking Truth, making Him the Ultimate Word.

When we continue to move deeper, we find that Christ is not only *literally* the Word, but His Word is also powerful and mighty, and He alone can create all.

Humans need supplies, resources, people, and time to create something. God, however, is the complete opposite. When God created, all He needed was the Word to speak and it was done. "By faith we understand that the world has been created by the Word of God so that what is seen has not been made out of things that are visible" (Hebrews 11:3 NASB).

By the Word, Christ as the Logos created what was within an instant. He did not need to learn or plan beforehand. He merely spoke, and what now is came to be.

Is it any wonder how God is the Ultimate Word? How His Word is the ultimate within our realm but transcends our realm? Who else can speak something out of nothing? Who else can declare for something to come into existence, and it happens within an instant without prior planning, preparation, objects, or help?

Truly, God alone is the Ultimate in everything, both within the realm in which that aspect finds itself and transcending beyond it! If it is so with the Word, it is with everything else.

What else is God the Ultimate in? Everything. He is Omniultimus. We might think He is the Ultimate in only specific criteria, but He is Ultimate in everything that corresponds to His Nature (since God cannot sin or do evil).

God is the Ultimate in humor, ideas, creativity, listening, being there for others, friendship, being a Judge, Authority, Ruler, as well as in sight, designing, paving paths, making ways, guiding, thinking, *Being*, supplying our needs, bringing people together, making all things work together for good, protecting, caring, and in strength, love, gentleness, holiness... everything that can be done and that is by God's Nature, He is the Ultimate.

What a blessing to know that God forever is the Ultimate Maximum of Infinite Measures! He alone is *The Infinite Omni* and cannot be triumphed over, brought down, defeated, or overruled. God has the Ultimate Say, since He is the Ultimate Word. God is the Ultimate Life since He is the One Who gives and extends life to all things. "I urge you in the sight of God Who gives life to all things, and *before* Christ Jesus Who witnessed the good confession before Pontius Pilate, that you keep *this* commandment without spot, blameless until our Lord Jesus Christ's appearing, which He will manifest in His own time, *He who is* the blessed and only Potentate, the King of kings and Lord of lords" (1 Timothy 6:13-15 NKJV).

Let us continually seek God for deeper revelations about how He alone is Omniultimus. Nothing can trump Him, conquer Him, destroy Him, or beat Him. God alone is the Absolute Supremacy, Sovereign Ascendent, and Endless Omni.

To *The Infinite Omni* be Glory, forevermore. He alone is Omniultimus.

God in Heaven, Who was, and is, and is to come, You are to be glorified and magnified. You, O God, are the One Who created the universe by

Your Word. You alone, O Lord, speak and it is done. You alone, O God, think and it is so. Who else can compete or combat Thee and triumph? Who can destroy You and begin to say You are in the wrong? God, You are Omniultimus. In all realms, dimensions, and realities, You rule and reign Supreme. You are the Unconquerable God Whose Strength and Power has no limitations! All that You are is All that You have ever been. You cannot grow, for You are Infinite. You cannot cease to be, for You are Eternal. O God, rule our hearts and minds. Draw us into Thy Presence that we may experience more of Thee. Captivate us by Thy Word. Teach us, Holy Spirit, to go to God in all things. For Who is greater than our Unending God? Who can bring to us what does not already belong to Him? Who can help us in such a way that God cannot? O Great Maker, design in us Thy plans. Holy Spirit, execute Your established plans by the Heavenly Father. Guide us, O Truthful, Immutable Word. Teach us Thy ways we pray, Lord Jesus. In Your Holy Name, Amen.

Afterword

I appreciate you taking the time to read through *The Infinite Omni: The Unending All Behind All Things (Volume I)*. I hope it benefited your growth in understanding more about the Might, Magnificence, and Splendor of Who God *Is* as *The Infinite Omni*.

If this was a blessing, it would be greatly appreciated if you took a few minutes to write a review on the platform you purchased the book (e.g., Amazon).

An honest review can go a long way and help make the book more visible to future audiences.

If you feel led to do so, I truly do thank you.

Lance D. VanTine

Author

Let's Connect

If you would like to connect with Lance D. VanTine, you can find him on the following platforms:

Facebook (Quotes): @lvtquotes

Instagram (Personal): @lancevantine

Instagram (Quotes): @lvtquotes

LinkedIn: Lance VanTine

Linktree: linktr.ee/lancevantine

Services: https://stan.store/ascendwithvantines

Twitter: @lancevantine

YouTube: Lance VanTine

About Lance D. VanTine

Lance VanTine came to a more profound knowledge of God when he realized it was only Jesus Christ Who could break the chains of sin that kept him bound.

He is passionate about diving deeper into the study of Who God is, His Attributes, His Nature, and His Being, and sharing the revelations he has received with all who have an ear to hear. His desire is for others to know God intimately. Not only as Father, Son, and Holy Spirit, but as Creator of the Universe.

His testimony is impactful, as it reveals God as the Deliverer. He was supernaturally set free from an addiction to pornography and masturbation at age 23, as a Non-Denominational Christian, and received the gift of tongues and discerning of spirits upon getting married.

Since the age of 25, Lance has consistently posted one video each day on YouTube containing apologetic, theological, or philosophical insight. He is an Entrepreneur, dedicated Author, husband to his wife, Jackie VanTine, and grateful to be a Dad.

Also by Lance D. VanTine

Infinite Omni (Volume I) is VanTine's seventh book. He has multiple books in the works expected to launch this year and in the years ahead.

Some of the books to be released soon (or are already published) that were mentioned throughout this book are the following:

- *The Realm Beyond: Spiritual Truths, Tongues, Demons, & Deliverance (pg. 26)*
- *The Infinite Day: Insight Into God's Middle-Knowledge (pg. 36)*
- *Maximum Mind: Understanding the Knowledge & Wisdom of God (pg. 38, 102)*
- *The Prophetic Voice: When A Man Is Guided By The Holy Spirit (pg. 79)*
- *Spiritual Gifts: What Can Only Come From The Holy Spirit (pg. 26, 84, 91)*
- *The Metaphysical Trichotomy of Persons (pg. 93, 148)*
- *Shadowed Realities: God's Vantage Point vs. Man's Vantage Point (pg. 192)*
- *In God Alone: Understanding God's Self (pg. 213)*

We hope *The Infinite Omni* was an edifying read that benefited your growth in understanding the One True, Living God and growing in the knowledge of the Holy One of Israel.

God bless you, keep you, guide you, and continue to lead you in His Will, according to His Word.

Made in the USA
Las Vegas, NV
05 March 2025

070c769d-b464-454c-a964-d52f35ffff90R01